The GHAN

The Ghan has become part of Australia's store of folk legends that permeate time, as stories of narrow-gauge rail travel between Adelaide and Alice Springs, and the Outback, are retold by generations.

Today, a standard-gauge line from Tarcoola to Australia's Centre provides an efficient, all-weather passenger and freight service inland. Meanwhile, the memories of the infamous old Ghan have never been forgotten, and are preserved in Rail Museums established at Quorn in the south, and Alice Springs in the Centre.

So too, the joy and challenges of travel by the old Ghan have been preserved thanks to Basil Fuller, who recounted his travels in the brake van, from Port Augusta to Alice Springs, and whose fascinating glimpses of railway life were first published by Rigby, Adelaide, in 1975. This new paperback is the latest reprint of this classic book.

Paul Fitzsimons
Alice Springs, 1996

The GHAN

The Story of the Alice Springs Railway

BASIL FULLER

LANSDOWNE

Distributed by Outback Books
PO Box 8412
Alice Springs
Northern Territory 0871

Published by Lansdowne Publishing Pty Ltd
PO Box 48, Millers Point, Sydney NSW 2000

Chief Executive & Publisher: Jane Curry
Art & Production Manager: Sally Stokes
Publishing Manager: Cheryl Hingley
Cover design: Robert G. Taylor

First published by Rigby Limited 1975
Reprinted in Seal Books 1978
Reprinted by Lansdowne Publishing Pty Ltd 1996
Printed by MacPherson's Printing Group, Australia

ISBN 1 86302 5251

Front cover photograph courtesy of the Ghan Preservation Society, Alice Springs.

CONTENTS

LIST OF ILLUSTRATIONS

FOREWORD

One evening in Melbourne I was the guest of Jack Moir, collector of Australiana and founder of the Bread and Cheese Club, at a P.E.N. dinner when Nevil Shute was the distinguished guest.

Someone asked a question about *A Town Like Alice* which had by then been well known for some nine years.

Towards the end of the ensuing discussion, the idea occurred to me that the Central Australia Railway, the line that goes to Alice Springs, would make a fascinating, if perhaps difficult, subject of research. For though it ranks as one of the world's glamour railways, this line—unlike the Canadian Pacific, the Union Pacific, and the Trans-Siberian railways—had seldom been described. Unless the facts were assembled, the story would be forgotten, as changes came and the railway to the Centre took fresh form. So I thought at the time.

Later the idea had still stronger appeal. It seemed to me that this was somebody's obligation. And if somebody's, why not mine? With an affection for the region concerned, and at least a little knowledge of its vagaries, I felt that the task would be congenial. So I began to prepare—gradually.

Years were to pass before an opportunity occurred. Then one day the opening presented itself and the job was on.

This was pleasing to me for, though no railwayman, I have a nostalgic leaning towards the days of steam. And for most of its years the Ghan has been steam-hauled.

It is a fact that with the coming of the diesel-electric locomotive a new interest has sprung up in the old steam engine. This interest seems to be very nearly world-wide, and in South Australia it is exemplified in the recently-formed Pichi Richi Railway Preservation Society.

To write the story without the goodwill and practical help of several organisations and a number of specially qualified people would not have been possible, however.

Chief among the former were the Commonwealth Railways, the

South Australian Railways, and the State Library of South Australia. These provided the means. By permission of the Railways, I was enabled to consult annual reports and many railway documents not generally available. In this regard, I should like to thank in particular Mr H.N. Turner, Secretary of the Commonwealth Railways, and Mr F.A. Stretton of the South Australian Railways. In the State Library the specialised knowledge and advice of Mr L.S. Marquis directed me to the brittle and yellowing pages of many old journals containing the facts and stories of early railways days, in particular the *Port Augusta Dispatch*, a valuable source of reference. I also owe much to Mr I.K. Winney of the Australian Railway Historical Society.

Perhaps the writer of a factual story may credit himself legitimately with hard work in research, some mental effort in selection and arrangement, and much hard labour in drafting and finalising his material. But always he is indebted to others.

In the present case the list of helpers is long. Indeed, to mention all would be to fill at least a page. So I name a few only, asking the others to accept afresh, this time collectively, thanks already individually expressed.

Thus I should like to acknowledge assistance given by Messrs A.R. Polmear, J. Averis, G.L. Stirling, A.G. Williams, G. Hall, L. Rose, A. Crombie, R.D. Kempe, D. Mercer, B. Evans, M.D. Farley, A.K. Johinke, G. Eardley, M. Khan, A.M. Khan, and Mrs Bebe Nora Bejah.

1

BEFORE THE RAIL: OPENING THE WAY

The South Australian sun blazed! A smell of dust hung on dawdling currents of hot air. Mirage—shimmering as a migraine—showed giant gum trees, butts uppermost, high over glittering water where, in fact, stretched sun-dried bush. A roadside notice warned of heat and sand-drift. And the Birdsville Track ran northwards towards the floodplains of Cooper Creek and the Diamantina River.

Hot stones toasted the soles of thin sandals so that I stood as a stork, first on my right leg, and then on my left, and stared into distance. To the west lay salt-pans, gibber plains, and Lake Eyre South; to the east sandy desert arranged in high, steep-sided ridges where—incredible recollection on that sweltering day—cold winds blow in winter; and to the south-east, perhaps ninety miles distant, the hill which Edward John Eyre—deceived by just such a mirage as plagued me now—named Mount Hopeless, thus spreading the "Torrens Myth", the belief that a horseshoe-shaped sea blocked the way to the north.

Arid regions in which to build railways! Yet, at times, the in-hospitable land bursts into bloom. Then blends of yellows, greens, and purples—colourful as patchwork quilts—form countless gardens, a circumstance that explains the conflicting accounts of explorers: Eyre and Sturt described a useless desert; McKinlay, Howitt, Davis, and Goyder saw a land of plentiful streams, of lakes and meadows.

Far off, a locomotive blared a warning and my thoughts switched to the purpose of our journey—to uncover the facts of an epic achievement, the brave enterprise of men who had challenged a continent. The plan was not new, but on this occasion we meant to learn the full story of the line that, running from the coast to the Centre, lies like a long slim finger pointed at Australia's heart.

Varying the toasted area, I sat down, turned from the flickering deceit, and looked back at Marree, now the important change-of-gauge depot of the Central Australia Railway, but once the "metropolis" of cameleers who ran the old-time camel communications network that linked the outback with civilisation.

Again the horn sounded. "Ghan must be running late," said my wife, Sally, and laughed because, the world over, people are amused when a train they do not need to catch is not on time. And, of course, there was the Ghan's reputation for delay. But as it happened, I had seen the Southbound pull out two hours previously. Besides, if all had not run smoothly that morning, stationmaster Len Hickey would not have been free to show us round town. So it was not the Ghan. Perhaps some shunter grown impatient!

Len grinned and pushed back his cap to mop his forehead. He must have read my thoughts for he remarked that the story of how the famous train received its name has several versions, not associated with unpunctuality.

I knew those tales—or most of them. One simply has it that the name "Ghan" arose because the railway supplanted the Afghan camel drivers working the country between Port Augusta and Oodnadatta. But others are more specific, especially those told by railwaymen.

Two stories originated in Quorn, an important railway junction for seventy years. In the first of these a porter, seeing picturesquely-dressed Afghan camel drivers board the first sleeping-car train to Oodnadatta, remarked to a mate, "The Afghan Express, eh?" And the phrase caught on in the odd way these things happen. In the second an identical situation is linked to a later event, the departure of the first passenger train to Alice Springs.

An Oodnadatta account slightly varies the theme. It says that in the early 1890s when there was much talk of extending the railway across the continent, Nabby Bux, an Afghan of distinguished appearance, owned one of the camel strings that worked the country to Newcastle Waters, transporting all that a railway would have carried. One day a local drover, watching Nabby transfer a crate from railway truck to camel back, guffawed and, slapping his thigh, burst out, "Bloody Afghan extension, that's what!"

A version that seems more convincing comes from Marree. This explains that in the mid-1880s, when the township was called Hergott Springs and the railhead was advancing slowly northwards, the construction train to William Creek usually was so crowded by Afghan camelmen—then some fifty per cent of the local population—that facetiously minded navvies named it "The Afghan Special" or, according to one account, "The Royal Afghan".

One railwayman assured me with a grin that every settlement on the line from Port Augusta northwards has its own explanation of the nickname. However, Mr George Williams of Port Augusta, who served the railways for forty-eight years, working his way from "swab pusher", or engine cleaner, through all relevant jobs to line inspector, told me a story that must be given weight in view of such long experience. He explained that he worked on the first through-train to Oodnadatta in 1923, and that when the train reached Quorn an old Afghan jumped out hurriedly. "He'd just about missed his sunset prayer," said George Williams, "so he was rushing off to a secluded spot at the west end of the station that sometimes was used by Moslems as a place to pray."

It seems the engine driver was a wag. When he saw the Afghan bolting so fast up the platform he turned to a crowd of people standing near by and remarked drily, " 'Struth, if that one's going through to Oodnadatta, we should call this the Afghan Express."

Authentic as this account undoubtedly is, some rival stories probably are equally well-founded on fact. So the question of which incident actually gave rise to the nickname "Ghan" perhaps must always remain in doubt.

But whether the popular description dates from early or comparatively recent railway days, it appears to have been applied in the beginning chiefly to the train known as "The Slow Mixed". But later, when a passenger through-train began running to Alice Springs, this became known as "The Flash Ghan". Then the slow supply train—among other less parliamentary descriptions—was called "The Utility Ghan". Finally the public appears to have confused the situation, using the nickname more or less indiscriminately.

We left the Track and Len drove to the railway yards where running repairs are performed. These yards adjoin an area that once was an extensive paddock where camel drivers rested their strings between outback journeys. With typical kindness, Len was sparing no trouble to show us the spots of interest and the way the railway works at this meeting place of the gauges.

We stopped near a guard's van that had suffered from a shunting miscalculation and was undergoing a minor skin graft. Other work in progress included adjustments to brakes and bogies, and repairs to water tanks. It was interesting to notice that the tanks were fixed at bogie level. If they were placed higher in rolling-stock, when the train was running to the Centre, the water would boil.

Fully-equipped workshops are maintained at Alice Springs, a popular spot where a large tradesman force can be kept more easily than at lonely townships on the plains. But all major overhauls are performed at Port Augusta. Narrow-gauge vehicles are taken there pickaback from Marree on specially fitted standard-gauge trucks.

For ninety years this spot had been a centre of railway activity. But, in the context of transportation, its importance had begun long before that. A quarter of a century earlier, in 1859, twelve water-giving mounds were found by an artist-botanist, J.F.D. Herrgott (or Herrgolt as the name was sometimes rendered), a member of the second northern expedition led by John McDouall Stuart who, three years later, made the first crossing of Australia from south to north.

In the following year the area of the springs became a Government water reserve and has remained so ever since. But near-by land was leased to pastoralists, brothers named Matthews, whose holding now forms a part of St Stephen's Ponds and a part of Mundowdna.

These events are important in the story of the Ghan. For from this time forward the country gradually prepared for the coming of the rail.

Some years later an interstate camel communications network, the first outback "train" in this region, became based on the Herrgott Springs district. And, though a railway was a talking point long before camels reached the colony in numbers, this network opened the way in the far north. Ultimately the railway, in conjunction with the motor-truck, replaced it. But it formed the background of life in early rail-building days, and Herrgott Springs was its pivot.

The water source at the future camel and railway depot of Hergott (one "r" was soon dropped from the spelling of the name) was noticed officially for the first time soon after the Matthews settled. Governor MacDonnell camped for a night at the springs. Recognising that the spot would become a staging point for drovers and travellers generally, he ordered that the springs should be fenced to prevent beasts from trampling the surrounding area into mud. From within this fence, water was piped to the first engine-supply tank in the station yard a short distance away across the plain when, years later, the railhead arrived.

Almost certainly, the springs near the future railway depot were in regular use 110 years ago. There was movement in the country then. A strong northwards advance of squatters followed a mistakenly optimistic report made by Assistant Surveyor-General Goyder, who had visited the region immediately north of the Flinders Ranges during an exceptional season.

Knowledge of reliable water points was vital to those young pioneer graziers. They desired the freedom of the lonely places and accepted big risks to achieve their ambition. Each bought a few horses, a flock of sheep, and rations enough to last for two years. Then he set out to find his fortune, and the lives of his beasts depended upon water found by the track he followed. When he arrived in country that pleased him he squatted and obtained a lease from the Government. And soon, if somewhat unreasonably in view of his wish for isolation, his thoughts turned to a northern railway. For in due course the southward movement of stock began. And, though droving was the expected procedure, the colony was becoming railway-minded and would shortly enter a period of construction described by many as "railway mania".

Drovers travelling from far northern stations to markets in the south spelled their mobs at Hergott Springs. They, together with explorers, prospectors, and surveyors, must have come to regard the spot as the beginning of civilised parts. For settlement in the Flinders Ranges began in the late 1840s, and it is said that by 1862—the year when the first cargo from England reached the head of Spencer Gulf in the *Ormelie*—more than 6,000 pastoralists and miners were living in the region north of Port Augusta, all people planning in terms of a future railway.

Exactly when camel drivers began to use the district of the springs as the centre of their far-flung operations is uncertain, though its situation at the division of the ways to east and west of Lake Eyre made the choice inevitable. No record was kept. Nor is this surprising. The camel drivers were Asiatics—usually described as Afghans, though some were Indians—people who could speak little English, let alone write it. And squatters appear to have kept their counsel, probably because they were greedy for land and so avoided advertising their knowledge of conditions and of what was happening in the country.

However, one may arrive at an approximate date for the first cameleer encampment in the neighbourhood that was to become of particular importance in the railway story.

Several sources state that in 1880, four years before the arrival of the line, Hergott was "a little Asia", the focus of camel strings that travelled the Queensland Road (later to become known as the Birdsville Track); the Strzelecki Track to Innamincka; the way through Blanchewater eastwards into New South Wales; the track to Charlotte Waters, and so to Alice Springs and other far northern stations on the Overland Telegraph Line. These were the chief routes of the camel communications network, though all—particularly those leading to the east—branched into many side tracks.

The trunk supply route ran from Port Augusta, through Beltana and the quaintly named Government Gums, later to become famous in the railway context.

Later, though not until the opening of the western goldfields, by which time the railway had arrived at Oodnadatta, Hergott cameleers pushed out another supply route, this time south-westwards to Tarcoola and Eucla, and so to Coolgardie and Kalgoorlie.

How the network of pre-railway supply routes developed seems relatively clear. According to a record in the Archives Section of the State Library of South Australia, in 1867 Sir Thomas Elder, whose firm played a historic part in the growth of the State, took up lease Number 1710—532 square miles of country in the Beltana district—just fourteen years before the coming of the railway. He established a camel-breeding station with 123 animals brought from India in the *Blackwell*. These beasts, together with saddles and other necessary furniture, were driven upcountry by twelve Asians who had brought them from Karachi.

Elder continually extended his interests. In the June following, for instance, he took up lease Number 1766, the Lake Arthur run which comprised 342 square miles west of Blanchewater. Eventually he held territory greater in extent than the area of his homeland, Scotland.

Perhaps Elder and Samuel Stuckey—a partner at that period and the man said to have proposed the use of camel transport—at first intended to employ the beasts solely for the supply of their own runs. But if this was the original intention, the purpose was extended. Soon some of the Beltana camels were being used in a general carrying service up and down the western plain and along the route of the future railway, transporting equipment to copper-mines in the Flinders Ranges and carrying the mined ore to Port Augusta for export. Others travelled northwards, far beyond Hergott Springs to Lake Hope and Cooper Creek.

In long northward hauls, Elder's cameleers certainly used the springs as a watering point, just as the drivers of steam engines were to do a few years later. Dry staging for distances of up to ninety miles faced travellers on the Queensland Road in those days, for the first Government bore was not sunk until about 1890.

Inevitably a time came when some of the camelmen wished to set up in business for themselves. Talk of a northern railway had increased, but there appeared to be little likelihood that building would begin for some years. In any case, they felt that a line would not end the cameleer's opportunities. Naturally they could not foresee the coming of the motor-truck. So they argued that they would always find work in serving stations far to the east and west of a main trunk line. Rewards were high for the man who ran an efficient camel string. Moreover, competition was slight. No white men then had experience in camel-handling or, for that matter, the inclination to undertake it.

Importing their own camels, these enterprising Afghans appear to have been the first of the company of independent drivers who opened the outback communications service and, in so doing, not only blazed the way but also helped to build a market for the coming railway.

News of what was happening seems to have spread to Karachi. Soon strangers, all experienced cameleers, began to arrive on their own initiative. Each of these independent operators brought his own camels.

In the days immediately before the rail, these men, together with the explorer, the surveyor, the prospector, and the stock owner, opened up the far northern tracks, camelways comparable with the ancient routes of Asia Minor.

So two firm dates emerge: 1867, when Elder started the movement, and 1880, when Hergott had become "a little Asia". It seems that the first tent camp of independent Afghan drivers must have appeared at some time during the intervening thirteen years. But the date may be fixed more exactly than this.

If those of Elder's drivers who set up for themselves stayed with their employer for from three to five years (a reasonable period in which to acquaint themselves with the country and to acquit themselves of their obligation, for Afghan and Pakistani were punctilious in such matters) one arrives at the period 1870–72, the time when the Overland Telegraph was built and the demand for camel transport grew. Camels were used both in survey and construction work on the Overland Telegraph Line. Perhaps most of these came from Elder's station at Beltana, but it seems probable that some belonged to small owners based on Hergott.

The Archives in Adelaide have an undated photograph captioned "The Mosque at Hergott". This shows a tumble-down thatched building by a pool. The picture is puzzling if one happens to know that the foundations of a mosque exist on the outskirts of Marree (the name Hergott was dropped during the first World War) for it shows a long, rectangular building, whereas the physical remains suggest a square structure. The obvious inference is that two mosques existed, one considerably pre-dating the other, and this is confirmed by an old-timer of the region, Mr Allan Crombie.

Allan Crombie was born in Hergott in 1899. He was reared on a station off the Birdsville Track and today holds the lease of country about the famous springs. Many years ago, when he opened up his property, he came upon the ruins of a mosque. He wrote in a letter: "There were two mosques; the first one did serve the tent camp, and the second one was built later, only a short walk from what is called the Afghan Town . . . The picture in the Archives in Adelaide would be that of the first mosque built. The one nearer the town stood right away from any other buildings. The first one was right near their living place." When he first settled near the springs he used to shear his sheep in an old mud building adjoining the first mosque.

What happened seems clear. When the railway arrived, the Afghan drivers abandoned their first camp—half tents, half mud houses—and moved the short distance to the railhead where one of their first acts was to build a second and far more substantial mosque.

All circumstances considered, it appears probable that the cameleers established the first camel communications depot near the strategically-placed springs between ten and twelve years before the arrival of the railway in 1884. So, gradually, a picture of conditions in the region in pre-railway days builds up.

The Department of Lands is unable to supply particulars of the local population at the time when the Government town was surveyed and proclaimed as Marree, shortly before the arrival of the railhead. But the fact that it was surveyed, though negative in itself, at least infers that considerable population existed.

Other notable centres of the camel communications network were Angle Pole, Bourke, Broken Hill, and Broad Arrow. But Hergott Springs was of most consequence.

It is said that at least a hundred strings were based at Hergott during the heyday of the cameleers, or until about the time when the railway arrived. Sometimes a string comprised as many as seventy pack animals. But let us suppose an average of twenty. Then some 2,000 camels worked in and out of this vital distribution centre, though this number would never have been assembled at one time. It seems likely that the figure is an under-estimate.

According to old records, drivers normally left Hergott by late moonlight so that their beasts might rest at noon and thus avoid the worst of the fly plague. So, early each day the camp resounded to cries of "Hooshta!", the cameleer's command when he required an animal to sink down to be loaded or unloaded, and to the groans and roars with which the camels invariably received the order. Then, linked by long lengths of tough cord—from the nose-peg of the hindmost beast to the crupper of the next ahead and so on to the first in line—the camels padded away into the wilderness.

With such picturesque scenes the way for the rail was opened in the north.

Meanwhile, beside the comparatively well-settled southern supply route, through Government Gums and Beltana to Port Augusta, conditions were building up in a different way in gradual preparation for the coming of the rail. But the slow progress satisfied few settlers.

In the year when the colony came of age, or two years before the discovery of Hergott Springs, impatient miners in the Flinders Ranges had pressed for a railway to serve their needs. To say the least, they were a little premature, for at the time construction had advanced only about twenty-five miles north of Adelaide. Predictably, repeated requests elicited unenthusiastic response.

Then there was much talk of horse-drawn "trains". But all proposals were dropped, usually because insufficient feed was available near the routes intended. The miners complained that if only roads were fair, then it might be possible to carry on business profitably until a railway arrived. And in this matter they may have had a point. At the time, William Rounsevell was driving a mail-cart weekly between Port Augusta and Copley, using a nine-horse team "to ensure passage on stretches where the sand was deep". Eighteen years later, when railway building did begin, some reports suggest that no improvement had taken place. On the western plain "the ground is so torn up in places, so boggy in others that one unfortunate who had loaded with wool could only make progress towards Port Augusta at the rate of five miles per day, and in the first six miles capsized and had to unload twice". And again, "Conway's mail from Mernmerna had to be driven over the plain at walking speed with a guide in front supplied with a lantern, and even then narrowly escaped several yawning caverns."

On the other hand William Jessop, a visitor from Britain who rode through the country to the east of Lake Torrens in the year when Herrgott discovered his springs, gave a different picture. In a book oddly named *Flindersland and Sturtland: or the Inside and Outside of Australia*, he remarked: "Rising and falling in a straight line before us was the road to the north, almost as well worn, though only formed by the tracks of drays, as a famous old military way in Scotland to which, in truth, it bore no bad resemblance." And some accounts say that the settlers' track, trodden out in the Willochra Plain and far into the ranges, was equally good. This track was later closely followed by the railway surveyors.

Probably the roads were patchy, fair and bad by districts, their condition regulated by the nature of the soil over which they passed.

Jessop, who was a shrewd observer, held a poor opinion of the miners who led the agitation for a railway. When staying at Wilpena homestead he met two of them, men then engaged in opening the Appilena Mine. "These men," he wrote, "are altogether different in habits and thoughts from the sheep-farmers or shepherds. They have one engrossing object, to dig for money. They care about nothing else. Their labour is hard, their feeling hard, and their speech hard."

Whatever the justification for so harsh a judgement, northern miners, clamorous and pushing, were the first to make a railway "news" in the region. The Great Northern Mining Company opened at Oratunga in 1860 and the directors found transport by bullock wagon both costly and inefficient. So, of course, they pressed for a railway.

However, the Government was unresponsive. It did not regard mining as good railway security. The official attitude appears to have been that no matter how rich the copper-mine, it must eventually reach a production limit, and then the district it had made prosperous would gradually decline. Thus mines ensured no continuity of traffic, and so afforded insufficient justification for expensive railway construction.

But in the south a railway had just been completed to the copper-mining settlement of Kapunda. Perhaps this led the directors to conclude that the Government did not really mean what it said, for now they engaged a civil engineer to survey a route for a northern railway, presumably supposing that this course would influence the authorities in their favour. The proposal was for a line up the western plain from Port Augusta to Parachilna Creek, where it would swing eastwards to Mount Samuel and so to Oratunga.

In submitting the completed survey to the Government, the directors pointed out—as indeed the Federal Government was to do more than ninety years later—that, in so far as grade was concerned, the route along the plain presented no engineering problems.

Months passed without a satisfactory reaction. Of course, the fact was that copper far out on a northern limb was less attractive than copper situated some forty miles from the capital. Furthermore, Government geologists supported Governor MacDonnell's belief—fully justified, as events were to show—that copper occurring in the north came merely in small pockets.

Eventually the Government did react, but in a manner which appears to have been an attempt to satisfy influential people without making any financial commitment. A land-grant railway was proposed. That is to say a promise was given to grant land to any responsible company that would undertake to build a railway and then operate it. But, as might have been anticipated, this proposition interested no one. Grants of western plain lands, which Eyre had thought worthless, proved to be no inducement to undertake the construction of 120 miles of railway.

However, the miners were not easily denied and in the event they were the first to introduce a "train" to the north.

One day the Yudanamutana Copper Mining Company bought the Blinman Mine, so named because it had been discovered by a shepherd, Robert Blinman, in 1859. Soon substantial quantities of copper were raised, but the directors found that transport costs to Port Augusta took most of the profit. At the time, bullockies were becoming increasingly avaricious. For the round trip, Blinman–Port Augusta–Blinman, their demands varied between £9 and £11 a ton. William Harcus, a historian of the day, remarked: "No copper-mine in the world, unless under very exceptional circumstances will afford a cost of £10 per ton for carriage to the seaboard." The need for a railway, he added, "has been admitted for years".

Knowing the strength of their position, the bullockies went further than levying extortionate rates. They withheld their labour as it suited them. They refused to work at all in times of even minor drought, saying that their beasts would suffer from the scarcity of wayside feed.

Camel transport was still five years in the future. The Yudanamutana management had no alternative—for the time being. It continued to pay the teamsters' ruinous charges in the belief that the pressure of the numerous petitions then reaching Adelaide would compel the Government to sanction a railway. But when at last it became evident that the authorities, though prepared to talk a great deal, were still determined to evade the issue, the miners suddenly resorted to an unexpected expedient.

The picturesque events that followed received full coverage in the Press of the day.

News leaked out that the Company's London board had placed an order for several steam traction engines designed to haul loads of up to fifty tons. Then the local management spoke up. Road-trains would transport the Company's copper, since the Government refused to perform its manifest duty.

Naturally, the teamsters who had supposed that their monopoly could not be challenged turned up in numbers to watch anxiously when three engines, each with a train of six wagons, were landed at Port Augusta. First trials took place at once.

It was 17 September 1863, a significant date in a railway context, for the Governor had just received the London dispatch announcing that the Northern Territory would be placed in the charge of South Australia. Thus it was the time when first thoughts were being given to the ambitious idea of a transcontinental line.

The *South Australian Register* described the scene on the wharfside that morning. "On Monday last an interesting experiment took place here in the presence of 70 or 80 persons, namely the trial run of the Yudanamutana Company's traction engines. At the first sound of the steam whistle nearly all the inhabitants of the township, together with a large number of draymen, congregated between Mr Hackett's store and the Yudanamutana Company's wharf to see the great novelty. And at about 10 o'clock steam was got up and the massive but by no means elegant-looking machine got into motion.

"Where the ground was hard and firm it seemed to answer very well and to travel at a very fair rate. But in some places where sand lay deep and loose it proceeded with great difficulty, and on several occasions came to a standstill to the intense delight of a number of bullock drivers who surrounded the engine and became quite enthusiastic when it met with any obstacle. From the short trial made, and the fact that the engines had only just been taken out of the ship and set up and could not be expected to work as freely as after having been used for some time, perhaps it would be unsafe to draw any conclusion as to the prospect of their proving remunerative. But it certainly strikes me that—taking into account the quantity of water and fuel they will have to carry, and their heavy expenses in other respects, the bullock drivers need not yet dispose of their teams."

However, the engines and their trucks were shortly put into service in the confident expectation that they would roar up and down the plain at a majestic five miles an hour. They worked, but roar along they did not, the road being in no condition to accept so high a speed!

A month later, The *Register* reported that a member had moved in the House of Assembly "That an address be presented to His Excellency the Governor praying him to sanction the expenditure of a sum not exceeding £1,000—for the purpose of supplementing an equal amount first expended in making and improving roads and sinking public wells between Port Augusta and the northern mines by persons interested in such mines."

The report continued that the engines had "proved themselves successful in doing their work supposing a reasonable road be made for them". It appeared that, after all, sand caused little trouble. The great weight of the engines compressed it and so the road-trains would prove an immense advantage to all settlers in the region.

So the engines worked backwards and forwards between Blinman and Port Augusta with reasonable success. Now and then one went as far as the Yudanamutana Mine itself. However, the Company found it necessary to continue using a few drays.

One wonders if the directors still hoped to force the Government's hand. No doubt they hoped the road-trains would boost the quantities of ore carried to Port Augusta and so finally convince Adelaide that the colony had a bonanza in the north. If then a railway were to be built, the Company's transport costs would be halved.

Despite the opinions of Government experts, the public had faith in northern copper, and much sympathy existed for the Company's determined stand. But misjudgement brought about an obstacle which proved insuperable. A Company official named Anthony, speaking, it seems, in some bitterness, explained what happened to the editor of the *Register*.

It had been Anthony who chose the road-trains in London. And afterwards, knowing the country in which the machines must operate, he had had the forethought to obtain the authority of the board to establish depots at intervals along the road. "Men were to have both wood and water ready at stated times," he explained. "My instructions on leaving England were to get these stations ready as I progressed with the straightening of the creek crossings." However, "By the ruling of a power superior to my own, the establishment of these stations was blotted out."

Apparently, the "power", whoever he may have been, was over-confident. He seems to have believed that the Government would authorise a railway shortly and that then the road stations would represent so much wasted money. Consequently, he economised—with disastrous results. For by the time the route had been made fit for faster travel, and transport ran smoothly, the engine drivers and their assistant "steerers" had used up wayside fuel supplies and found it necessary not only to draw water from deep wells (a time-consuming chore) but also "to cut wood at such places as were found to be most convenient on their way".

Gradually wood became harder and harder to obtain, and the men had to search farther and farther afield. So it happened that "the real time of steaming in the journeys made amounted to about one-fourth of the time taken to run between two points, the remainder being occupied in getting wood and water". One imagines the exasperation of the engineers!

Finally, the country within practicable distance of the road became stripped of fuel. So through force of circumstance, not to mention mis-management, the Company "wearied of the experiment". Then the cumbersome traction engines were stored in Port Augusta. Eventually, they were sold—one suspects as old iron. So ended the first "steam train" ever to travel in country north of Port Augusta.

The Yudanamutana Mining Company must be regarded as having been unfortunate in its timings. For before long South Australians were to experience dreams of grandeur that caused them to view with equanimity proposals for a railway fifteen times the length of the line the copper-miners had so greatly desired.

Leaving the repair yards, we drove back to the railway station and Len's office, where hung a notice concerning, I supposed, the irritations of train marshalling: "No swearing aloud; lady present." I liked that "aloud".

At the time, Len was awaiting transfer to Whyalla, but he still occupied the stationmaster's house. That evening we left the brakevan, which the Commonwealth Railways had provided for us, to dine with the family. It was a cheery occasion. Ronda, Len's wife, was happy in the thought of returning to civilisation after years spent at outback stations, a view loudly endorsed by the children—Steven, Jo, Cathleen, and Bridie.

Later Dave Miller joined the party. Dave is Managing Director of the firm employed by the Railways Department to control the transfer of goods from standard-gauge to narrow-gauge lines, and vice versa. I had watched the procedure on the previous day. Two trains stood on either side of a platform. Some goods were man-handled, but the greater part of the operation was performed automatically.

Stores consigned to destinations north of Marree are packed in eight-foot, fourteen-foot, or twenty-foot "lift-over" containers that are handled by fifteen-ton overhead electric gantries. If necessary, the gantries operate in unison to lift units of up to thirty tons, provided they can be brought close enough together to achieve even weight on each hook.

When gantries are not used, goods are palletised and handled by forklift. On the southwards run, this applies particularly to bagged copper concentrates from the Peko Mine at Tennant Creek.

Perishable goods are carried in a refrigerated container large enough to serve the needs of all halts between Port Augusta and Alice Springs. Originally this special container was merely an ordinary icebox. But today refrigeration is controlled by a diesel motor. A lift-over of the entire unit is performed at Marree.

The transfer work force varies in strength, but averages thirty men. It seems that accidents seldom happen. Perhaps this circumstance and the healthy climate explain the framed prayer that hangs on a wall in the local hospital: "God bless our mortgaged furniture."

2

AT HOME IN A BRAKEVAN

If breakfast in the brakevan kitchen had a holiday atmosphere, it was, in fact, a business occasion, for we were committed to a definite objective—the story of the Ghan. And as this was an angle of the railway past that had been very little explored, probably we were making ourselves something of a nuisance to busy people whose practical purpose was to handle a railway in the present. Perhaps these people, in allowing themselves to become involved in our project, had incurred more work than they bargained for. However, tolerant people all, they had started us well in this travelling metal-sheathed home which, for obvious reasons, we had christened Silverskin.

It had all begun the previous week when, for a second time, we had called on Mr A.R. Polmear in his office at the railway station in Port Augusta.

Bob Polmear, then Superintendent of Passenger Services, had regarded us so seriously across his heavily-loaded desk that I had felt guilty of interrupting a busy man on a particularly busy day. But he was unruffled. "We thought a brakevan," he said, "and the Slow Mixed."

The Slow Mixed (sometimes called the Marree Mixed), the supply train of the Central Australia Railway, is the counterpart of the "Tea and Sugar" of the Trans-Australian line. But since thirty-five years separate the birthdays of the "Central" and the "Trans", the supply train of the former takes precedence in railway records. In fact, the departmental classification of the Tea and Sugar is "Slow Mixed".

On both railways the principal traffic occurs between the terminal points. But slow trains are needed to maintain the places in between.

The Slow Mixed leaves Port Augusta each Friday afternoon, its length dependent upon the number of general transport trucks that happen to be required. The basic components seldom vary, however: a pay van in charge of a pay clerk; an accommodation van for the use of semi-trailer drivers; beer and bread vans; a refrigerated container; a sit-up coach for inter-halt travellers; and a guard's van. On special occasions a brakevan may be included for V.I.P.s. Apparently this time it was to be laid on even for itinerant writers: Bob, in touch with Melbourne, had set official wheels turning. The outcome was appreciated.

So now, tucked away in a corner of an historic railway siding, we sipped coffee, pictured Hergott as it had been in days before the coming of the first railway navvies with their primitive track-laying equipment, and discussed the day's calls.

It had seemed a good move to start work by making contact with a few railway families, people who form living links with the outback communications network that led up to the railway, before the early days of construction. In Marree one may still talk to ex-camel drivers and ex-drovers, men who once followed the old tracks for a living, albeit they knew them only in the latter days. When the motor-truck, complementing the rail, terminated an era, some of these men joined the railway and, according to opportunity and length of service, became fettlers, gangers, checkers, or roadmasters.

An overhead fan maintained an agreeable temperature, though outside the day advanced sweatily. We drank third cups, looking out at the sun-scorched marshalling yards. Here, before the coming of the rail, the old-time drover had spelled his mob plodding southwards in days when the Queensland Road stretched all the way from Birdsville to Adelaide, a distance of nearly 800 miles. Here the turbaned Afghan, with his cry of "Hooshta!", had eased his camels of their towering loads of baled wool. But all we saw were stones, some rails and, just below our window, a dog that scratched with much content in the shade of the van.

For those without experience of brakevans, perhaps I should say here that any who lay store by "gracious holiday travel", as described in some tourist pamphlets, would probably consider the mod. cons ungraciously limited. But for people like ourselves whose work is travel and whose leisure more work—or very largely so—the *de luxe* accommodation of a crack express compares unfavourably with such individual journeying.

Our van comprised seven compartments linked by a window-flanked corridor. First came an entrance hall, with a corner dais and a chair of such cushioned dignity that it could be only the seat of authority, perhaps of touring inspectors; then a luggage compartment—generous for Royalty, ridiculous for us; two sleepers, each fitted with twin bunks and a table; a shower; a loo; and the diner-cum-kitchen where now we sat. For our odd needs, this was far better than plushly-upholstered, manna-scattered ease. Then there were concealed assets such as a satisfying sense of the unusual, and a gratifying impression of worldly consequence! Someone had said that a brakevan was the style in which the Railway Commissioner himself occasionally made inspection tours.

So here were we achieving Establishment status and indulging—for once with some cause—illusions of Big Brass. To make brakevan grade is nice going for the layman.

Our winning card had been the writer's need to stand and stare at frequent intervals when collecting his material. We required transport a shade more flexible than an express train, and a brakevan hitched to the Slow Mixed exactly filled the bill. Given a little shunting—and the Mixed is never too proud or impatient for this—our van could be uncoupled in a siding where local colour was to be found, and there forgotten for a while.

The dog, ending his scratching, sighed gustily. I sighed, too. The V.I.P. routine was the life, but work pressed. Stacking dishes, I urged Sally to "hooshta" and slid out from under, preserving my shins from assault.

Heat struck as we climbed down to the yard. Marree was thought to be the hottest spot in Australia until Marble Bar registered its claim. And there are some old identities who still dispute the record. On occasions in midsummer, when the north wind drives a haze of hot dust across the gibber plain, few can feel disposed to argue with them. However, contrasted with some regions of comparable trials, this is good country. Malaria, blackwater fever, and bilharziasis are unknown, and if flies are many, mosquitoes are few.

We followed the yard, and a strip of fencing near the station office recalled a tale of murder, a hot-blooded affair of the eternal triangle in the late 1880s. The killing took place by the turnstile, erected, says an old report, at a cost of £6 8s 10d.

Did the killer choose this public place fortuitously, or deliberately to advertise a deed that, doubtless, he regarded as an act of justice on his wife's lover? According to the story, he shot his enemy as the man arrived to catch a train. The turnstile was dismantled long ago, but the dim memory of the vengeance lingers.

Our first objective was the Marree Stores, once known as Northern Enterprises. Business was brisk and we passed through the main shop, a large, low-ceilinged chamber, to a bright sitting-room beyond.

Mormin Khan and Abdul Mutheen Khan, ex-cameleers, were born in Port Augusta. Naturally they recollect only the latter part of the camel era, a period when the railhead still rested at Oodnadatta. But their father, Mullah Assam Khan, an Afghan from country near Kabul, landed in South Australia in the early 1880s. Since he died at the age of eighty-four in 1949, he was then in his teens. Yet he brought with him three camels and so, by the standards of the day, was considered comparatively well-off.

Work on the railway had begun by then, and perhaps the railhead had reached the neighbourhood of Hawker. So Assam Khan began life in Australia by working for the contractors, using his small string of camels to transport sleepers, rails, and supplies for the construction camps. Later he became one of the independent camel owners who worked the outback communications network, then perhaps beginning to be affected by the slow advance of the rail. Probably, when he first went north, the tented camp at Hergott Springs had been transferred to the new township.

Long afterwards, the brothers—each at about ten years of age—joined their father as camel drivers. They carried supplies from the railway to stations round about Marree. But the principal business then lay between the railhead and Birdsville. Usually the journey of 307 miles occupied three weeks with pack camels. But, at need, it could be done in a fortnight, though this meant pushing the string hard. Fourteen miles was a comfortable stage. However, a good riding camel made little of the journey. Once Assam Khan travelled from Birdsville to Marree in three days.

Occasionally dust storms disorganised journeys. A bad storm might blow for most of a week. Then days were so dark that lanterns were carried to light the way.

I asked Mormin Khan about the "smash", popularly supposed to have been the worst tribulation of the cameleer. He seemed to have no strong feelings in the matter. True, camels ran into clumps when frightened. And then loads might become loosened, or even slip to the ground and tangle with the animals' legs. But often ropes caught on bushes and dragged nose-pegs. Then pain and impeded movement usually quietened the beasts so that they could be brought under control with little difficulty.

Though generally docile, camels occasionally were of savage temper and dangerous. I came upon the account of the death of a railway worker who joined a police camel-party travelling south. One morning he went out to bring the animals into camp and did not return. He was found "much bitten, mutilated and quite dead". A camel named Jemadar had his beard, chest, knees, and hobbles stained with blood.

He had knocked the man down and deliberately killed him.

Marree children seem to have enjoyed the arrival and departure of camel strings as much as the movement of trains. They used to run out for three miles when a convoy was expected, for the joy of riding the beasts back to town. Although even today here and there a camel may be found at work on a station, for practical purposes camel transport ended in the late 1930s.

Both Khan brothers worked on the railway when they gave up camel driving—Mormin as fettler, and finally as acting roadmaster, for a total of thirty years; Abdul as fettler and then checker, for eighteen years. They enjoyed every day of it. "Good bosses, good mates," said Mormin.

Guided by a large date palm, we reached the home of Mrs Bebe Nora Bejah, daughter-in-law of Bejah Dervish, the best known of the cameleers. Nora Bejah is the widow of Abdul Jubbah Bejah, who was a member of the 1939 Simpson Desert Expedition and who was as familiar with the Birdsville and Strzelecki tracks as with the railway on which he worked for twenty-seven years.

The room seemed cool after the oven heat outside, but the welcome was warm. Scarcely had my sight adjusted to the shadows before coffee and cakes appeared on a table.

Bejah Dervish became famous after L.A. Wells' expedition to the Great Sandy Desert. Two members left the party in search of water and did not rejoin. Bejah Dervish made five forays into the desert in search of them, but they died of thirst before they were found. Some maps of the region between Lake Way and the Fitzroy River mark Bejah Hill. Wells named this feature for the man he called Bejah the Faithful.

Now Nora Bejah handed me a brass-bound pocket compass bearing the inscription: "Calvert Exploring Expedition. Bejah. 24.5.96." Weighing the little box in my hand, I wondered what a psychometrist would make of its vibrations.

When he settled in Hergott, probably a little before the turn of the century, Bejah Dervish obtained railway contracts. For many years he shared in the wide-flung outback carrying trade, keeping his string moving constantly between the railhead and Birdsville and stations in north-western Queensland. In due course he was joined by his son, Abdul, born in Hergott in 1909—almost exactly a quarter of a century after the railway reached the township. In regions remote from the line, camel transport was still as important as ever. So "Jack", as usually he was called, continued his father's carrying business for nearly twenty years until the time of the Simpson Desert Expedition.

At this period the motor-truck, speedier adjunct to the railway, had obtained a stranglehold on the old, slow-moving trader, and camels were less plentiful. In fact Dr C.T. Madigan, the expedition leader, failed to fill his needs at Oodnadatta and at Alice Springs. But at Marree —the name Hergott was now long forgotten—a large pool of pack-camels was kept, no longer for use on the lonely tracks of the network but for employment on outback fencing jobs.

Madigan needed a cameleer as well as a string. As Bejah Dervish was too old for the work, he realised that nowhere would he find anyone more suitable than Jack, a man of powerful build and wide outback experience.

I asked Nora Bejah if there had been some particular memory of the expedition that Jack had liked to recall in later years. "No, not really." She smiled, suddenly. "Except his little arguments with Dr Madigan about camping sites. He always won these, being in the right." Then I smiled, too. Years of experience of desert ways gave cameleers an irrefutable advantage, and Madigan appears to have recognised this, for on the cover of Jack's copy of his report he wrote: "To Jack Bejah, who played so great a part in our successful crossing."

In early middle life Jack Bejah gave up his string and wagon to take a job as roadmaster's clerk on the railway.

Others made the change at about this time. The Dadlehs, for instance. Today Dene and Charlie Dadleh, whose father came from Karachi, work in the railway repair yards at Marree. We met them there one afternoon when walking with Len. They became camel drivers as boys in the early 1920s when they supposed that they would remain cameleers for the rest of their working lives.

In those days goods arriving from the south by rail paid £12 a ton for carriage to Birdsville. The job was worthwhile.

Merchandise manhandled from the railway trucks was stacked in the siding where it was made up into loads, each consisting of two parts of equal weight. The sections were roped across a camel's large, padded saddle, but were not fixed to it. This procedure permitted the cameleer to make adjustments while his beast was moving, and prevented a slipping load from dragging the saddle.

Edwin J. Brady, author of a *magnum opus* called *Australia Unlimited*, visited Hergott when Dene and Charlie were lads. He described the scene in the railway yard when loads were being made up for a waiting string—the stony ground littered with oil and kerosene drums, tin buckets, bundles of brooms, spare buggy shafts, bags of chaff, biscuit boxes, cases of hardware, bales of drapery, and dingo traps.

An average load weighed five hundredweight. But it was quite common for a strong bull to reach the rail with ten hundredweight of greasy wool. Apparently in the rutting season a heavy load was given to a cantankerous bull; it kept him occupied.

We paused on the shady side of the knife-edge of sunlight in Nora Bejah's front door and looked out at the date palm which recalled a story that, frankly, I had disbelieved. The tale told of a cameleer named Abdul Kadir, who, wearying of wandering the deserts in the service of railway and station owner, decided to grow dates commercially. He took up some ten acres of land a short distance outside the town, not far from the spot where the second mosque then stood. And there he built a mud-brick house and planted a date grove, irrigated with water brought by trench from the springs.

My scepticism regarding this story arose from the knowledge that the fly that pollinates the date palm in North Africa, South-East Asia, and parts of India just does not live in Australia.

True, the story covered this point by saying that Abdul, apparently not discouraged, performed the arduous task of pollination by hand. He would take a stamen, white and powdery, from the male plant and then, carrying a ladder from palm to palm, painstakingly insert this into each female flower. It appeared that his enterprise and patience paid off handsomely, for he supplied the township with fruit and sent consignments to Adelaide.

Well, that's as maybe, I had thought, and put the matter out of mind. But now, as we stood in the doorway, Nora Bejah stepped forward and picked for us—a bagful of dates.

Naturally I made enquiries, and it turned out that the story of the date grove is factual. Abdul did pollinate by hand and he did supply Marree and still have surplus crop to ship away by rail. Nora Bejah has one palm only, but she grows a most excellent date.

Today nothing remains of Abdul's grove. But the tall stump of a solitary palm marks the site of the second mosque, which served the religious needs of the cameleers for about sixty years from the time of the coming of the railway onwards.

Reports say that certain necessities for this building arrived from the south on one of the first trains to reach Hergott. The small building was fronted by a verandah where worshippers removed their shoes before entering, and the windows are said to have been latticed and painted silver. The interior was sky-blue, and here and there hung religious pictures, including one of the minarets of Mecca. In an alcove, the Mihrab, stood a low stool on which lay a silk-covered copy of the Koran.

Writing at the turn of the century when this mosque was some sixteen years old, J.W. Gregory remarked, "Though the Afghans at Hergott cannot get the heavenly coolness of a well-built Arab mosque, they have erected the coolest building in the town."

Len had made the unexpected proposal that we should search for "gems" in the foundations of the walls. It appeared that recently the family had come upon a small treasure of garnets, deep-red and transparent.

A local story had it that sometimes precious jewels such as rubies and emeralds were introduced into the fabric of a new mosque that was to serve a wealthy community. However, cross-desert journeys in the service of outback stations were not so profitable that the Hergott faithful could afford to endow their mosque thus richly. So they did the best they could in the circumstances, offering garnets which, though of small intrinsic value, can be nearly as beautiful as rubies. So garnets, perhaps contained in small bags, are said to have been placed in the fabric of the Marree mosque.

Later, at the mosque of Adelaide—an attractive minaretted building standing in a peaceful, walled courtyard off Little Gilbert Street—I made enquiries of the Imam. It appears that no traditional practice requires the use of jewels in the construction of a mosque. But local customs vary, and probably the camel drivers of Hergott followed the way of the regions from which they came. In any case, the desire to give some article of value to their mosque is universal among Moslems. Incidentally, the camel drivers are likely to have come upon garnets in the course of their travels. In the Harts Range, for instance, the beds of watercourses are covered in "ruby" sand, a beautiful sight.

We were solitary drinkers and he extended a thick hand. "Sam," he said, and offered a beer.

Sam was an ex-drover who had been familiar with the railway at Hergott for more than sixty years. He might, I thought, have been a mate to Donald Hogarth, once stockman to Sir Sidney Kidman and well acquainted with the railway in early days, the Birdsville Track, and the Channel Country. I had met Donald in Queensland when he was in his eighty-fifth year, a grand old man, six feet tall, straight, and still keen of eye and wits. He told many tales of trucking mobs at the railhead, and in between there crept in odd little threads of philosophy. In relation to a recent bush tragedy he remarked that people who fail to take adequate precautions in desert country show no faith in God. Perhaps I looked surprised, for he took me to task instantly. "Given powers to reason, warn't they?" he demanded. "Well, then! People who don't use their gifts show no faith."

An unusual man, I had thought, but over the years I had become less sure of this. Now I watched Sam and found similarities. Not that he resembled Donald physically. He was, perhaps, four inches shorter and his voice lacked the booming quality the other's had possessed. So it must be a matter of occupational stamp!

Sam had worked for a time as a fettler on the line. "Back quite a bit, that. In twenty-one. The Commonwealth had taken over from S.A. about ten years before, an' they was thinkin' of scrapping the stretch from here to Oodnadatta and building a new line through Birdsville. Reckoned they might make a link with the Territory east of Lake Eyre and the Simpson 'stead o' west. Pity they never done it. Better country that way." He grinned. "From over the border meself." He drained his beer. "I recollect they sent round a bunch o' fellers asking questions of everyone."

He was talking, I knew, of the journey made by the Sub-Committee of the Parliamentary Standing Committee on Public Works that prepared an important report on the Central Australia Railway for the information of the Federal Government in 1922. I set up a fresh round.

"Yeah, a pity," he said. "Except fer timber and rails, all they needed was on the spot. An' floods that way wouldn't have been so bad as what they've suffered on the Finke. O' course, when she floods, she floods. The Cooper will spread out—mebbe ten mile. But there's a natural stone crossing above Kopperamanna. I've always reckoned there's a lot o' bull talked about floods in them parts. Floods never worry the stock. Water just rises gradual and the beasts walk away. Then they walk back agen on to rich country and fatten good in three-four months." He nodded across his beer. "Yeah, they should've done that line."

Sam was an old man, perhaps nearly as old as Donald had been at the time of our meeting. He would stare into distance. And his thoughts seemed sad, though perhaps this was no more than the melancholy most of us feel when we watch familiar manners pass away.

He talked of "good" days before the first World War when the big runs that sent mobs to the rail at Hergott lay chiefly in the districts of Camooweal, Cloncurry, and Burketown. These ranged from 2,000 to 5,000 square miles in area and carried between 10,000 and 50,000 beasts. At that time, Queensland herds totalled about 5·5 million animals, principally beef cattle.

Sam pictured the scene of an arrival at the railhead—the mob debouching from the Track; the riders circling to form a turning wheel of cattle; the dust hiding half the balling herd; the first sight of the rail; the rake of trucks moving into position.

An interesting point emerged. One is apt to think of mobs moving straight to holding yards. It appears, however, that first the animals were classified for size, a precaution against injury during the coming railway journey.

Halting his mob on the gibber plain outside the settlement, the boss drover, assisted by his riders, would weave ways through the cattle, cutting out light animals and drafting these apart. Later the divided mob was yarded in separate herds.

Sam's description of the condition of the drovers on arrival at the railhead was forthright—"sweatier'n hell". He explained that a drover always slept in his clothes. "Had to, mate. Come a clap o' thunder, a shower o' sparks from the fire, the crash of a dropped plate even, and they could be up an' running." He chuckled. "No time then to slip into pants—specially if they happened to head through camp."

Mobs of "fats" on the way to meatworks usually comprised three train loads, or about 650 steers. Normally a boss drover handling a three-train mob employed two young riders, an elderly cook, and an Aboriginal horse-tailer. Such a group was known as a camp.

Sam said that a problem of the railway authorities was that a drover might sustain losses on the road and so they could never be sure of receiving the full tally of beasts for which trucks had been booked. Once Jack Clarke—a noted drover and a contemporary of Donald—left Warenda with 500 "fats" for the rail at Hergott. He trucked seventy beasts only. The rest had perished during a dust storm that blacked out a wide region for five consecutive days.

Unpunctuality in delivering mobs at the railhead was a frequent cause of disorganisation and loss. In driving stock along a watered route, a drover's reckoning allowed for seven miles a day, and an estimate of time required became an obligation as soon as the manager of the cattle station handed him his waybill. This was the moment of contract, of recognition that arrangements had been made with the railway for trucks to be in readiness on the date stated.

So punctuality at the railhead went far to decide a drover's reputation. But often circumstance made the attempt to live up to his responsibility extremely difficult. Once Donald and two mates camped at a spot near Kopperamanna with a herd of 150 horses, which in the first years of the century were worth about £3,000. The animals were booked for entrainment at Hergott in three days and with about eighty miles still to travel there was little time to spare.

Shortly before dawn Donald awoke to a crashing roar. A fast-travelling storm had burst overhead and the camp had exploded in turmoil. Stark white flashes lit a frenzied scene as thunder banged. Screaming horses milled and reared. Some, down already, were rolling, their hoofs thrashing.

In moments the herd would be gone, stampeding into the sandhill country. Donald leaped on to a seasoned saddle-horse hobbled near by and rode into the mêlée. And, as he rode, he yelled, for the frantic animals knew his voice.

Cannoned constantly, he bore on one rein, circling. Quickly the nearest horses followed this lead. Others fell in behind. Then horse after horse joined the string. The circling continued until the storm rolled away. The herd reached the railhead intact and was entrained on time.

Punctuality was more than a matter of business to the railway; it was a necessity if traffic schedules were not to become hopelessly disorganised. For, customarily, heavy pressure built up on the line in the droving season. One record of the early 1920s quotes a contractor as stating that some 40,000 cattle travelled the Birdsville Track annually for trucking at Marree. The Birdsville police constable who then was acting inspector of stock was more specific. He gave the figures for five years—1917, 6,136 (sheep, 7,650); 1918, 7,472 (sheep, 16,600); 1919, 8,847 (sheep, 2,339); 1920, 22,929 (sheep, nil); 1921, 31,249. However, the final figure represented ten months of the year only, so probably the contractor's estimate was nearly correct for that year.

During the second World War most of the cattle from the Channel Country reached markets through Windorah. Consequently the railway yards at Marree lost business. But by the late 1940s traffic down the Track had recovered part of its pre-war importance. Then, for a time, the numbers of cattle entrained settled down to rather more than 6,000 steers in a winter-spring season, or about 670 truckloads. In those days twenty-eight vans was the usual load for a class NM steam locomotive, so there were about twenty-four cattle trains in season.

Sam took a long pull at his beer and then exploded wrathfully. "Bloody beef-roads!" he growled.

To read his thought was simple. The movement of cattle and sheep on the hoof has virtually ceased throughout Australia. The day of the drover has ended. Now road-trains have taken over and beef-roads have been constructed for their use.

Until 1958 the Birdsville Track was still just that, an ungraded route. In 1960 the Highways Department allocated $10,000 for minor works such as repairs to creek crossings. But in 1971 no less a sum than $679,760 was spent on the Track. This figure included a Commonwealth contribution of $350,000.

Sam said sorrowfully that the only cattle on the hoof to pass down the Track in recent years had been a mob of 200 beasts which reached the railway yards in 1970. He complained that "the two wars ruined the far back", for all the world as though this was the only harm they had done. "Except fer them, we'd have been spared diesel-powered prime movers fer another fifty year, I reckon," he muttered. He appeared to feel that the drover, not to mention the railway, had been defrauded. But then Sam decried all change.

"You recollect 'The Queen o' Marree'?" he demanded abruptly, and did not wait for me to shake my head. "Used to sing it, riding herd on the road to the rail." He stared into distance.

And there we left it—on a note of nostalgia. Nostalgia, be it noted, for the ways of the drover, not for those of the cameleer. Sam had kind thoughts of one camel only, a beast that was the chief actor in a favourite yarn. "First good camel I ever knew—and the last. She'd carry her boss to the pub, wait like a patient wife till he got good and plastered, and then see him home."

That evening when we reached the brakevan, the top edge of the sun rested on the rim of a wide sweep of desert that looked hard and black in the waning light. Suddenly, as we prepared to climb aboard, four small figures stood beside us. One held out an envelope. Inside lay a generous handful of gleaming garnets. Better treasure hunters than we, Len's children had come to share.

3

GIVE US A RAIL!

They were the best of times, they were the worst of times. So Charles Dickens might have described them had he lived to visit South Australia during the late 1870s. The period was one of abundance for the few, of something less than abundance for the many. But considered from either viewpoint they were great days. Well-to-do and just hopeful alike, men were ambitious, filled with a flowing confidence born of belief in their young colony. Had they been less than this they would scarcely have attempted—unaided and with scant resources—so heroic a task as the construction of nearly 1,800 miles of railway through the heart of an untried continent.

Often to be referred to as the North-South line, the railway was planned as a double operation. Construction was to advance from south and north simultaneously, and the two portions were to meet somewhere in the centre. So the record of what happened in the far north has a place in the story of the Central Australia Railway though, as events turned out, clearing and grubbing for the formation of earthworks in the Territory did not begin until about seven years after building had started in the south. But the story of the line begins in the north.

Probably South Australians began to think of Alexandra Land, or the Northern Territory, as a natural extension of their colony when they learned that John McDouall Stuart had reached the centre of the continent and planted the Union Jack on the summit of a high mound, Central Mount Stuart. Indeed, shortly afterwards, Governor MacDonnell made an application to the Home Government. But this was set aside for the time being, with the implicit advice to wait until one of the colony's explorers had made the complete crossing from south to north.

In 1862 Stuart accomplished this feat, and the colony settled down to wait. Now, surely, the transfer would be made automatically!

This must have been the time when thoughts of a transcontinental railway first intrigued the imagination of many of the colonists.

Parliament placed on the statute book the Port Augusta and Overland Railways Act. This authorised the Government to treat with syndicates interested in building a railway northwards on a basis of land-grant. No destination was specified, but clearly the men who framed the Act had the northern coast in mind. An approved contractor was to be granted two square miles of land for each mile of line built. These ungenerous terms attracted no offers, nor were any received when, two years later, a new Act doubled the consideration.

Meanwhile the communication from London, so confidently anticipated, did not arrive. Finally the Government began to wonder whether a fresh application should be made. And then it transpired that, while Adelaide procrastinated, Brisbane had acted.

It happened that Sir Charles Nicholson, first President of the Queensland Legislative Council, had been in London on business for the Colonial Land and Emigration Commission of which he was Chairman. He took the opportunity to visit the Duke of Newcastle and urged him to provide at once for the government of northern Australia. He followed his call with a letter. "Within a very few months," he wrote, "the desire of occupying new country will tempt many persons, with their servants and flocks and herds, to locate themselves in this new district. The probability also is that many individuals who may have made themselves obnoxious to the laws, will, for the purpose of escaping the pursuit of justice, betake themselves in the same direction."

These, and other considerations, had led Sir Charles to recommend either that a new colony should be established, or that the country should be placed under the guardianship of Queensland. The Home Government referred the matter to the Emigration Commissioners, and the outcome was that control of the Northern Territory was offered, not to Adelaide, so confidently awaiting an approach from London, but to Brisbane.

This development was more than South Australians could tolerate in silence, for it was a period when the colonies were jealous of each other's progress. The Government in Adelaide drew up a series of resolutions in Executive Council. These were sent by the new Governor, Sir Dominick Daly, to the Duke of Newcastle.

Nine months passed. Then a dispatch arrived from London. By Letters Patent, dated 6 July 1863, and signed by warrant under the Queen's sign manual, the Northern Territory was attached to the province of South Australia, but power was retained "to revoke, alter, or amend the Letters Patent annexing the said territory".

Not all were pleased, however. A few politicians—whom time was to prove to be far-seeing—opposed proposals to colonise the Territory. Chief among these was George Fife Angas, the originator of the South Australian Company and one of the founders of the colony. Angas forecast loss and ultimately failure, because the colony lacked the resources necessary to accomplish an undertaking of such magnitude. But despite his great popularity, he addressed a coldly silent House when he urged that, should Parliament decide to proceed, it should not try to establish a sub-colony, but rather should encourage squatters to take up land, and simultaneously form a company to cultivate tropical products.

This advice was ignored. Such slow methods ran contrary to the climate of the times. It was argued that the compact with the Home Government required prompt action and the construction of a railway as soon as possible. So counsels of caution were put aside, and the concept of a great northern dependency linked to the colony proper by a transcontinental railway became firmly fixed in the public mind. However, another project was to receive priority.

As early as 1854, the Government had established a Magnetic Telegraph Department under the Minister of Public Works, and four years later a telegraph line to Melbourne had been completed. Now overseas cable companies showed a desire to include Australia in the world communications network, and South Australians awoke to opportunity. Here was a chance to obtain a first link with their newly-acquired territory, while securing a world telegraphic tie-up which all other colonies would be obliged to support.

So the Overland Telegraph Line was built, almost along Stuart's track.

Meanwhile efforts were made to survey and settle a northern capital. Eventually Palmerston, the township of Port Darwin, was selected. Approximately half a million acres of land were sold to Adelaide and London companies, and to certain enthusiastic albeit disastrously ill-informed settlers, and pastoral and agricultural activities were encouraged. The colony had begun its great task.

Naturally the public experienced a sense of pride in high accomplishment. Now, riding the flood-tide of success, many persons insisted that a transcontinental railway was the proper and indispensable corollary to the Overland Telegraph Line. South Australia should pursue this second project immediately and so doubly justify possession of its new territory.

Promptly adapting to the trend in popular feeling, certain Adelaide financiers floated a company for the purpose of constructing a north-south line. The empire-builders in the community exulted. Action! This was the spirit! But when the promoters, asked for details of their proposal, calmly announced that the land-grant they envisaged was 200 million acres, public enthusiasm waned.

The demand was considered outrageous and may have prejudiced the chances of five competitive submissions advanced shortly afterwards. These also were territorially ambitious, and all originated outside the colony.

Pressing local advantage for all it would carry, the Adelaide company succeeded in arranging for a Bill to be introduced to Parliament. But, because of the terms proposed, there was considerable opposition and the Bill failed to command serious consideration. In fact the distaste for the land-grant system that later developed probably dated from this period.

Clearer understanding of all that a transcontinental railway involved enabled those who had opposed the acquisition of the Northern Territory to exert some influence in the matter of a railway. They said that, for the time being, the colony had spent all it could afford in building the Overland Telegraph Line. And with this point of view many people agreed. Indeed, an opposition party grew up. This party adopted the slogan that a line would never pay, "not even for axle grease", and rebutted the indignant retort that such pinchbeck reasoning had been employed by opponents of the Union Pacific Railroad with the rejoinder that the American line had had to be subsidised by huge Federal grants, and that it was unrealistic to suppose that South Australia could support such outlays.

If the camelmen in the first tented settlement at Hergott Springs had felt anxiety for their monopoly in outback transportation, they now probably concluded that for many years nothing would come of the railway talk, and put the matter from their minds. As one columnist ironically remarked, they were concerned "with the deserts of reality rather than with the wastes of words".

Incessant arguments about the railway wearied most Members of Parliament. However, a few kept the topic simmering with support for the land-grant system, though scarcely on more realistic terms than any so far advanced. In brief, they wished overseas financiers to assume the risk at bargain rates to the colony.

Writing in the 1880s, Edwin Hodder described what happened. A number of "standing dishes" came before Parliament for session after session, the chief among these being the question of "the formation of a railway to Port Darwin". "In August 1873," wrote Hodder, "the oft-mooted subject of a transcontinental railway was brought before the Assembly by the Chief Secretary. It was proposed to grant a quantity of land in alternate blocks of not exceeding ten miles, laid out upon a chess-board system. The line would be open to tender, and the tenderer required to deposit £10,000, and the successful tenderer a further sum of £20,000. The line would have to be constructed in fourteen years, and at the rate of not less than one hundred miles a year; and a train would be required to start from each end of the line at least once a week."

Wordy speeches followed the introduction of a Bill. Supporters pictured the advantages which must accrue from the settlement of "tens of thousands of good, sound, healthy workers in the waste lands". But opponents—far more vigorously determined—denounced the alienation of territory and prophesied disaster from the grant of the fee simple of so great an area as 100 million acres.

Much talk of "bubble companies" and of "the madness and iniquity of such prodigious construction proposals" followed. And, amusingly enough, three determined opponents adopted the "holier-than-thou" position that the House was proposing to set a trap for unwary capitalists.

The debate was resumed from time to time, but the session closed without the question coming to a vote on the second reading.

Finally, several years later, the decision was taken to finance a railway by means of loans. This step was the outcome less of political drives than of agricultural pressures.

A glance at a graph showing the acreage under wheat in the early 1860s will reveal a sharp upward trend. The removal of the British corn duties in 1847 had made possible the export of South Australian wheat. This led to a movement that, among other effects, was to shape the pattern of railway development.

No issue was then more subject to emotional overtones than the rivalry between farmer and grazier. The fathers of the colony had laid down as a general policy that the community should be based upon freehold farming. Thus, in theory, the farmer received first consideration, and from early days the squatter felt himself aggrieved.

Nevertheless the abdication of the "shepherd king"—to use the farmer's satirical description—came about only gradually. The beginning may be dated by the invention in 1843 of a mechanical reaper, John Ridley's "stripper", which placed wheat ahead of wool as a staple product. From then on, the farmer, not the wool-grower, received the consideration that counted. Within twenty years South Australia led the colonies in wheat production.

So when a great drought burned up the countryside from 1864 to 1866, causing enormous loss, the interests of the farmer rather than those of the grazier prompted the instruction that sent Surveyor-General Goyder into the north "to lay down on a map, as nearly as practicable, the line of demarkation between that portion of the State where the rainfall has extended and that where the drought prevails".

The boundary Goyder then established was accepted officially as closely indicating the natural division between desert and arable land.

His "Line" became famous overnight. The grazier now hoped that he might regard the country outside the line as his own. There, he concluded, the State would be unlikely to resume his lease, since it had been established that for the wheat-farmer to plant in this country would be folly. At the time, his assumption appeared to be justified, for then plenty of unoccupied land remained inside the line, which passed through Melrose, south-east of Port Augusta. But this situation was not to last.

In January 1869 the Waste Lands Amendment Act, popularly called the Strangways Act, made land available on credit terms for the first time. By helping the small man, the Act gave an enormous impetus to wheat-growing. Now so many people took up land that by 1874 the entire region which the Surveyor-General considered suited to wheat-raising had been occupied.

That same year a magnificent harvest convinced everyone that the colony must become one of the chief wheat-sacks of the world. Applicants no longer asked for land; they demanded it.

Told that no suitable country remained, they went north to look for themselves. They crossed the Line, now become unpopular, and found great stretches of fine grassland, for again the season was exceptional. The soil, they decided, could be tilled with ease. Comparing notes, they assured each other that where grass grew, there wheat would grow also, and reached the conclusion that here was great farming country.

They had no means of knowing that eighty-two percent of South Australia receives a rainfall of under ten inches annually, and so did not understand that in the region they liked so much, the fall was always unpredictable. If they had realised this, probably they would merely have shrugged their shoulders. For in those days the belief was widely held that tilled soil drew rain even in regions originally arid.

Few of the would-be farmers paused to consider the withering effect of the hot winds. Nor did they pay sufficient regard to the likely depredations of locusts which were, according to a contemporary account, "one of the most serious calamities with which we have to deal".

Finally they did not perceive, as Goyder had perceived, that though attractive-looking soil erratically watered might be worked usefully when the price of wheat was high, when the price fell, uncertain rainfall placed the region beyond the margin of profitable cultivation.

It is possible that some of these men, so determined to grow wheat, were misled by reports brought back by members of the teams surveying and constructing the telegraph line. Many years later an elderly witness, giving evidence before the 1922 Commonwealth Parliamentary Standing Committee on Public Works, quoted from a letter written by his brother, a member of one of Charles Todd's teams during the survey of the Overland Telegraph Line. "On parts of the MacDonnell Ranges millions of bushels of wheat will be grown in the future," wrote the surveyor, adding that the rainfall would be sufficient to grow crops like those grown in the wheat districts of the south. Apparently, fifty years later, the witness still placed faith in his brother's findings, for he concluded his evidence testily with the comment that money should have been spent in "opening up the interior instead of fooling about the cities with suburban railways that do not pay".

Seemingly well-informed opinion such as that of the surveyor may have gone far towards discounting Goyder's warnings. Many young would-be farmers loudly proclaimed their belief that they were being fobbed off with the half-baked notions of elderly and over-cautious theorists. Given proper support, they announced rashly, wheat could be grown all the way to the Centre.

With hindsight, it is difficult for us to see the situation through their eyes. Perhaps their chief reason for placing little reliance on Goyder's opinion was their knowledge of the manner in which he had been deceived by appearances in 1857, when he had written his misleading report on the region north of the Flinders Ranges. Many thought that the Surveyor-General was now playing safe. Just as once his optimism had been unfounded, now his pessimism was without substance. He was, said some, "a scared old man afraid to take a calculated risk".

Goyder, in fact, was not yet old, but they wrote off his advice contemptuously because it did not fit in with their desires. Some even claimed that the "rainfall line" had been laid down as a guide to graziers and without regard to agricultural interests. The "people's grass", they said, had been leased at too low a price, and thus the squatters were able to make fortunes in short order.

Wanting land, the farmer demanded that the pastoralist should be pushed back farther still. "To the Territory border," cried a few. So the bitterness grew.

Sensing uncertainty in the Government, some prospective farmers advanced their demands. They would transform country north of the Line into "a wheat-grower's golden glory". But they must have support.

The railway the miners had sought for so long should be built. Given the land and a railway, they said, wheat would be raised in sufficient quantity to compete with that grown in California.

The farmers knew that in the matter of a railway they had the support of the public. For despite the warnings of a few people who talked portentously of "the malignant grip of the railway mania", the extension of existing lines was discussed constantly, and the thought of a transcontinental line to develop the Northern Territory was in everyone's mind. Mass meetings were held in White's Rooms in Adelaide, for the purpose of forming an association for the promotion of railways. In short, wheat and railways were the topics of the day.

So it is not surprising that a northern railway continued to be a political "standing dish". One day the House of Assembly directed the printing of a petition signed by the people of Cadnia, a mining settlement known until recently as Sliding Rock. This petition requested a railway from Port Augusta to Beltana, "or any point north".

Here again was the old story. The directors wished to invest in promising northern properties, but were deterred by the high cost of transport.

It happened that the Cadnia petition coincided with "a flowing stream of demands". The general tenor of these suits was that South Australia would become of world importance agriculturally, and that in restricting the northward advance of wheat-farming, and in failing to build a railway to assist the supporting mining industry, the Government showed itself blind to the common good. No opportunity was lost to point out that Charles Sturt had been mistaken when he had said, soon after the founding of the colony, that hot, dry summers would prevent the growing of wheat in the Adelaide region. Originally Gawler had been set as the northern limit. After that, the hills of Clare. Later still, the Burra. And so on. Now Mr Goyder and the squatters blocked the path to riches. And, of course, the miners were still without a railway.

Newspaper writers joined in the clamour. Headlines shouted, "Away with Goyder's Ridiculous Line!" and "Goyder's Line of Rainfall all Nonsense!" A leader talked of a galling hindrance to progress that the people should tolerate no longer. A humorist proposed that the Government should present the Line to the Territory where, said he "they have the elevation to give it the treatment it requires". Of course the farmers agreed. Sure! Shove the Line across the Territory border along with the squatters!

Throughout the uproar, the Surveyor-General appears to have remained unruffled. He agreed that much land north of the Line appeared to be good agricultural soil. Then he repeated his warning. Hitherto rainfall had been unpredictable. In the circumstances, to farm the region would be a hazardous experiment. But the farmers merely charged him with wishing to help the wealthy squatters.

Suddenly the Government surrendered, abandoning the Surveyor-General. A new land bill, that certainly influenced the future decision to build a northern railway, was brought before Parliament. The Chief Secretary opened with a statement of the arguments in favour of removing the restrictions imposed by Goyder's Line.

To many graziers this statement represented disaster. Some instantly charged that among the farmers seeking to cross the Line were some who well understood that properties in the north would be useless as farms and desired possession only so that they might obtain payment to leave. Such men, it was angrily suggested, proposed to make the Government a pawn in a game of blackmail.

Promptly the farmers counter-charged that the graziers were drones who spent their time drinking and gambling in town clubs.

In general, all the charges were groundless.

Records of the debates that occurred reveal the continuing intensity of feeling. Perhaps the squatters' extravagant reactions influenced Members who were still undecided. Anyway, when Goyder's views were raised afresh by the Commissioner of Crown Lands, etiquette collapsed. Jeers and catcalls greeted each fresh reference to the "line of rainfall".

And so a new Waste Lands Amendment Act became law. This opened for credit-selection unappropriated land "situated south of the twenty-sixth parallel of south latitude" (in other words the northern border of South Australia). The Line had been shoved into the Territory in very fact.

Then began a northwards movement which many level-headed people described as a "land panic".

A railway was now only a matter of time. For having forced the land issue, the farmers pressed their demands for cheap transport for the fabulous crops they announced they would raise. In this they became aligned with the miners and even with the distant graziers, who were unlikely to be soon affected by the advance of farming. All wanted a railway.

Action came surprisingly quickly. In the following month, a Railway Commission was appointed to "estimate the probable direction of traffic and the requirements of the country for railway accommodation" and to make recommendations. Ironically the Chairman was G.W. Goyder. His feelings must have been mixed when he took his seat at the head of the Board.

The Commission's report was submitted in August 1875. It covered an unexpectedly wide field and must have caused headaches to the

Government.

Realising the intense rivalry that existed between districts, and knowing that everyone could not be satisfied quickly, the Commission wisely prepared a list of "priorities". This schedule was divided into four sections, arranged in order of urgency. In the first section there appeared a recommendation for "a long line deep into the northern interior from Port Augusta, via Pichi Richi Pass and the Willochra Plains, to the Yudanamutana copper district".

Though he still wished to dissuade wheat-farmers from settling in the north, Goyder favoured outback railways because he believed that these would secure for South Australia a share of the interior trade of neighbouring colonies. Thus, in the fourth section appeared a recommendation for two lines from Mannahill Well, one north-easterly and the other easterly, running respectively to the borders of Queensland and New South Wales.

Immediately the Commission's findings became known, a cry went up from the farmers: "Give us the rail!"

Simultaneously, Goyder became as unpopular with the people of Port Augusta as with the northward-pushing farmers. For the second section of the report contained a recommendation to link the Adelaide–Gladstone system with the proposed far northern line by means of an extension running due north to Willochra. Acceptance of this proposal would have resulted in a line that by-passed the little port at the head of Spencer Gulf, thus frustrating its ambition to become "the Liverpool of the south", a description already adopted by its enterprising inhabitants.

As it happened, the by-pass was to follow a different and equally displeasing route.

A Bill for the construction of a northern railway was sanctioned by Parliament early in the following year.

Act No. 26 of 1876 authorised "the formation of a line of railway from Port Augusta to Government Gums", 200 miles of narrow-gauge track to consist of iron rails each weighing forty pounds a yard. The Act contained a number of interesting and, in places, entertaining provisions.

It may be hard to credit nowadays, but the basic conditions laid down in Clause 3 were accepted cheerfully by the people of the time: "Trains carrying goods, or goods and passengers, shall not travel at a greater rate of speed than fourteen miles an hour; and trains carrying passengers only shall not travel at a greater rate of speed than twenty miles an hour."

One is reminded of a story of the Royal Train in Queen Victoria's time which, of course, was the time of the Act. Should it appear to the Queen—a nervous traveller—that the fields were sliding too rapidly past her stateroom window she would send an urgent message forward: "Mr Driver, not more than twenty, please."

The charges that the Commissioner might levy appeared in Clause 5: "(i) In respect of the tonnage of all articles conveyed upon the said Railway, or any part thereof not in this Act otherwise particularly specified, the rate of Ninepence per ton per mile. For wool, measurement goods, fruit and furniture, One Shilling per ton per mile. For every description of carriage, not being a carriage adapted and used for travelling on a railway, and not weighing more than one ton, carried or conveyed on a truck or platform, One Shilling and Threepence per mile; and for any ton or fractional part of a ton beyond one ton which any carriage may weigh, Eightpence per mile.

"(ii) In respect of passengers and animals conveyed upon the said Railway in carriages whether belonging to the said Commissioner or otherwise as follows: For every person conveyed in or upon any such carriage, being a first-class carriage, or compartment of a carriage, Fourpence per mile. For every person conveyed in a second-class carriage or compartment, Threepence per mile. For every horse, mule or ass or other beast of draught or burden conveyed upon the said Railway, Sixpence per mile; and for every ox, cow, bull or meat cattle so conveyed, Twopence per mile. For every calf, sheep, lamb, pig or other small animal conveyed in or upon the said Railway, one Halfpenny per mile. Provided always that for every fraction of a mile a full mile may be charged, and that for any shorter distance than three miles, three miles may be charged."

Clause 9 detailed the tolls that might be levied for small articles and packages. "Notwithstanding the rates of tolls hereinbefore prescribed, the said Commissioner may lawfully demand the tolls following, that is to say, for the carriage of any parcel not exceeding twenty-eight pounds in weight, One Penny per mile each; for any parcel not exceeding fifty-six pounds in weight, Three Halfpence per mile; for any parcel not exceeding one hundred and twelve pounds in weight, Twopence per mile; for the carriage of any one boiler, cylinder or single piece of machinery, or single piece of timber or stone or other single article the weight of which shall exceed four tons the said Commissioner may demand such sum as he shall think fit."

The Act closed with an interesting provision: "The Railway by this Act authorised to be constructed shall be, and is hereby declared to be, exempt from all rates and taxes whatsoever whether local or general."

Obliged to think in terms of limited outlay, the Commissioner planned a cheap railway that would cope with the light traffic expected to pass, within a few years, between the southern and northern coasts of the continent.

Much still remained to be done before construction could begin on the "P.A. and Gee-Gee Railway". The odd name—perhaps inevitable in view of the speed of the trains—appears to have been employed affectionately, but it dropped out of use when the name of the temporary terminus, Government Gums, was changed to Farina.

First, arrangements were made for the survey of the route of the railway. Then orders for building materials and rolling-stock were placed, in the knowledge that many months must pass while the goods were shipped across the world from Britain and landed in Port Augusta for the use of contractors. Tenders were invited, but it took time for interested companies to examine the country, and then for the resulting proposals to be considered. It was a long process.

The orders included thousands of tons of rails and fastenings; twelve turntables; five weighbridges; switches, crossings, and signals; bridging; engines; and wagons. The tender finally accepted was for £578,944 7s 6d, including contingencies of £52,631 6s 2d. The successful tenderers were the firm of Barry, Brookes and Fraser, and they signed their contract in October 1877.

The new contractors appear to have been businesslike people for, according to the Engineer-in-Chief's report, they began excavation, clearing, and grubbing within a few days of signing the contract which divided the project into three phases, with dates fixed for the completion of each.

Generally, the first phase is said to have ended at Hawker, but the Engineer-in-Chief's report for 1877 gave the termination as Wonoka, beyond Hawker. Wonoka was a new wheat town, the only one surveyed to the north of Hawker, and sometimes it was known as Hookina, despite the fact that the original Hookina was situated lower on the creek and had been surveyed some five years previously.

The first section was a few chains short of sixty-five miles, and the completion date was fixed for 1 October 1879. The dates for the second and third phases were: Wonoka to Beltana, seventy-four miles, 1 October 1880; Beltana to Government Gums, fifty-five miles, 1 October 1881.

Unquestionably, the man in the street regarded this contract as the first move in the construction of a transcontinental railway. He believed then that in twenty years at the most Adelaide and Darwin would be linked by rail. Had not the Overland Telegraph Line, despite some major problems, been built with efficiency and dispatch? A similar outcome might be anticipated in this new and greater enterprise. It was, indeed, a courageous viewpoint for a colony of slender resources and a population of 225,677!

The Survey Department had been enlarged in the previous February.

So, in August, a few days after the Act became law, the railway survey opened from headquarters in Port Augusta.

Many people had supposed that the line would follow the western plain where, long before, steam road-trains from the Blinman Mine had puffed their heavy way. Indeed, recently, part of this track had been surveyed afresh. But now it was set aside—partly because the Commission had recommended a route through the Willochra Plain, but perhaps chiefly because the Engineer-in-Chief, H.C. Mais, advocated the way through the Ranges. Later, Mais said, "I brought considerable blame on myself by so doing." However, there seems no doubt at all that the wheat-farmers, then establishing settlements in the northern Willochra area, influenced the decision.

Thus the survey teams set out towards Saltia and the Pichi Richi Pass, following a road surveyed by George Goyder nineteen years earlier. Some surveyors rode horses, others camels. One snapshot shows four men standing with camels, riding and pack beasts. Probably the photo was taken that Christmas. In any case, the occasion appears to have been a celebration for each man holds up a mug which—judging from cheerful expressions—held a liquid more convivial than the tea or coffee proper to it.

Another print—faded and crinkled—pictures a surveyors' camp. Rough poles, supporting leafy branches laid cross-wise, make an adequate bush office. A tarpaulin, slung over a rope pulled taut between two conveniently-spaced trees, affords rain-proof if not dust-proof sleeping quarters. A bucket, suspended from a pole supported on forked uprights, hangs over a log fire.

One knows instantly that this picture, unlike the snapshot, was taken for the record. A waste-bin, placed obtrusively in the foreground, suggests a set scene. Five surveyors stand in self-conscious poses, each with the air of strained expectancy that seems always to have attended the click of the early hooded camera.

These were the men who are said to have sought the advice of local Aborigines respecting the ancient ways of the region. The Aborigines' pads were known to follow routes least subject to flooding. So in considerable part the railway survey was shaped by the path once taken by the red-ochre trade.

William Jessop described the old Aboriginal track. He wrote that it left a gorge near Aroona (an important source of the sacred red earth) to wind southwards across the site of Port Augusta and on to the Noarlunga district. The Aborigines, who were numerous in the Ranges in the 1870s, used the ochre to paint their bodies with ceremonial designs in preparation for corroborees and other tribal occasions. It appears that trading parties from distant tribal grounds were allowed unhindered passage, provided they passed back and forth within agreed periods of time. Boomerangs, lost or discarded, are still found near the route the railway surveyors mapped.

Trading camps, said Jessop, were spaced at intervals of about 150 miles. Here the coloured clays were exchanged for shields and spear shafts made from woods unobtainable in the Flinders Ranges and southern regions. The red-ochre track continued northwards—the future route of the railway through Parachilna and the Hergott Springs district. Afterwards, it struck north-eastwards to Boulia, with a branch through Kopperamanna to Charleville.

When barter was completed, visiting parties (never, it seems, more than three strong) left at once, each man carrying on his head a square block of ochre weighing up to fifty pounds.

Travelling with such burdens, the Aborigines naturally took pains to find the most reliable routes. The railway surveyors turned this circumstance to advantage.

Wonoka became headquarters for the second phase of the survey. Its hope so far pinned to the wheat drive, the settlement now added the coming railway to plans for an ambitious future. A wheat-raising centre and an important railway depot! The *Port Augusta Dispatch* remarked at this time that: "Wonoka bids fair to become one of the great commercial centres of South Australia." Already the settlement had saddlers' and bootmakers' shops, a post office, a hotel, and a boarding-house, which was then a signal distinction. But one wonders if the editorial comment was made in irony or simple faith. For today Wonoka is no more.

Clearly news of the coming railway was rippling through the north in waves of optimism. A dozen new settlements dotted the route of the survey to the Government well, situated at a bend in Leigh Creek, where a lonely clump of gum trees gave rise to the odd name of the future temporary railway terminus. But only at Wonoka was there a boarding-house. The hopeful township appears to have prinked itself out to receive the surveyors who, for a brief period, found the boarding-house a welcome change to camp life.

However, of all the future railside settlements, Quorn was progressing most rapidly. The *Dispatch* noticed its surprising growth. One day a hotel-keeper and three friends drove out from Port Augusta to choose a site for the Par Excellence Hotel. The hotelier and one companion left the buggy and promptly became lost in the bush. Much cooee-ing failed to locate their friends with the vehicle. So, uncertain of direction, they set out to tramp to the head of the Pichi Richi Pass. By chance only did they find the track.

Six months later two hotels, a large stone flour mill, several shops, and a number of dwellings had been built. Quorn had the best position of all and its future advance reflected this advantage.

The railway surveyors came and went through Port Augusta, their activity coinciding with a period of rapid development in the little gulf-side settlement which, with a population of about 600 persons, had been incorporated as a town in the previous year.

Built on a bank of red sand that blew in clouds on windy days, The Port had experienced twenty-five years of doubtful prosperity. The whitewashed walls of a few stone buildings shone in the blazing sunshine and scorched the dust-whipped eyes of the inhabitants so that ophthalmia was common among them.

Long ago, the surrounding country had been swept of the pine and black oak that had grown in modest profusion when A.L. Elder had named the spot after Lady Augusta Young, wife of Deputy-Governor Sir Henry Fox Young. At that time thick undergrowth stabilised the sand. But this had been cleared by herds of goats which, according to one account, camped at night in the streets, made all corners stink, and turned the settlement into a goat-yard.

But a town seemingly destined to become the southern terminus of a grand trunk railway spanning the continent was a place where capital might be invested safely. So in the year the surveyors arrived two hotels replaced the old wooden Dover Castle pub; a newspaper-cum-printing business was established; and a police station was built. During that year the telegraph line linking South Australia and Western Australia was completed. Thus The Port became the meeting place of two overland telegraph systems—one to Perth, the other to Darwin.

The population now rapidly increased to over 2,000 and, suddenly grown self-conscious, the community enforced a new by-law that imposed fines upon goat-owners who allowed their animals to stray in public places.

Hitherto eight short, ramshackle jetties had handled the export of small quantities of wool and copper. Now the decision was taken to build a railway wharf suited to "the huge wheat outflow" so confidently anticipated. To make room for this wharf, five jetties were condemned, though demolition was delayed until all railway materials from Britain had been landed.

Such were the beginnings of the railway, which some people already described as The Great Transcontinental.

4

BUILDING BEGINS

Oddly enough no record appears to have been kept of the October day when the earthwork gangs moved out of Port Augusta. Clearing and grubbing in the direction of Saltia, a teamsters' settlement twelve miles distant, they left town, if not unnoticed, without an official gathering to mark the importance of the occasion.

Of course, there was a good reason why the ceremony of turning the first sod was not held at this time. But, in the circumstances, the start of work might have passed without special notice even in the local Press, save for a murder and an attempted murder—happenings which hit the headlines.

On the afternoon of Monday 26 November 1877, Patrick Bannon, a construction navvy, was found battered to death in a dry part of the creek at Saltia. He lay in a pool of blood with his head in his swag. A fellow navvy, Hugh Fagan, was arrested.

Reporting the crime, The *Dispatch* writer stated: "The prisoner when taken in charge and cautioned made no statement but afterwards said, 'I hope that this will be a caution from the South Australians to the Victorians.' "

Three weeks later the newspaper reported further violence on the line: "We have had a narrow escape from having to chronicle another homicide among the navvies on the railway." At the Saltia inn "an Italian was set upon. In the scuffle, he picked up a pair of scissors used for trimming lamps and stabbed a navvy named McGrath." The injured man was taken to Port Augusta. The Italian escaped.

Christmas and the New Year passed without further news of what was happening in the country outside The Port. And then, on 19 January 1878 the first sod of the railway was turned—officially.

Wide publicity was given to this event. Perhaps editors had felt that it would be incorrect to comment upon progress on the line until after the Governor of South Australia, Sir William Jervois, had made his visit. However, it is clear that the earthworks had advanced into the entrance to Pichi Richi Pass by the time Sir William arrived to give official sanction to the proceedings. The Governor had not been dilatory. The explanation of the unusual state of affairs is to be found in a succession of unexpected events in Adelaide.

In January 1877 Sir Anthony Musgrave, who had assented in the name of the Queen to the Act authorising the railway, had left the colony to take up an appointment as Governor of Jamaica. Justice Way had filled his post until the end of March when the new Governor, Sir W.W. Cairns, landed. But within four weeks of his arrival, ill-health compelled Cairns to resign. Again Way became acting-Governor until Sir William Jervois arrived at about the time when the contract for building the railway was signed. So the new Governor had been in the colony for three months when he made his first visit to Port Augusta. The pressures of taking office had prevented him from performing this important ceremony earlier, and probably he felt that since construction was well away already the delay made little odds.

Governor Jervois was a decisive person. Whenever an occasion appeared to him to drag he took the initiative. This trait caused some amusing incidents when the long-anticipated ceremony took place.

At eleven o'clock in the morning the *Governor Musgrave* made fast in mid-channel. At once the Mayor of Port Augusta, supported by the Town Clerk carrying an address of welcome, prepared to put out to the vessel. But His Excellency, who appears to have assumed that a small boat with a deputation aboard would have been waiting at the anchorage, frustrated their purpose by coming ashore.

The meeting thus took place on a crowded jetty hampered, according to an irate editor, "by a few snobs who endeavoured to obtrude themselves upon His Excellency's attention and succeeded in preventing His Worship from formally introducing the members of the Council".

However, the brass band performed well, "considering that they had been in practice a few weeks only".

Then, again, the Governor upset carefully planned arrangements. For the party set off "pell mell to the Institute", while the Town Clerk, who expected a procession to form, was left behind. "So," continues the account, "there was to be seen the apparition of an excited Town Clerk flying up Commercial Road." Apparently, the distraught man, hurrying through an arch hung with flowers, plunged, breathless, into his address which described at length a railway that would "form a speedy means of communication between this colony and its possessions on the northern coast".

Responding briefly, the Governor was off once more. Now the procession that the Town Clerk had awaited at last formed in front of the Institute, with the Mayor himself driving Sir William in an open carriage. But still the desired formality was missing. For "it is no joke to wade through Port Augusta sand, and it is not at all to be wondered at that the procession was not as originally intended. Those who could made as short a cut as possible to the rendezvous."

At a spot where already the railway earthworks disappeared towards the east, about 2,000 persons had assembled. Here the official party was met by "Mr Barry with his manager, Mr Tidy, and a portion of the extensive staff connected with the work". Barry presented the shovel, a gift from the contractors. It was nickel-plated and had a blackwood handle.

Attended by the Engineer-in-Chief, Sir William performed his task in "a most businesslike manner". Indeed, so prompt was he first in wielding the shovel and then in delivering his address, that he disorganised the Mayor's timetable. "His Excellency, having got his work done very expeditiously, waited for what was to happen next. It was scarcely 12 o'clock when the party returned to the town and, as the luncheon was not to be ready till 1 o'clock, His Worship the Mayor entertained His Excellency and the Parliamentary party at his private residence."

Already disturbed by unexpected changes in his carefully planned schedule, the Mayor suffered further annoyance immediately the guests —numbering about 140—had returned to the Institute and taken seats in the main hall. For now a water-carter, a well-known local character, who, perhaps, had been drinking a fluid stronger than that he purveyed, found an opening between two visitors. Suddenly leaning forward, he seized a turkey from the table and, in the words of the newspaper report, "began the study of anatomy". Fortunately, "when informed by the Secretary to the Committee that he had made a mistake", he left quietly.

The speech that the Governor delivered consorted well with the sentiments of the time. An extract from the report that appeared next day illustrates the tenor of his remarks. "He believed it was Trollope who said that this railway was to go through a desert to nowhere. But he ventured to say that it did not go through a desert and that it went everywhere. If it only went to Port Darwin it would be worth constructing. But in going there it went to Java, India, Siam, China, and also shortened the communications with Europe and America. The line would ramify eventually to Queensland and New South Wales, and who could tell the full benefits which would accrue from connecting all these colonies with the iron band of a railway?"

When the Governor had finished, the applause was prolonged. Such views as these were sure to win approval. Many speeches followed, for the luncheon appears to have been an excellent one. Among the speakers was the Premier, J.P. Boucaut, who had introduced the policy of railway expansion. A forceful, popular man! None the less, he appears to have been apt to trail his coat. As reported, he now remarked in respect of the importance of the task about to be undertaken, "We may reply to Victoria's threat of annexing South Australia that we should be more likely to annex Victoria."

The Governor embarked at four-thirty after having taken only five-and-a-half hours to inaugurate a project which he described as being of greater importance than any that had been introduced in other colonies! But the people liked his hustling ways. In a phrase to become popular many years later, he made them feel that they were "going places". A Beltana settler summed up the popular feeling in a letter to the Press. "The turning of the first barrowful of soil, sand, or sea-shells at Port Augusta of the Port Augusta and Government Gums Railway has been hailed with pleasure. All speed to it, and may it never cease to extend until it reaches Port Darwin and becomes the Transcontinental Railway."

Meanwhile, the Governor—seemingly as confident in the privacy of his study as on the public platform—wrote to the Earl of Carnarvon in the Colonial Office, London: "The immediate object of my trip to Port Augusta and Port Pirie was the ceremony of 'turning the sod' of an extensive railway which is about to be constructed . . . Port Augusta is the harbour to which all the pastoral, agricultural and mineral resources of the country to the North, North-east and North-west will converge. It will, ere long, be the port of the produce of a large portion of the Western part of New South Wales and the South-western portion of Queensland. It will be the Southern terminus of a Transcontinental Railway, about 1,800 miles in length, which will ultimately be carried through the Province of South Australia to Port Darwin."

Optimistic, brave words from a capable man with little talent for prophecy!

Soon after the ceremony at Port Augusta, Barry, Brookes and Fraser established a main camp with workshops and offices at Woolshed Flat in the Pichi Richi Pass. By this time clearing and grubbing had reached a spot about ten miles beyond the camp. Now the contractors' men were strung out in large parties at more or less regular intervals along twenty-five miles of roughly prepared track.

These workers included many Cousin Jacks, Taffies, Jocks, and

Paddies, as well as about 200 non-European labourers, who were carefully assembled in gangs of their own.

It is sometimes supposed that the contractors were placed under an obligation not to engage coolie labour, that the Darwin to Pine Creek Railway—commenced some years later—was the only line in Australia on which such labour was permitted. That this assumption is mistaken is proved by a leader published in the *Dispatch*: "The fact that we have now in the neighbourhood about one hundred Chinese labourers, a small instalment of the number likely to be introduced for carrying out the railway work between here and Government Gums, is a subject we think worthy of serious consideration."

The editor discussed the topic at length, on the whole favouring the move, provided care was taken to balance the sexes. He concluded: "The Government of South Australia have invited competition for the purpose of getting their railways built as economically as possible and have accepted the lowest tender for the work. The contractors then have the right to employ the kind of labour which will suit them best."

None of the Chinese was skilled in any trade. They worked as labourers, carrying materials in large baskets to form embankments and the track bed. Their first camp was situated near Port Augusta. From here, they worked forward up-line in parties, care being taken to site their camps apart from those of European workers, for there was strong feeling respecting the use of Asian labour. It is said that for a time resentment was so keen that some of the European navvies threatened to burn down the tents of the Chinese labourers. But nothing came of this.

Though at Woolshed Flat and later at other important construction camps some wooden hut accommodation was provided, generally speaking the navvies lived in tents. A picture of camp life may be formed from stories of a practical joke usual among young men with a primitive sense of humour. The frequent practice of these types was to tiptoe round the lines at night untying the ropes of tents on one side and then pushing the canvas over on top of the sleeping occupants.

As news came in of the advance of the line, many young men sought railway work, drawn by the romance of the undertaking and by stories of Union Pacific adventures. In this respect the situation was soon to change, but for the time being plenty of labour was available.

Though the line was planned as the opening phase of an epic operation comparable with American transcontinental construction, the building did not proceed in so flamboyant a style. Rough characters were present in the gangs, as frequent outbreaks of violence proved; but compared with the polyglot rabble of multi-national labourers who blazed the roaring Union Pacific trail, the navvies who built the

Australian railway were a law-abiding assemblage. There was good reason for this.

As a community the South Australians of 100 years ago were a family-based, middle-class society of regular church-goers. Until the turn of the century books on religious subjects obtained higher sales than serious novels.

South Australia had been fortunate. The outlook of the people was unaffected by traditions of penal servitude, and so unclouded by shadows of unhappy memories. The colony had no Prinsep to write sadly in *Letters from Van Diemen's Land*: "If the histories of every house were made public you would shudder; even in our small ménage our cook has committed murder, our footman burglary, and our house-maid bigamy."

Some records have it that the colony was planned "as a paradise for Nonconformists", that the Colonial Missionary Society considered it "a sphere of labour for Independents". So, probably, "independent" rather than "turbulent" is the description that most fairly pictures the navvies of the northern construction gangs.

However, the wild element was present, and the Government took no chances when instructing Barry, Brookes and Fraser. The contractors received orders similar to those issued nine years before to the organisers of the Overland Telegraph Line. Charles Todd had been placed under an obligation to do everything possible to ensure the morals and general good behaviour of the men under his direction —the camps of Aborigines were to be placed out of bounds; no communication whatever was to take place between the workers and Aboriginal women; and so on.

There is no doubt that in the early days the people were in love with the idea of their new railway, the first phase of the Great Transcontinental. Popular feeling was on the up-and-up. The new wheat-farmers establishing themselves north of Goyder's Line were confident—even, according to some accounts, exuberant. Not that the Government was popular on account of its recent compliance. On the contrary it was energetically attacked in many quarters. One newspaper spoke scathingly of "the *vis inertiae* of the leaden brains of our shopkeeping lawmakers". And, contemptuously, of "Our colonial statesmen—save the mark!"

But events appeared to be moving once more in favour of the colony, and few people were disposed to heed the warnings of croakers, especially those of George Goyder who, maintaining his equanimity, still talked of the risks of an unpredictable rainfall and a withering hot wind.

Advanced construction headquarters at Woolshed Flat had just been finished when the main part of the railway supplies began to flood in to Port Augusta from Britain.

Now a dozen vessels were sharing the work of transporting equipment across the world. Most were small ships. The *Glaramara*, the *West Riding*, and the *Royal George*, all three-posters, carried the greater part of the traffic. A record says that in the month when the railway contract was signed, a seaman, Benjamin Smith, was charged with desertion in Port Augusta Police Court and ordered aboard the *Glaramara*. It appears that Smith's purpose had been to enrol as a navvy on the line.

Barry, Brookes and Fraser had opened two large yards on the wharves. In one, huge stacks of rails and sleepers were rising steadily; in the other, recently-landed rolling stock was marshalled.

The locomotives were 2-6-0 W Class engines, Numbers 19 to 23, and 25 to 28, built by Beyer, Peacock and Company of Manchester. Apparently, the Railways Department sold numbers 22 and 23 to the contractors as soon as they came ashore. A little later four more were hired to them for use in the early stages of construction, for these were not listed officially as working the railway until June 1881.

Rolling stock was of the primitive type then in use overseas. In Britain, at first rail travel had been thought to be "low class", perhaps because no washing or lavatory accommodation was available on early trains. The original first-class coaches were four-wheeled and had three compartments, each fitted with six seats. For some years doors were locked on leaving stations, lest nervous passengers should jump out. Usually second-class coaches had side walls to waist level only. (Apparently it was considered unimportant whether or not these lower-paying passengers leaped out.) Third-class carriages were just open wagons without seats. These vehicles comprised the greater part of the accommodation on the famous "Parliamentary train", introduced when the Cheap Trains Act obliged railway companies to run a proportion of trains providing inexpensive third-class fares. The "Penny-a-miler", as it was also called, stopped at all stations and travelled at about the speed of the first South Australian trains.

The rolling stock landed at Port Augusta included some improvements on these early arrangements, but it afforded few amenities and little comfort. There was no internal means of passing from one coach to another, and staff had to shuffle precariously along the running boards while trains were in motion. Lighting was provided by dim, evil-smelling kerosene lamps.

Deliveries from Britain had been arriving punctually. The contractors' organisation moved smoothly. Then suddenly trouble developed, and for a time it seemed that construction might be halted.

By now rails had been laid beyond Saltia, and a work-train had begun to move up and down the short stretch of line between Port Augusta and the railhead. Then, one day, a ganger reported a fault in materials his party had handled. Later the Engineer-in-Chief stated tersely: "The rails which have been received for this section are of a most inferior quality, and the majority will be unfit for use."

Following this disturbing discovery, some 1,500 rails—a part of the materials landed from the *John Patterson*, the *Jessie Osborne,* and the *Andes*—were taken at random from the huge stacks in the yard and tested. The test consisted of dropping a wedge-shaped iron block weighing about 500 pounds, from a height of sixteen feet on to a rail placed across iron supports three feet apart.

Only about 250 rails were considered to have withstood the test satisfactorily. About 140 broke in halves. Many of the others became so seriously bent as to be useless until re-rolled.

However, excellent results were obtained with 500 samples taken from stacks assembled from cargoes landed from the *West Riding,* the *Steelfield,* and the *Oban Bay.*

The test merely enabled engineers to estimate the percentage of defective rails likely to be present in the stocks held. It was not used as a means of dividing good from bad in those dispatched daily to the railhead, or in those already laid.

An enquiry was held in the Courthouse at Port Augusta. The proceedings were *in camera*, but details soon leaked. It seems that the Government had instructed the Agent-General in London to appoint inspectors to examine the rails before they were shipped. This had been done, but the examiners had been incompetent or corrupt. It was decided to demand compensation on an estimated 6,000 tons of rails at £6 per ton.

A funds-saving procedure was adopted. It was ascertained which cargoes held doubtful materials. And experts decided that most of the defective rails could be used safely in sidings and on sections of line that were free of curves.

In the upshot the defaulting firm was declared insolvent. It seemed that about £36,000 had been lost. However, eventually a refund of £20,000 was secured. Since the faulty rails were retained and, in large part, utilised, the colony was little out of pocket.

Meanwhile a temporary holdup in the supply of rails to Woolshed Flat delayed construction, already slowed by engineering problems encountered in Pichi Richi Pass. Descriptions left by J.F. Hayward, a pioneer grazier whose drays were the first to bring wool down to Port Augusta twenty years earlier, give an impression of the nature and extent of these problems. Hayward wrote of capsized wagons, of steep slopes in a winding gorge where bullocks were lamed and dray wheels smashed. No more than a bed load—or five bales—could be taken through the pass at a time. Even then, double-banking (two teams yoked together) was necessary. Hayward had camped at Saltia to rest the exhausted oxen, to wedge tyres loosened from wheels, and otherwise repair a greatly damaged outfit.

Since Hayward's time Goyder had built a road. But railway construction here was hard going. And now, down past the sweating navvies, other wagons came, the bullockies cautiously leading their beasts. Had catastrophes similar to those of twenty years ago overtaken these vehicles, the results would have been far more disastrous. For this time the loads were not wool but wheat.

An astonishing situation had developed. On Port Augusta waterfront, near the newly-established railway yards, large sheds had been built and these were filled to capacity with great stores of grain. The wheat came from the newly-opened agricultural districts. The *Dispatch*, in its capacity of "Voice of the North", observed confidently: "It was only a few years ago when the idea of wheat being shipped at Port Augusta in any quantities would have been scoffed at as the chimera of an over-sanguine brain. But this season will surely convince the most sceptical."

And so, indeed, it seemed. The Waste Lands Amendment Act had been followed by two magnificent seasons. Just then, most of the townspeople would have given odds that the railway now approaching the new wheatlands would secure the sustained support of an immensely rich far northern wheat-growing region.

Now, between railway and wheat, so many vessels were sailing up the wedge-shaped gulf that insufficient berths were available at The Port. Some ships swung at moorings, while a two-way lighter service handled both inward and outward cargoes.

But perhaps it was not until work began on a railway station—no imposing building, just a low, board platform with a few wooden sheds to serve as ticket-office and stores—that the people fully realised that their town had been chosen as the terminus of a future transcontinental railway. Always provided, of course, that Adelaide, in its selfishness, did not obtain a main line that would by-pass Port Augusta and carry the greater part of the trade southwards.

It was at this time that first tests were made over the telegraph line between Port Augusta and Semaphore of a new instrument, shortly to be put into use by Barry, Brookes and Fraser at all their important railway camps—the telephone recently patented by Alexander Graham Bell. A letter from Beltana gives a picturesque account of the form taken by this test and the other tests that soon took place across the continent along the length of the Overland Telegraph Line. "On Easter

Monday a party of gentlemen were entertained at the Telegraph Station by an experiment with the telephone." It appears that "conversation, music, songs and bell-ringing were exchanged" with another party of gentlemen gathered at Strangways Springs, 200 miles distant. " 'Auld Lang Syne' was sung at Beltana," continued the writer. "When Strangways was asked 'How's that?' the reply was 'First rate'. The gentlemen at the Springs sang 'Coming through the Rye' in response. And so on the amusement went with flute, fiddle and horn to the delight of all present."

This incident occurred early in April when the railhead was approaching the top of the Pass. Soon the earthworks gangs were headed for Quorn, a settlement now sufficiently advanced to hold a cricket match—shearers versus non-shearers.

There followed a period of violence, uproar, and riot of a kind that was to be the experience of settlement after settlement as the railhead advanced. Trouble appears to have started in fights between railway navvies and shearers. "We require police protection as the wineshop is in full operation," wrote one disturbed settler. "Sunday is mostly given to drunkenness and fighting. The peaceably disposed think that as the Government will thrust wine shanties upon us, whether we like it or not, they ought to protect us from the lawlessness and violence which are the fruit of the same. But, as usual, we suppose there will have to be a coroner's inquest or two over violent deaths caused by the poison which is being sold as wine. Then our wants in this respect will be attended to."

Quorn's ordeal seems to have ended by June 1879. Then a correspondent wrote cheerfully: "The railway engine may now be seen in the centre of our township, and the time may be counted in weeks when it will be at Kanyaka. Hurrah for the iron horse! Advance Australia!"

A fortnight later a historic event took place. The first goods reached Port Augusta by rail down the Pichi Richi Pass. The shipment comprised 300 bags of flour from the Quorn mill. "This looks as though the line were in a fair way to be open for goods traffic at an early date," noted the *Dispatch*. "It will be an advantage to the public if this portion could be opened previous to the completion of the first section to Wonoka." A later report shows that this is what happened. "Messrs Bignall and Young have received per railway trucks since our last issue over 2,000 bags of Cowan's flour from Quorn . . . A considerable quantity of stores have been sent up to Quorn during the week, and the goods traffic is now fairly open. We need not expect many teamsters to find employment now through the Pichi Richi Pass."

Track-laying having passed through Quorn, the time had come for a railway station to be built there. Tenders were invited for this job, and in August an announcement was made that the contract had been won by J. Wishart. The building was to be of wood and the cost £900.

Because of the bumper harvest, the carriage of which the railway was now taking over from the teamster, a letter written at this time by a Blinman settler may not have appeared as mere whistling for a wind. "About 2,000 acres were taken out last week," he said. "Give us cheap transport and we will send to your port breadstuffs in abundance and stop the voices of the croakers for ever."

In point of fact the farmers themselves were doing much croaking just then, most of it, unreasonably, against the new line. "Until the railway from Port Augusta to Willochra is fenced we shall be in imminent danger of accidents which may result in a fearful loss of human life," wrote one irate agriculturist a trifle absurdly. What had happened was that one of this man's horses, ambling along the permanent way in front of a train, had been pelted with coals by the driver and fireman in an effort to shift it and, when this form of persuasion failed, it had been frightened by shrieks from the whistle.

Another farmer, living at a spot where the line was fenced for a short distance, complained angrily because it was enclosed. Two of his horses, having entered at one end, were unable to leave when a train came and had galloped ahead for some distance before finally turning in front of the engine.

Then for a short time wheat, complaints, and railway were forgotten. Gold was said to have been discovered near Quorn! The sensation was immense. A prospector claimed to have found some small nuggets on the fringe of the new settlement, and excited farmers demanded that "an examination by a competent person be made without delay". But only a seven days' wonder came of all the fuss.

Meanwhile surveyors laid out townships ahead of the advancing rail. Gordon! Wilson! Hawker! Only Willochra was long-established. It had been surveyed in 1860 on land settled by John Ragless, an early immigrant. Lately, the Ragless run had been resumed and divided into holdings for wheat-farmers who openly disbelieved the stories told by Ragless and other dispossessed graziers—tales of drought when the country became a dustbowl. Such yarns were regarded as transparent lies told in a last-ditch hope of discouraging agricultural enterprise.

At this time the contractors began to experience difficulty in recruiting labour. They hoped to obtain men from other States, but newspapers there were often unhelpful. For instance in Victoria the *South Eastern Star* reported: "Messrs Cook and Company advertise for fifty navvies. Only twelve applied. Men said they would sooner starve in Melbourne than go. It appears that the line is being made through tracts of desolate country, badly watered."

TOP: Excavating a cutting on the approach to Rumbalara (the extension from Oodnadatta to Alice Springs). BOTTOM: Twenty-nine miles north of Oodnadatta during construction of the line to Alice Springs. (*Both photographs courtesy Commonwealth Railways*)

Promptly, the *Dispatch* tried to correct the damaging impression created by this and other reports. "We are grateful to the *Star* for this information," observed the editor sardonically. "We did not know it before. Neither have the men on the line discovered this grave fact yet."

In the matter of advertising, the contractors were in poor case compared with the builders of American railways. In Willochra there were no travelling saloons served by high-kicking cancan dancers and barmaids of fragile virtue; no women of the type who had followed the camps all along the route during the construction of the Union Pacific Railroad. Reports told merely of dust, poor water, and heavy labour.

It is said that an attempt was made to introduce travelling diversion on the American pattern. If this is true, the move was prevented.

Again, though the occasion offered plenty of scope for the adventurously-minded it held out no attractively thrilling hazards. Here were no wild skirmishes with yelling, hard-riding Indians. Track-laying in the region of the Flinders Ranges and later in that of Lake Eyre did not require navvies to toil with rifles at hand, ready to beat off flying raids by scalp-hunting redskins.

Had it been required of them, those first navvies would have been well qualified to perform the double service. They were seasoned men, most of them accustomed to hard living on the fringes of the outback. And great reliance had to be placed upon them, for unskilled labour was an important factor in all construction work in those days of simple tools. Problems mounted for the contractors now that labour was in short supply.

But the men available were tough, and certainly a sense of rivalry and a determination to outdo if possible the performance of the builders of the Overland Telegraph Line inspired their efforts. A high standard of achievement had been set. And now, once more, all Australia was watching. The transcontinental railway must be pushed through resolutely. So thought the track-layers, alive to colonial rivalries.

When anyone asked, incautiously, where the money was to be found for so tremendous a task, he was condemned as a no-hoper. They could borrow, couldn't they? Britain was bursting with wealth! A bit-by-bit policy would work the trick. First, Government Gums. Then an extension to Lake Eyre. Later, to Central Mount Stuart. So would a link be established with the line from Darwin. A matter of a few years, they said. None added that it would be "a piece of cake", but had that phrase been current then it would have expressed the popular feeling.

Considered from the angle of time occupied, the building of the Port Augusta and Government Gums Railway was scarcely an impressive performance. But, having regard to the tools available, it was a creditable feat.

TOP: Railway navvies about 1885. These are probably men who worked on the Port Augusta and Government Gums Railway (*Archives of the State Library of South Australia*). BOTTOM: A typical construction camp, 87 miles north of Oodnadatta, May 1928 (*Commonwealth Railways*)

Several industrial revolutions separate that period from our own, and the contrast between the implements available then and now is startling. Particularly since the turn of the century, each decade has witnessed the invention of new labour-saving devices. But in the days when the line was first built out of Port Augusta, work was almost entirely manual. The techniques employed were little more advanced than those used in Britain during the great rail construction era when some 200,000 labourers were engaged in the huge operation of building the nation's railway network. It was then that the term "navvy"—a simplification of the earlier "navigator"—was first used. Immigrants introduced it to Australia.

Early pictures show the railway navvy as a strong man with the implements of his trade draped about his person—pick-axe, shovel, water-jar, and lantern slung from his shoulders; a wheel-barrow strapped to his back; an iron crowbar gripped in one fist. He had a great fondness for whisky, which he called "white beer".

Country people are said to have been bewildered by his rough appearance and hard speech, and in particular by his passion for plush waistcoats. None the less they considered him a king among builders for the railway was regarded as the classic building achievement. But, mighty man as he was held to be, the navvy toiled with his hands alone.

His method of constructing a railway cutting affords an example of how slight was the assistance at his disposal. Horsepower, no more! First he dug, pitching out earth on either hand. When he reached a depth from which he could no longer throw dirt to the surface, he built a timber runway up one graded bank and set a post, topped by a pulley-wheel, at the crest of the slope. Then a rope, tied to the front of his barrow, was passed over the wheel and hitched to a saddle worn by a cart-horse. When the horse was led forward, the barrow, heaped high with earth and rock, was drawn up the wooden walk, with the navvy guiding it from below.

But the slope was usually steep, and the motion of the horse not always smooth. So sometimes the barrow overturned, and the navvy slid back into the cutting beneath a scattering of rock and soil.

The P.A. and Gee-Gee line was built by shovel-gangs using horse-drawn scoops to help them clear the way. A plough-style scraper was also employed, but this scratched rather than dug hard surfaces.

For the rest, the men used double-ended picks; gympie hammers, short-handled with heads about six pounds in weight; crowbars; levers with hardwood shanks, up to seven feet long, and iron shoes with up-tilted toes to grip and lift the track when packing sleepers to correct levels; long drills called "jumpers" because the navvies raised them two-handed, dropped them into holes, and twisted the blunt chisel ends as they struck bottom; jiggers; mauls; broad-axes; long spanners to turn the bolts of the fishplates; spiking hammers to drive dog-spikes into sleepers when fastening rails; sledge-hammers, called "sloggers", up to fifteen pounds in weight; and stone-dressing hammers, perhaps five pounds in weight, for cutting and splitting, each with one end short and blunt, the other tapered to axe-shape.

The wheel-barrows used were unusual in build. Sometimes called "Cousin Jack barrows", they had no sides and were without feet. Long handles extended under a solid floor to the stopper-board that was fixed behind and above the wheel. The barrow was used for shifting rock rather than earth.

Repairs to such simple implements as these were effected on camp or in the tool factory that adjoined the blacksmith's forge in settlements like Beltana, where the smith hammered out iron tyres for wheels and built drays and buggies.

Could they return today, the navvies of those times would stare, unbelieving, at bulldozers and front-end loaders. As things were, they toiled heavily, whistling, singing bawdily, and swaggering. According to accounts of the day, the navvy carried his shovel as an infantryman his rifle, and called it his "banjo" because of a similarity in shape to the musical instrument.

As in building earthworks, so in laying rails. Hand labour was the only means available. More than thirty years later, when the time came to build the Trans-Australian Railway, a track-laying machine was used for the first time in Australia. But now rails were off-loaded, often from the backs of camels, and then man-handled into position.

Glimpses of the routine and clothing styles of the construction gangs may be had from a few surviving photographs. One of these shows ten navvies gathered at a trackside camp. A huge tarpaulin slung across a line stretched between two desert oaks is pegged at all corners. Before one open end is a hearth—a gravel square spanned by a cooking-pole supported on forked sticks.

Seven of the party wear cabbage-tree hats, probably made from fan palm, but three sport very battered billycocks. However, the chief surprise is that six of the navvies wear coats, while three have buttoned waistcoats as well. It was a sunny day. And the season, judging from flowering trees, was summer.

Another old picture shows a dozen railwaymen gathered about a locomotive and tender, and all wearing bowler hats. The bowler—round or square, black or grey—appears to have been upgraded to foreman wear at about the turn of the century. Some pictures taken during the building of the Trans-Australian Railway show navvies in soft felt hats while foremen assert authority with black bowlers.

Recognising the unsuitability of much of the clothing of the colony, the editor of the *Dispatch* published a leader on the topic. One paragraph ran: "The Chinaman—who receives a garment as a pattern whereby to make a new one—produces an excellent copy, including the patches, darns and frays of the original. So we South Australians, in copying the social usages of the Mother Country show little of the power of adaption to altered circumstances so necessary here where, in many respects, the customs of England are glaringly inappropriate. With the thermometer at 110 deg in the shade, 130 deg in the sun, the South Australian deliberately invests himself in a black chimney-pot hat and black coat on all occasions of ceremony or public importance."

So, in wearing coats and bowlers despite the heat, presumably the railway navvies were merely—in the words of the song—doing "what came naturally". One must suppose that at the work site many men flung clothes aside and laboured naked to the waist, though this assumption gains little support from pictures of navvies at work on the Nullarbor Plain during the building of the East-West line. However, it is possible that the photographs one sees today were taken for the record and that, for this purpose, naked torsos were not approved in front of the official camera.

Generally speaking, the workers appear to have worn trousers of twilled cloth, garments soft to the touch like the coat of a mole and so called moleskins. Braces, not belts, were used. Boots—about 15s a pair—were usually worn. And bowyangs (knee-straps) were popular. Few seem to have understood in those days that by enclosing the body closely and so adding to its heat the chances of heatstroke were increased.

Clothes worn by camel drivers bringing materials to the camps were more colourful than the garments of the construction workers. Men like Assam Khan and Bejah Dervish continued to wear the dress of their homeland—full trousers made of white calico and fastened with bands at the ankles, a shirt that was allowed to hang free and billow in the wind, and a turban.

Following in the tracks of the Aboriginal trader and of the early teamster, the gangs worked their way up the Willochra Plain, toiling in coarse, red, sandy soil, and bridging dry creek beds bordered by magnificent gum trees. One correspondent thought little of the country, which he described as extremely commonplace and monotonous. But he did notice "two bridges built of very handsome stone".

The attractive stonework of the railway bridges is one of the features of the line. In this connection interesting facts are told by Mr George Williams who had the unique experience of working on the last Ghan train from Quorn to Oodnadatta on 31 December 1925 as a member of the staff of the South Australian Railways, and returning on the first Ghan train from Oodnadatta to Quorn in 1926 as a member of the staff of the Commonwealth Railways. The changeover in administration had taken place during the journey.

George Williams' father worked with a man named Paddy Casey, one of the party of stone-masons and stone-dressers from the British Isles who built the mortarless stone retaining walls along the embankments and perfectly-fitting stonework in the bridge abutments in the Pichi Richi Pass and in many places along the line as far as Oodnadatta. (It is in part to preserve fine work of this kind that the Pichi Richi Railway Preservation Society was formed, when news spread that the old line was to be demolished.)

But the correspondent of 1879 had little time to spend on writing of the excellence of the bridge work that was being done. He was more interested in the transformation that was taking place around Willochra. Until recently the country had been pastoral land comprising huge, dry runs. Now wheat-farmers were looking skywards for the rain which they had fondly supposed would fall regularly once they brought their ploughs northwards.

Lacking any especial sympathy with the ousted graziers, the navvies can scarcely have noticed their deserted homesteads except, perhaps, Kanyaka, "the place of the stone"— which had become known in the course of thirty years. Tales told of this spot, in particular an inconclusive murder story, must have caught the passing interest of the railway construction workers.

Before the recent change to farming land, Kanyaka had run some 40,000 sheep and supported about seventy families. A staging point on the dray route into the Ranges, the station had been opened by Hugh Proby, third son of the Earl of Carysfort, an admiral who served under Lord Nelson. But Hugh had not lived long to enjoy his enterprise for he was drowned on a day when the Willochra Creek came down suddenly in flood.

The murder occurred some years before the gangs arrived, but it must still have been a talking point in so lonely a community. A thirty-one-year-old hawker, Thomas Smythe Holyoake, sold household goods, clothes, and small luxuries at homesteads and mining camps. One night at Kanyaka he died by violence. No details of the crime are remembered today. But, doubtless, the navvies were told the full story. Thomas was buried in a small graveyard close to the ruins.

Hans Mincham in his deeply researched book *The Story of the Flinders Ranges*, tells stories of some of the people buried at Kanyaka. One particularly pathetic tale concerns a tragedy that took place shortly after the gangs had passed through the district. James Bole, the two-year-old son of a wheat-farmer, wandered from his home. Three months later, his remains were found. He had been killed by dingoes. The story throws light on conditions in the region at the time when the railway was built. It was infested by wild dogs and shepherds needed to be constantly watchful.

One gathers that the navvies made themselves as unpopular at Kanyaka as they had done earlier at Quorn. According to a letter written in June "disorderly persons" had become a nuisance. The writer employed a phrase that by this time had become familiar in correspondence: "The presence of police is much required here just now." He went on to speak of numerous robberies. "Some clever fellow managed to cut the side of our butcher's tent taking a box of old clothes but leaving another box containing the monthly payments for meat. I would like to have seen that coon's countenance on opening the clothes box. I hear since that one of the Chinese storekeepers lost about 50 lbs of bacon that night."

The next affair was more serious. "They burgled the store, taking a considerable sum in money and stamps. But they must have been disturbed as they left the cashbox unopened."

However, some at least of the offences appear to have been misdemeanours rather than crimes. "Some ruffians made a raid on the publican's pantry, taking several pies, tarts and a jar of lard." It seems, though, that they were caught in the act, for "One fellow was floored by a lady help of the house with a brass candlestick; she gave him a good kicking."

All the trouble may not have been attributable to navvies, however. Tramps "and other disreputable characters" followed the gangs for whatever they might pick up, not in hope of any jobs that might be going. The letter refers to "drunken men prowling about at night". No direct reference is made to women among the camp followers. But it seems clear that there were some of these.

On the day when this letter was published in Port Augusta, Barry, Brookes and Fraser announced, somewhat belatedly, that goods would be accepted for carriage between The Port and Quorn. Probably the facility, practised unofficially for some time, was now recognised publicly so that a condition might be imposed. Goods would be carried only at the owner's risk. "This is necessary because the contractors have not sufficient storage accommodation." Passengers might travel on the same understanding. The fare was 6s 6d each way.

At about this time news on a sensitive topic reached Port Augusta. The report stated: "A deviation will not be made in the railway from Terowie to connect with the township surveyed on station 500, Hundred of Coonatto." The rub of this information lay not in the fact that no deviation would be made to include a place in which few had any interest, but in the reminder that a railway to link Terowie with the far north was to be built. The junction for this new railway would be Quorn.

Understandably the people of The Port opposed the railway centralisation policy pushed by Adelaide. They feared that they would be by-passed and much of their trade siphoned southwards when a direct link was established between Terowie and the new line to Government Gums. The Port Augustans preferred the old system of disseminated outports so that their town might become, in the grandiloquent phrase of the day, the "undisputed entrepôt and emporium of the north". In hope of this development, they had begun work on a ship canal—150 feet wide and eighteen feet deep at low water—to serve the new railway wharf.

Perhaps particularly bitter was the thought that Quorn (until so recently a patch of land indistinguishable from any other patch in lonely sheep country) would become an important railway junction, filching much of the traffic proper to Port Augusta.

On this matter, the *Dispatch* had been particularly outspoken, clearly revealing the feeling that then existed in The Port: "This country has hitherto been occupied only on the margin of its sea coast except for a few settlers in the interior who live in continual dread of being cut off from their source of supplies by an unfavourable season when traffic on ordinary roads would be out of the question because animals of draught could not be supported . . . Our railways should, therefore, be constructed in such a manner as to pierce the interior as much as possible in every direction . . . It may be a grand conception to form a great trunk line of railway connecting the Far North with the Metropolis of South Australia, but it is by no means a wise one at present. Our first care should be to give the farmers, the miners, and wool-growers facilities for shipping their produce and then, when this is accomplished, we may indulge in the luxury of an easy and speedy method of travelling from the outlying districts to Adelaide.

"But stay! Our readers must pardon our use of the word luxury in connection with railway travel in South Australia as the term is altogether inapplicable. Our system of railway management, founded as it has been upon the experience of older countries, with their examples to guide and their mistakes to warn us, ought to have been one of the most perfect in the civilized world whereas we have no hesitation in saying that it is one of the worst. It is entirely a disgrace to the intelligence of South Australians. It has been well said by a gentleman who went from South Australia to America, when comparing our railway management with that of Brother Jonathan, that no foreigner could have supposed that the two systems had been originated by people of the same race under somewhat similar circumstances. In America every facility is given those who wish to make use of the railway and every possible freedom allowed, and the travelling itself is a continued pleasure. In South Australia the preliminary arrangements for a trip by railway are rendered as difficult as possible, while the journey, if a protracted one, can only be compared with a few hours in purgatory. In speaking thus we refer to the Government railways."

It was a time of considerable bitterness. While each of many small townships constantly pressed its peculiar need of a railway extension, towns already satisfactorily served raised the old cry of "railway mania". Indeed, the facts seemed to justify the fears of the latter. A railway report of the time stated that Bills had been introduced for the construction of no fewer than nine lines—among them the Terowie to Pichi Richi extension—for which Parliamentary surveys had been made. A footnote added that preliminary surveys had been made for six additional lines.

Fifteen new lines in preparation! This, surely, was a tall order for a young colony already deeply committed to railway expansion.

The traders of Port Augusta sought to insure themselves against the time when "the ruinous process of centralization" would rob them of much trade. They demanded that a north-eastern branch should be built from the northern line. Such a branch, they hoped, would collect the trade of south-western Queensland and north-western New South Wales for their "natural outlet", Port Augusta. This was a move in which they were sure of the support of George Woodroffe Goyder who, after all, was still Surveyor-General.

Meanwhile they probably consoled themselves with the thought that the trunk line would suffer a break-of-gauge at Terowie. Port Augusta should continue to attract the business of all northern producers who needed to ship their products with a minimum of delay, in particular wheat-farmers who, if they hoped to compete with Californian growers, would need to ensure that their grain reached distant world markets as rapidly as possible.

The navvies had moved out of the Kanyaka district on the way to Hawker when the first fatal accident occurred on the new line. An eighteen-year-old navvy, travelling on a train loaded with sleepers, tried to pass forward, clambering from truck to truck. Slipping, he fell to the line. Before the train stopped the wheels of sixteen trucks had passed over him. His left foot was cut off, the leg shattered, and his right arm severed from his body. The train changed direction and took him to Port Augusta, where an operation was performed. He died there that night.

Though construction failed to meet the deadline for the completion of the first section, the Government appears to have been well satisfied with the contractors' performance. A report stated: "We are informed that this line is now virtually completed as regards the first section to Wonoka. The only part of the work which remains undone is the timber girders over some of the large culverts. We may, therefore, reasonably conclude that the formal opening of the Wonoka section will take place in a very short time."

Earthworks were now built as far as Hookina and construction was advancing at the rate of about two miles a week. Only the unfinished culverts held up the completion of the first section, and here the contractors were not at fault. Some unexplained delay had occurred in Western Australia, preventing delivery of the necessary timber.

Whether or not in celebration of the occasion, on the day in June 1880 when the line to Wonoka was freed to traffic a mass meeting in the Adelaide Town Hall demanded the opening of public houses on Sundays.

5
STEADY GOING

During the first week in July 1880, the General Traffic Manager of Railways visited the contractors' camp at Hookina.

At this time 900 men were working on the line. But many more were needed. The problem of recruiting sufficient labour for the gangs was one of the reasons for the visit.

Construction had now entered the region of the Yappala and Elder ranges. A member of the General Traffic Manager's party wrote enthusiastically: "The grand Wilpena Pound Range, the Arkaba Range, the 'Three Sisters' and the Mernmerna Pass! The course of the railway through the gorge beyond Wonika [*sic*] is more serpentine than it is through the Pichi Richi. The scenery is very bold. To the westwards stretches away the vast Western Plains, and here you come across the overland telegraph line, along which it would have been far easier to take the railway." Clearly, here was one of those who had opposed routing the line through the ranges for the benefit of would-be wheat-growers.

The railway passed along steep hillsides of quartzite and slate and sandstone. The permanent way had to be dug deeply, in places blasted out with dynamite, invented thirteen years before by Alfred Nobel. There were sheer drops and many hairpin bends.

One pictures the scene at dusk, with the navvies lounging about glowing cook-fires, waiting for the evening meal. This was eaten at long trestle tables in open marquees or prefabricated wooden sheds, which were easy to dismantle and move to the next camp. But the season was dry, though cold, and so probably many ate in the open.

It is likely that some men who worked for small sub-contractors fended entirely for themselves, cooking in camp ovens. There would perhaps be talk of the difficulty of keeping meat in summertime, of dry salting and hanging in bags.

Water for everyone had to be trucked to the main camps and carried forward to advanced work sites, sometimes in drays, sometimes on the backs of camels. Though every care was taken to avoid wastage, the tanks and canisters in which it was transported sometimes leaked.

It appears that no account remains of the food provided at base and advanced camps. However, William Jessop, always observant of detail, wrote of the rations allowed to shepherds in these same hills. Basically, the shepherd's weekly portion consisted of ten pounds of flour and twelve pounds of meat, usually old ewe mutton. Additionally, he received two pounds of sugar, a quarter of a pound of tea, and extras such as salt and goat's milk. And Anthony Trollope noted that the average labourer ate meat three times a day. "He is provided as a matter of course with rations . . . Fourteen pounds of meat, eight pounds of flour, two pounds of sugar, and a quarter pound of tea are allotted to him weekly." That Trollope was writing of Queensland matters little: the allowance in either colony would have compared closely. But, considering the heavy nature of his work, the railway navvy may have received somewhat larger rations. Meat was obtainable readily, steers and sheep being driven regularly to construction headquarters and to major camps. During the building of the Overland Telegraph Line, mobs comprising thousands of beasts had been driven distances of up to 500 miles to supply the working parties.

The navvy drank his tea black. Afterwards, a pipe consoled him for the lack—at least officially—of ardent spirits. Tobacco then cost 4s 6d a pound. Clay pipes are said to have cost twopence each. One wonders if these were imported from Sydney—the short-stemmed dudeen, first manufactured some forty years earlier in Skinner's pipe factory on the bank of the Tank Stream, sold for a penny.

Liquor was obtainable in the settlements on the route of the line but was forbidden on camp. A contemporary account remarked that because of this rule the average navvy "was apt to long with a longing passing all understanding for a blank good drunk". Perhaps this was an exaggeration. Many hip-flasks must have been carried for replenishment when opportunity served. And the majority of the workers appear to have been reasonably temperate. But any strongly inclined towards drink were able to appease their longing more frequently than might be supposed, having regard to the loneliness of the region.

Apart from the wood and iron hotels that had been built in several settlements—there were two of these at Beltana—rough shanty taverns dotted the northern road. An old letter describes one of these. "For some years, this pub had done a reasonable trade with drovers, teamsters, camel and mail-cart drivers, miners and travelling graziers. But when the railway gangs drew near enough for the men to knock down their pay— !" It appears that the publican coped with the sudden rush of business by placing a row of buckets outside the back door. Parties of fresh arrivals for whom there was no room inside collected a bucket apiece, passed it through a front window to be filled, and then squatted in circles in the dust, each man dipping the mug he carried hooked to his braces.

According to this account, at any one time between twenty and thirty buckets might be in use along the track outside the drinking house. At that time the cost of two gallons of liquor was 6s. Since the navvy's wage was then 6s a day, and he was paid fortnightly, he seldom lacked the cash to lubricate a thirst built up by loss of body liquids during pick-and-shovel work performed in dust, scorching sunshine, and, often, parching dry wind.

But if some navvies drank to excess and fought occasionally, most seem to have been relatively sober, hardworking, and cheerful. Several accounts speak of the men of the gangs joking and singing at their work—besides cursing.

Many, perhaps most, of their songs were bawdy. The unexpurgated versions of "The Road to Gundagai" probably strike the note that the majority adopted. Here the railroad itself offered plenty of opportunity. It appears that by this time the line was variously described—affectionately or ironically according to mood—as the Port Augusta and Government Gums Railway; the P.A. and Gee-Gee Railway; the Great Northern; and, for short, the Great Gee-Gee, or sometimes the Gee-Gee Run. As will be understood, the men found little difficulty in knocking out indecorous jingles round certain of these titles.

But songs of other kinds were popular also. About six years before the earthworks pushed out from Port Augusta, Gilbert and Sullivan had opened the long period of co-operation which resulted in their many light operas. The first of these to make a hit outside Britain was *H.M.S. Pinafore*, which opened in London in 1878. Its more famous songs appear to have reached Australia very quickly, and one in particular seems to have caught the fancy of the railway navvy. So it is not out of place to picture sturdy labourers swinging picks or "banjos" while bawling raucously, "I'm called Little Buttercup, dear Little Buttercup,/ Though I could never tell why . . . "

The next international hit came in 1879, soon after the railhead had left Quorn. Shortly, the gangs were yelling with feeling "A Policeman's

Lot is Not a Happy One". Very like the sailor, the outback worker is often sentimental. Thus, each in its turn, "I Cannot Tell what this Love may be" and "Twenty Love-sick Maidens We" had a period of popularity. And, eventually—though this not until the line was half-way between Hergott Springs and Oodnadatta—came "The Flowers That Bloom in the Spring".

It was at about the time when construction moved out of the hills that an altered feeling among northern wheat-farmers became apparent. The run of good seasons had ended and the face of the country was changed. Reports of the time describe the weather at this period as "variable—one day a regular brickfielder, and the next cold enough for overcoats". Then one journal stated plainly what many people had begun to think: "These conditions are a repetition of the great drought." It described the country beyond Quorn: "Most desolate! Instead of the bright green patches of growing crops which should be stretched out in smiling promise of many bushels to the acre nothing was to be seen save dried-up looking bushes, and parched, red ploughland." The newspaper did not say so, but the fact was that the men who had settled the Willochra and country northwards with springing confidence had lost their faith. They knew now that the dream of golden harvests all the way to the Territory border was as insecurely seated as a northern mirage, that their belief that rain would follow the plough was just another old wives' tale.

Their first reaction to this bitter disappointment, still not openly admitted, appears to have been the very human one of further fault-finding with their chief support, the railway. Some complained that the whistling and snorting of locomotives scared their livestock. Others—and this surely was the extreme of unreason—asserted that the money being spent on the railway should have been used instead in direct farming subsidies. The situation must have been infuriating to those graziers who had been dispossessed of their lands to so little purpose.

In the south the wild land speculation of the past few years was still in flood; Adelaide street property was changing hands at double the prices of five years earlier.

Now work-trains, running a shuttle service out of Port Augusta, steamed through stricken lands on their way to and from the railhead, where the materials they brought were fed forward to advance camps by means of camel and bullock transport. These camps included several picturesque features characteristic of bush life of the day—for instance, the tinkle of bells, a pleasing background sound that probably went unnoticed until occasions when it happened to be absent.

Surveyors, boundary riders, prospectors, all outback travellers used the horse bell. A straying horse might cause the death of a lone rider, and so the bushman hung a bell about his mount's neck. His first act on waking was to listen for the clink of hobble chains or the note of a bell. To simplify the recovery of a straying bullock, teamsters also belled their beasts, choosing for the purpose the mellow alpine cow-bell. Once established as a precaution in outback regions, the use of bells continued as a custom in settled districts.

The first bells used were imported from Switzerland, where they were designed to be heard from far away. Eventually, bells made to the Swiss pattern were beaten out in Australia, principally in New South Wales and Queensland. Old pit-saws and cross-cut saws were the materials commonly used. Horse-bells were small and light; bullock bells large and heavy.

Australian bell-makers were usually blacksmiths. Perhaps the best known were Mennicke and Mongan, whose bells were called after them. The Mennicke, a horse-bell, had a high note; the Mongan, a bullock-bell, was deep-toned and massive, weighing anything up to eight pounds.

Both these bells were in manufacture at the time when the Port Augusta and Government Gums Railway was being built and their distinctive tones must have been familiar sounds to the men of the construction gangs. At first light the tinkling of bells mingled with other camp noises—the rattle of pots and pans, rough voices, the hooting of a work-engine, the roaring of camels kneeling to receive their loads. An odd medley!

Easier going was encountered in the plain. Having left the new wheatlands far behind, the line now advanced in pastoral country where men still lived very simply, even though they might be wealthy in terms of flocks and herds. Jessop described a dwelling of the better sort, and conditions had changed little since his day. "As the roof was of the angular shape—the angle being acute—three rafters of slender poles ran from side to side and so tied the whole together. There was thus overhead something like the cock-loft, or room over the garret."

Comforts were minimal, refinements altogether lacking—save in one minor and curious particular. A common practice was to divide an emu's egg and have the halves set in silver for use as cups. The delicate, dark-green shell and bright metal base must have contrasted oddly with a rough board table, lit by guttering candles or a stable lantern.

The railhead lay deep in this country when one day a Quorn resident sat down to write a letter. "The early part of this week the horses, drays and men engaged on the Terowie line arrived here making the township look lively. For once the storekeepers seem to be satisfied and say they are doing a lively trade. We understand the main camp of the contractors (Messrs. C. and E. Miller) is about fourteen miles from Quorn, smaller camps being formed within that distance to the Quorn end of the line."

No wonder the shopkeepers were satisfied! Their settlement was about to become an important railway junction. It is likely that the traders of Port Augusta, on the other hand, were proportionately cast down. Perhaps the only really cheerful office in town was that of the *Dispatch*, about to assume broadsheet dignity in place of magazine-style format: sensational stories were plentiful just then, for this was the time of the trial of Ned Kelly.

Nevertheless The Port was making notable progress. By this time the population had grown to about 2,700 persons. Four banks and a flour mill were in business. Furthermore a start had been made in secondary industry, for an ostrich farm of about 5,000 acres had been opened. The birds thrived on the natural herbage of saltbush and mulga, while their feathers found a ready market in Europe. Thus Port Augusta had outgrown Clare, long called the "Northern Capital", though its geographical situation, some seventy miles from Adelaide, made this title ridiculous.

When the railhead was nearing Beltana, the people there appear to have suffered an attack of nerves. Reports of violence at Quorn and Kanyaka had, of course, reached them and undoubtedly the stories had become exaggerated on the way up-country. At the time the alarming tales first began to arrive, a disturbed settler had written to the *Dispatch*: "I don't know how long it will be before the navvies get this far with the railway works. But, as we may reasonably expect a few roughs amongst them, what provision will the Government make for their safe-keeping in case of rowdyism? This is supposed to be a permanent township, unlike those at the different mines in the north, so that we may reasonably expect to have a police-station built and a lock-up."

Events were to show that the settlers had cause for some apprehension. The construction gangs were over a thousand strong by this time, and the lonely little township must have felt as if it were about to be taken over by an invading army.

At this time Beltana was nine years old, for it had begun as a settlement on the Overland Telegraph Line. However, the district had been opened up in earlier days. Edward John Eyre, the first arrival, had named it Mount Deception, and in the early 1850s, several pastoralists had taken out leases. Later, these leases had been included in Thomas Elder's camel-breeding station.

An impression of the settlement as it was shortly before the coming of the rail emerges clearly from news items of the day. The settlers included several enterprising traders. For instance, there was Thomas Pearce, who owned a many-sided business which he seems to have pushed with energy. One day he advertised as follows: "Thomas Pearce, Boot Manufacturer, jeweller, tobacconist etc., begs to thank his friends and the public for their patronage and support since he came to this locality and to inform them that, having secured a proper supply of Horse Fodder, large stockyards, a Well of Water with force-pump and long troughs, Teamsters and others will have conveniences afforded them free of charge. The public pound is also under the charge of Thomas Pearce, Poundkeeper."

Characters such as Pearce constantly emphasised the importance of Beltana as a northern township, and as soon as the railway survey made clear that the transcontinental line was to pass through the settlement, Beltana began to make its presence felt. Then opened, for example, a succession of complaints concerned with "the folly and incapacity" of the postal authorities. "A coach comes here every Sunday night at 9 o'clock and every alternate week it brings mail. Why it cannot do so every time is a mystery to all residents. The coach remains here till one o'clock Monday and then mail from Blinman arrives just when the coach takes its departure, leaving no time to read and answer letters. Such a stupid arrangement should be altered."

This protest appears to have brought results, for five months later a certain John Moses was appointed "the north-west mail man". But John, making his deliveries on horseback, seems to have failed to give satisfaction. One reads: "John Moses tried to cross Warrioota Creek. He was washed from his saddle and then horse and rider were carried some six hundred yards. Several by-standers were unable to help. The current cast man and horse among timber growing in the middle of the creek. He regained the bank exhausted when he returned back two miles to Thomas Elder's station."

One pictures the frustration of the several by-standers as they watched John depart, their letters—probably soaked through—still in his mailbag. No doubt they thought that the coach would have got through.

At the time when the railway was approaching across the plain, Beltana had "three stores; an assembly room with a raised stage and drop curtains and seats to accommodate two hundred people; butcher, baker, saddler and barber" and, of course, Thomas Pearce's multiple establishment. On Sundays the assembly room was used as a church, one of the storekeepers reading the service.

There was also a school which on several occasions afforded the settlers a further opportunity to protest their new importance. "The school is certainly no credit to the Government or School Board. It is kept in a rough building owned by the blacksmith where local courts are also held. So there can be no school on court days." And again, at a

Early power tools: TOP: A "Marion" shovel at work in 1928, half-way to Rumbalara. BOTTOM: A "Keystone" excavator at work on the S.A.–N.T. border in 1928 (*Both: Commonwealth Railways*)

time when school had been closed for three weeks and thirty children had been running wild: "One thing is very necessary, a residence for a school teacher. How can it be expected that a person will leave his family in town to accept the appointment of teacher when he has to make his shakedown in the school room? Yet such has been the case here during the whole time the school has been opened."

Judging from frequent references to illness, Beltana seems not to have been a healthy settlement at that time. "There has been a very great deal of sickness," said one report on this topic. "Bunged eyes are as plentiful as shrimps upon the sea shore. The women seem to get off the best, and it is a tie between the men and the children who fare the worse. Dysentery, slow fever, inflammation of the lungs and all kinds of ophthalmia have been prevalent." But "that fever should take root in this place is quite to be expected because sanitary labour is begrudged".

Meanwhile the district continued to be an important camel centre. From time to time fresh batches of animals were landed at Port Augusta, swelling the number available for use on the line. Some of the beasts went to Beltana, others to private owners.

Some camel drivers brought wives with them. A tale is told of two navvies who set out from the railhead to shoot bustard for the pot. Unexpectedly they came upon a camel camp and three Afghan women, unveiled. When the women saw the navvies, they hastily veiled themselves. Then a camp attendant hurried across the clearing, gesturing angrily. "Master—in town," he shouted. "You go—quick!"

Camels brought considerable amounts of railway material from the hills where foresters were sent to cut light timber and quantities of sleepers. The drivers were unpopular with bullockies because they cut charges, and with saddlers, blacksmiths, and wheelwrights because they had no cause to call upon their services. But, of course, they were most unpopular of all with those who worked horses. No one could explain why horses became terrified at the sight of camels, although the fact has been recognised since ancient times. Herodotus noted it and Cyrus is said to have used camels to rout the otherwise unbeatable Lydian cavalry.

No record remains of the day on which the railhead entered Beltana. But it is likely that the rails arrived in time to honour the contract date, and clearing and grubbing parties would have passed through three weeks in advance.

The official opening of the line took place on Saturday 2 July 1881. By this time, the earthworks of the final phase were well on the way to Government Gums.

The ceremony was short and simple. A Government train, carrying "one hundred and fifty passengers—taken on a free excursion—and a

TOP: The busy Brachina Crushing Plant (*M. D. Farley*). BOTTOM: A graphic view of the railhead at Oodnadatta in 1905 (*Archives of the State Library of South Australia*)

valuable cargo of merchandise", arrived late in the afternoon. It passed under an archway with "Welcome" spelled out in flowers of several colours, and pulled up in a little station decorated with flags and evergreens.

When the Mayor of Port Augusta and five Town Councillors had climbed down from their coach (there was no platform) a circle was formed around the engine. Then a magnum of champagne was handed to Mrs Blood, the wife of the postmaster, who declared the second section of the railway open for traffic and smashed the bottle on the fender of the engine.

Following the cheers, everyone walked to the township, which was situated on sloping ground facing Beltana Creek, about half a mile from the railway.

At eight o'clock everyone gathered in the Hantke Assembly Rooms where, said a newspaper reporter: "The local ladies turned out in grand style, and the visitors were two deep with their wives and their sisters and their cousins and their aunts." Clearly the Press was familiar with the latest Gilbert and Sullivan opera.

The toast of the evening was "The Port Augusta and Government Gums Railway Contractors and Staff". The chief Director of the contracting firm, D.M. Barry, responded. Then "dancing was resumed with great spirit and was kept up till the bell tolled midnight".

Next day the visitors attended a corroboree arranged for their entertainment by the many Aborigines who still lived in the district. On Monday morning the train returned to Port Augusta, "comfortably in time for tea".

Now a three-a-week train service started, leaving Port Augusta at 7 a.m. and arriving at Beltana at 6.54 p.m. The return journey took place on alternate days, with trains leaving at 6.15 a.m. and arriving at 6.10 p.m. Two-way fares were £2 14s 6d first class, and £2 5s second class.

Evidently the opening ceremony at Beltana—a "mid-course" occasion—was not thought of sufficient importance to require the presence of the Governor. However, Sir William made a flying visit to the construction camps at this time. On the way he stopped at Quorn, where he reminded a reception committee that just three years had passed since he had turned the first sod of the railway. Perhaps he wished to see for himself the progress that had been made in establishing the junction, for he supported the policy of a metropolitan railway focus.

A resident wrote of this visit: "His Excellency, attended by various members of the Houses of Legislature, walked to Mr Greenslade's Transcontinental Hotel where a substantial breakfast had been provided. At about 9 a.m. he proceeded northwards and returned about 6 p.m. I do not know whether rightfully we, the Quornites, are voted a dull lot, a one-horse township, because we did not present an address to Sir William. But, having no intimation that Sir William wished to be bored—!"

There he left it. One feels sure that for once Governor Jervois, a crisply-spoken, forthright man, sighed thankfully as he went his way.

6

THE GUMS

The people of Beltana anticipated advantage and disadvantage from the coming of the gangs—profit and violence. Both expectations were realised.

Extra money began to flow as soon as the earthwork navvies came within striking distance, so to speak, of the township's two bars. And when in due course the railhead arrived and supply trains regularly reached the newly-built station, Beltana was invaded. The township was to remain the seat of operations until the completion of the final section to Government Gums. So, for a considerable period, a large part of the pay of many construction workers was spent in Beltana.

A newspaper correspondent wrote in great satisfaction: "Beltana owes its present prosperous condition to the large number of railway hands now stationed here. Messrs Barry, Brookes and Fraser have removed the whole of their large workshops from Hookina and erected them, together with their blacksmiths' and engineers' shops. And the numerous other employees, in various gangs, all stationed here, give a lively appearance to the town."

This was one view of the situation. Another was less pleasing.

Today, it is not clear just how soon the trouble started. The first recorded case concerns the arrest of four navvies for drunkenly disturbing the peace at Blackfellow Creek. The men were fined and discharged. Then one was re-arrested as he left the courthouse, and charged with robbery.

The case had ludicrous aspects and in this respect was typical of many others, for plenty of the culprits were childish in their misdemeanours. By this time a mounted police post had been established in the district, and the constable called to the scene of the disturbance had found himself at a loss to decide which of the two men before him was the more intoxicated—defendant or plaintiff. According to the record, he faced a situation calling for the judgment of a Solomon. "The prosecutor had handed his purse to the accused to see how much was in it. The purse was handed back. Three sovereigns and two half-sovereigns were inside. One sovereign was said to be missing."

The constable's dilemma lay in the fact that the owner of the purse was in no fit state to know how much money should have been found in it. The constable seems to have scratched his head in perplexity. But someone in the crowd that had gathered quietly gave him a tip. He ordered the accused man to pull off his boots. Giggling drunkenly, the man obeyed. A sovereign fell out. Next day the thief was convicted and sentenced to two months' hard labour.

One day a disturbing report came over the wire from Wilson, twelve miles south-west of Hawker. A young man had been thrown out of a train by larrikins, men recruited as railway navvies and on their way to base camp. The youth, who had been found lying by the track, was disfigured for life. This report caused alarm in Beltana. No one was arrested.

Soon the settlers were disturbed by a new and unexpected situation. Men began disappearing from the gangs. Why large-scale desertion should have started at this juncture is hard to say. Perhaps the circumstance that Beltana was the terminal for the second phase of building suggested to navvies who were discontented that this was the place to quit. Perhaps arrival at a settlement of some size unsettled men who found life in the gangs monotonous. Perhaps the thing just became a fashion. Whatever the cause, many labourers simply walked off the job.

Those deserters who were experienced bushmen were able to look after themselves and were not seen again. But there were others without outback experience. These men usually lost themselves. It thus became customary for a ganger to allow a few days to elapse before reporting a man missing. This allowed for a change of mind on the part of the deserter, and gave him time to find his way back to camp. In many cases this proved to be a sensible course, and many men returned to duty and a few hard words.

But some deserters—probably awaiting a suitable opportunity to board undetected a southward-bound supply train—lurked in the bush outside Beltana and raided stores and houses in the township for food and money. A typical case of this kind was that of an Irishman caught in the act of breaking and entering. He resisted arrest violently.

Carried off to the lock-up, he was charged with being a rogue and a vagabond within the meaning of Clause 63 of the Police Act, 1869.

When he appeared before the Court in the blacksmith's shed-cum-schoolroom he admitted that six months previously he had been convicted at Wonoka of being an idle and disorderly person, after deserting railway duty. He was sentenced appropriately.

The whole situation seems to have been surprisingly foolish. Presumably, any man who wished to do so might give notice, serve out whatever time remained under the terms of his employment, and then receive free transportation back to civilisation on the contractors' supply train. However, numbers seem not to have viewed the matter in that light.

A curious and unusual case was that of a deserter who, following arrest as a suspicious character, was charged with "being a lunatic". The prisoner, who came from a camp fourteen miles north of Beltana, had been missing from duty for a week. His absence had been reported two days before, the usual interval having been allowed prior to making a thorough search of the surrounding bush. The railway doctor who examined the man said that his condition was due to over-excitement caused by want of sleep and the fear that he would die in the bush. The case was dismissed, and the man returned to his gang.

Perhaps the grimmest and most puzzling of all the incidents that occurred at this time was one that took place at Galloping-Out Camp.

One night, Bert, a member of a plate-laying gang, disappeared. At first there seemed no reason to suppose that this disappearance was different from the many others that were happening. Then rumours that an accident could have taken place caused a search to be mounted more quickly than was usual. The missing man was not found, and so a message was sent to the police at Beltana. Two constables with a black tracker rode out to investigate.

Without hesitation the tracker led the way for about five miles through bush country. The party reached a clearing and there they found the missing man, lying on his face, left arm across his chest, right extended. He was dead, but no injury was visible.

However, in view of the rumours, the constables were not satisfied that Bert had died naturally. They took the body back to Galloping-Out Camp and began to take evidence.

The first witness, Bill, a navvy, said that he had overheard a quarrel between Bert and a fellow plate-layer, Roger. Bill had seen Bert at tea-time on the evening of his disappearance. Bert had been sober then, but Roger had staggered as he walked.

Later, when in his tent, Bill had overheard a second quarrel. An angry, menacing meeting had taken place outside in the darkness.

"What took you to my tent when I was away?" demanded Roger, furiously. And to this Bert replied: "Upon my word, Roger, I wasn't there." It had then become clear that Roger was accusing Bert of seducing his wife. Nor would he listen to denials. "I'll perish you," he threatened. "I'll put a half-moon in your belly."

Then they tusselled and fell, cursing each other. Presently, there was silence. Then Roger's voice came again. "Wish I'd perished you, you bastard. Could perish two like you any day."

In further evidence, several men spoke of quarrels, and a woman said that Roger's wife had come to her because Roger had grown threatening and possessed a gun.

However, the railway doctor who performed a post-mortem found that peritonitis had been the cause of death. Nevertheless the local Court held Roger responsible and sent him in custody to Port Augusta. And there, unsatisfactorily, the story ends. No record tells how the matter was decided.

But the story makes one point clear. Wives were allowed to live with their husbands at major camps on the workings. At least two women were present at Galloping-Out Camp. And later, several reports of child disappearances confirm the matter. One of these said: "A child, two years old, belonging to a man named Penny, working on the line, was lost on Saturday evening, having strayed from the camp. The search party found him about four miles out at 5 o'clock on Sunday morning." A child of this age would not have been allowed to live on camp, when the father was away all day, unless the mother had been present.

The contractors were watchful and did all that was possible to prevent unauthorised women from reaching the camps. But there is some reason to suppose that a number contrived to avoid their vigilance. Not all did this for purposes of prostitution. Some tried for jobs as navvies: on several occasions women dressed in men's clothes were detained aboard construction trains on the way to the railhead. It is difficult to understand how women could have passed themselves off as men for long periods in the conditions of camp life. But a spirit of adventure may have prompted a few to attempt this, as has happened on a number of occasions, in not dissimilar circumstances, in recent times.

A letter written in Government Gums on 5 August 1881 shows where the railhead lay at that date. "The railway earthworks are within two miles of Farina, and the plate-laying is now as far as Sundown Creek, ten miles north of Beltana. This bids fair to seeing the train at Farina in about seven months. The great topic of interest to the Farina business people is the probable whereabouts of the station and terminus of the Port Augusta and Government Gums Railway. Of course, each man declares in turn that he must have it opposite his own door."

If far ahead of contract with earthworks, Barry, Brookes and Fraser were behindhand with plate-laying. Supplies had lagged behind delivery dates, so, whenever opportunity served, the contractors hastened consignments from Port Augusta. In so doing they appear to have disturbed the minds of people living in settlements along the completed section of the line.

On the day the letter from Farina was published there appeared a complaint from Wilson. "How is it that the railway contractor is allowed to run trains past the sidings at such a fast rate of speed? One of the Company's trains passed down by this station this morning at the rate of fully 30 m.p.h. Some say it was 40 m.p.h., which is altogether too fast."

While the plate-layers were in the vicinity of Sundown Creek, the railway grapevine brought rumours of disaster in the south. Crops had failed completely in the new wheatlands, which were to have been extended steadily to the Territory border. Soon rumour became hard news. A report from Quorn stated: "Very little wheat will come from the Willochra Plains, there being nothing to reap. Some paddocks are particularly destitute, so much so that the corn stalks may be counted on the lands. 'Do you want a reaper?' I heard asked this morning. 'Thanks, no; the grass-hoppers have taken over the contract and just completed it' . . . " And Kanyaka reported similarly: "The farmers are busy gathering what little wheat there is left after the depredations of grasshoppers and kangaroos . . . Few will get so much as the seed they put on the ground."

And so it went. All the country to the north of Goyder's Line had dried up so much that the ground was too hard to plough. Crops not entirely discouraged by drought and grasshoppers had withered in hot winds, just as Goyder had predicted they would.

The situation appeared to be a catastrophe not only for northern wheat, but for the North itself. The plough, which was to have drawn life-giving rain, had done much to destroy the land. The farmers had removed the natural vegetation, and when this had not been replaced by wheat, the dry surface-soil had drifted. Now with saltbush and other herbage gone, land proved at last to be useless to the farmer had also been spoiled for the grazier.

Not all the people now facing ruin had been foolhardy. Some had understood the sense of Goyder's reasoning, but had believed that scientific methods would enable them to win out. In this they were sixty years ahead of the times. Nowadays new agricultural techniques, based on many years of rainfall records, enable the farmer to advance to the ten-inch rainfall line, and Goyder's barrier is outdated. This was not so in the 1880s, though. Then the Line constituted a reliable guide, and those who disregarded it did so to their cost.

Now panic came to the failed wheatlands. The new settlers appealed to the Government. The great wheat drive had ended.

On the railway workings the men recalled with wry grins that Government Gums had been renamed Farina because it was to be the hub of a northern agricultural region. With reason, they feared for their jobs.

Hitherto they had assumed that the line would be pushed on beyond The Gums. After all, Darwin was the objective. But if times were bad and money was short, what then? Already the word was that work was hard to get in the south.

Soon another rumour spread through the camps. Whatever the Government's railway intentions, Barry, Brookes and Fraser would not renew their contract.

Now each construction train brought fresh tidings of disaster—drinking water was being shipped from Port Adelaide to the stricken areas; subsidies had been refused to desperate farmers on the grounds that if help were given them, then graziers might reasonably claim compensation for their heavy stock losses; southern farmers were being canvassed for seed wheat which the State railways agreed to carry free of charge. And so on.

Eventually the Commissioner for Crown Lands spoke out, stating roundly that far northern country had been resumed only after strong pressure from men claiming to know their business. The Government could not be held responsible for the mistakes of those who blundered with their eyes open. After that, many indignant farmers demanded their money back and release from obligation. Eighty of them packed up and walked out on their commitments.

Emigration figures appear to reflect the lack of confidence at this period. Whereas in 1876 emigrants leaving South Australia numbered 4,995, in 1881 the outflow from the colony leaped to 16,800 persons. One must suppose that the families of many disillusioned wheat-growers contributed to the increase.

Unrest grew in the railway gangs. The men argued that a line to the northern end of the Flinders Ranges would satisfy miners and most graziers. The Gums would be the terminus, they said. But still a few optimists talked of "South Australia's golden spike", in allusion to the final rail of the Union Pacific Railroad set in place thirteen years previously. They insisted that the Territory was the mark of the planners, that pay was safe until the golden spike had been driven in a completed transcontinental line. The optimists proved to be in the right—for the time being.

On 18 November, Act No. 226 became law. It authorised "the formation of a line of Railway from Farina Town to near Hergott Springs". The provisions were similar to those of Act No. 26 of 1876. Gauge, speeds of travel, and tolls remained as before, the chief point of difference being that steel rails were to replace iron. At once the hullaballoo over "railway mania" broke out afresh and was continued into the New Year.

On the morning of 18 April 1882 the contractors' work-train entered The Gums for the first time. Ten days later a two-way construction train service began between Beltana and the railhead, carrying passengers at "reasonable rates".

The railway was now complete except for a little consolidation work. In his report, the Engineer-in-Chief said: "The first section (sixty-five miles) has been maintained by the Government during the year; the second section (seventy-nine miles) for nine months; and the third section (fifty-five miles) has been maintained by the contractors. The line through to Farina was opened for traffic on May 17th."

However, the ceremony did not take place at Government Gums. Two lines were to be opened together—the Port Augusta and Government Gums Railway and the Terowie to Quorn extension. It was therefore decided to hold the official event at Quorn, the junction, with minor ceremonies at Port Augusta and Farina.

The manner of the opening was described at length in the *Dispatch*, the editor taking the opportunity to deplore the choice of the three-foot-six-inch gauge: "We accept the narrow gauge in the same spirit as the beggar receives the half loaf." But his long account of the ceremony was filled with touches of humour and for once the pontifical style was abandoned.

As on the occasion of the turning of the first sod, a little over four years previously, the Governor arrived at Port Augusta in the *Musgrave*. It was the afternoon of 16 May. Once again hitches occurred in the programme. First a misunderstanding arose respecting the time of the vessel's arrival. As a result, the Rifle Company, attending as a guard of honour, was caught out of step. The order was to muster at the weighbridge at 5 p.m., but this turned out to be just an hour too late, and so only a small part of the force was on parade.

However, this time Mayor, Town Clerk, and Councillors were successful in boarding the vessel before the Governor came ashore. Thus everyone was formally introduced before "the gang-plank was run out and the Vice-regal party and Corporation stepped onto the jetty". Then a band struck up, a salute was fired from the *Musgrave*, and those enthusiastic riflemen who had turned up early presented arms.

A reception was held "in the wharf store of A.D. Tassie and Company where a dais had been erected and seats provided for the distinguished visitors". These included the Chief Secretary and Treasurer and the President of the Legislative Council.

One gathers that from the outset the proceedings were marked by a certain atmosphere. It is clear that the guests soon became aware that all was not just as it should be on this sort of occasion. And certainly the Governor, an unusually perceptive person, noticed this instantly. But if the behaviour of the hosts was, perhaps, a little restrained, still the occasion advanced smoothly enough.

When the time came for the Mayor to make his address in welcome, he opened with the somewhat surprising comment that he "would not allude in any way to an absence of loyalty on the part of the people here". Indeed, the fact that "they were prepared to accord the fullest respect to Her Majesty's representative was apparent from the number who had assembled to meet and greet him. The loyalty of the people of The Port was in no way less marked than that of the residents of other places in the colony."

By this time the Governor must have wondered what lay behind these protestations, and just what, when at last it arrived, the big "but" would be.

And then the Mayor came to the point. He said that he must be candid and say plainly that the people of Port Augusta had been slighted, in fact neglected by the Ministry. Their claim to participate in the great event, the opening of the railway to Government Gums, the first sod of which His Excellency had turned in this place, had been ignored. The Port had peculiar claims to share in this matter. However, though all were conscious of a slight, they had not allowed, and did not intend to allow, this consciousness to interfere with their expressions of loyalty.

Now the cat was out of the bag with a vengeance. So, no invitation had been sent to Port Augusta! It was bad enough that Quorn, the upstart township, should have been chosen as the scene of the opening ceremony and banquet, but that Port Augusta should have been overlooked entirely . . . ! The Governor must have started to think very fast indeed.

The Mayor could not resist a final prod that would push the point home conclusively. So at the end of his address he said that the oversight in not inviting the Councillors of The Port to take part in the festivities could probably be explained, but the slight was still keenly felt. Then on behalf of Port Augusta he bade a hearty welcome to Sir William Jervois.

Accepting a copy of the address in welcome, which had been printed on vellum, Sir William read his prepared speech in reply. Then he spoke informally, apologising simply and sincerely for the mistake "in holding over the invitations until the last day almost". As though conscious that this was a somewhat weak explanation, he went on to say that he was positive that his friend, the Chief Secretary, and his friends, the members of the Ministry, had nothing further from their thoughts than such a neglect, and reminded everyone that such accidental omissions occurred occasionally even in private life. Then he remarked smoothly upon the surprising growth of Port Augusta. He spoke of the large and handsome buildings and congratulated the people upon their energy and foresight. Finally, he said that he was pleased to see the Rifle Company present and appreciated the honour of their attendance.

This final comment brought cheers from the riflemen who, by this time, had turned out in force. Now everyone was happy and not particularly concerned whether or not the invitations were in fact on the way, for it had been made clear that Port Augusta would be adequately represented at the ceremony on the following day. So the Mayor called for three cheers, the riflemen presented arms, and the Councillors escorted His Excellency to the waiting carriage.

Sir William spent the night in Poyston House, and at 11.15 next morning boarded a special train of eight coaches hauled by two engines. In addition to Sir William's suite and members of the Ministry, the party included reporters from Adelaide and country newspapers and many guests, among whom were now included the Mayor and Town Councillors of Port Augusta.

When the train pulled up at the junction and the party alighted, an amusing incident took place. All three members of the Quorn band had assembled, their instruments a drum and two brass horns. Their instructions were to strike up the National Anthem the instant they saw the Governor. But since none of them knew him by sight, they found themselves in some uncertainty because of the size of the visiting party. In fact, according to one report, they were about to honour the representative of an Adelaide journal when someone a little more knowledgeable stopped them just in time.

The band having done its part, the Quorn Rifle Company escorted the Governor to "a large and handsome triumphal arch of evergreens" where two addresses were presented. Sir William then opened the railway with a very short speech: "Ladies and gentlemen, I will reserve any remarks I have to make about this grand railway until after we have refreshed ourselves at the banquet, and I will now hereby declare this line open to Government Gums. May many trains and much produce pass over it, and long may it be a success to the people of South

Australia. I now call for three cheers, and one cheer more for the railway to Government Gums."

He used the old name, and according to the record the cheers were loud indeed. More cheers followed, this time for the Governor himself, and yet others for Lady Jervois. But still the guests were not free to repair to the elaborate lunch that awaited them. For now the Governor was led to "a carpeted dais" beneath yet another arch of evergreens, this time within the Railway Reserve. Here two addresses were read while about 500 people listened and the Rifle Brigade stood at attention.

The Chairman of the Quorn Reception Committee was verbose in the manner of the day. After many expressions of loyalty and confidence in South Australia's Vice-Regent, he said: "We desire to express our great pleasure in meeting Your Excellency on this important occasion, namely the Great Northern Railway, which, in common with Your Excellency, we consider to be the first step towards accomplishing that grand project a transcontinental railway connecting South Australia and Port Darwin. We congratulate Your Excellency that this part of that important work has been accomplished during Your Excellency's administration, and we feel sure that when in future the work of through communication shall have been completed Your Excellency's name will always be associated therewith." He continued in this vein for some time.

Sir William responded briefly, and then the Secretary of the Quorn Branch of the South Australian Farmers' Association offered afresh the customary assurances of loyalty and attachment, which frequent repetition must have made very tedious to the Governor. On this occasion the formality was lengthened by the addition of a rider expressing satisfaction that the Queen "had been saved from the hand of the assassin", for an attempt had been made to shoot Victoria as she drove through Hyde Park.

At last the speaker came to the point: "With unmixed pleasure we congratulate Your Excellency on the completion of the two lines of railway from Terowie to Quorn and Port Augusta to Farina; on Your Excellency's arrival here at the grand junction for the purpose of opening these extensive lines; and on the progress and advancement of colonial interests. We venture to observe that the present railway lines which Your Excellency will open today, and which we regard as largely the result of the settlement and enterprise of agriculturists in the Northern Areas, will greatly facilitate the transport of farm produce to the seaboard. While we deeply deplore the present distress among the northern settlers owing to the almost total failure of their crops during the past three years, we still have confidence that the North, with suitable legislation in regard to the land laws, will prove remunerative in production of wheat and other cereals."

One has sympathy with the Governor who, no longer young, had to listen wherever he went to prepared speeches—always long and fulsome. Each address began with the same form of words: "To His Excellency Sir William Francis Drummond Jervois, Knight Commander of the Most Distinguished Order of St Michael and St George; Companion of the Most Honourable Order of the Bath; Governor-in-Chief in and over the Province of South Australia and its Dependencies . . . " He must have wearied of his own distinctions, announced perhaps as many as three or four times at each formal occasion.

He now returned thanks for "the flattering and hearty address" that had just been read and added, a little desperately it seems, "And now, I think, we will proceed to our banquet."

Two hundred guests attended this function. A contemporary account speaks with respect of "four glasses, three plates, a napkin and a button hole" provided for each person. Clearly, the correspondent was impressed.

More than the usual number of toasts appear to have been drunk. And each time the three-instrument band cut in appropriately, if noisily, with "The National Anthem", "God Bless the Prince of Wales", "For they are Jolly Good Fellows", "Fine Old English Gentleman", and so on.

One of the last speakers, D.M. Barry, responding to the toast of "The Contractors", remarked that there had been times when he had thought that he might never finish the line.

Shortly after that, the proceedings ended. Sir William and party returned to Adelaide by special train.

Five days later the railway station at Farina was opened. This appears to have been the occasion when the official description of the line was changed from the Port Augusta and Government Gums Railway to the Great Northern Railway, for after this date the old name disappeared from official records. However, many people—perhaps wishing to keep fresh the ambition with which building had begun—preferred to use the title of Transcontinental Railway.

Now traffic began throughout the entire route, passenger trains travelling at a speed of twelve miles per hour. The rate of travel became as great a source of inspiration to facetiously-minded persons as the new name of the temporary terminus—Farina, "the great granary of the North". It was popular then to recall the proposal of Mark Twain, who had urged upon railway managements the desirability of attaching the cow-catcher to the guard's van instead of to the engine.

But slow speeds mattered little to the people of northern settlements. The convenience of railway travel, compared with the available alternatives, was so great that they saw no occasion for serious complaint.

Some accounts described passengers as rocking gently on bench-like seats that ran the length of either side of a coach, and staring out at the passing scene over the shoulders of the persons opposite, while dust seeped in at ill-fitting windows and sand sifted under the doors to mix with their paper-wrapped sandwiches. Small wonder that the train emptied at any halt where there was a clapboard pub! The practice was to stay at the bar until the whistle blew. Even then nobody hurried. For train crews came to feel that it was a matter of honour to ensure that everyone was aboard again before the journey was resumed.

The Engineer-in-Chief announced in his report for the year ended June 1882 that the twenty-five-mile stretch between Port Augusta and Quorn had been fenced and steel rails substituted for iron. It was in this report that Hergott Springs figured for the first time in railway records: "The extension of the Great Northern Railway from its terminus, Farina, to Hergott Springs was authorised last session. Tenders are invited for the construction of this line. To be received by 23rd October."

Beneath this statement appeared a list of no fewer than sixteen preliminary surveys recently completed. Among these were two surprises—Hergott Springs to Stuart Creek, and Stuart Creek to Strangways Springs. This appears to have been the first public announcement of the Government's intention to push the railway still further north without delay. It was underlined by the final item in the list—Port Darwin to Pine Creek, Northern Territory.

Also included in this list were announcements of surveys from Farina to the Queensland border, and from Hawker to the Barrier Range. Clearly these surveys were variants of those proposed by the 1875 Railway Commission. At the time nothing came of them, but they were not forgotten. Later a line was built to the Barrier Range through Peterborough (then Petersburg), but the idea of a Queensland railway was shelved until the turn of the century.

An odd touch in this report was the statement that the average number of maintenance men employed on the railway was ·66 to the mile, a figure giving a total of about 130 fettlers between Port Augusta and Farina.

The fears of the railway navvies respecting the future intentions of the contractors turned out to have been well-founded. Barry, Brookes and Fraser did not submit a tender for the extension to Hergott Springs. This is made clear by two unrelated announcements. The first of these—an advertisement inserted by a firm of general dealers and dated 7 October—stated: "We have purchased the whole of Messrs Barry, Brookes and Fraser's railway sleepers. Suitable for well timber, and fencing posts. To be sold in large lots." The second—a news item published just three weeks later—said: "Three tenders were opened at the Chief Engineer's Department on Monday for the construction of a railway from Farina to Hergott Springs. That of Moorhouse, Robinson and Jesser was the lowest."

Probably the comment made by D.M. Barry when responding to the toast of "The Contractors" during the luncheon at Quorn had been intended as notice that his firm would not seek further Government business. Had he tendered for the Hergott Springs extension he would doubtless have been awarded the contract, if only because of the experience gained in laying 200 miles of line in outback conditions. As matters were, the Government bought back the locomotives originally sold to the contractors to work the construction trains.

On 10 November Moorhouse, Robinson and Jesser announced that they proposed to commence work at once. They had made a fortunate and unexpected purchase of plant and so were able to start operations earlier than had been anticipated.

Five days later the Chief Secretary laid on the table of the Assembly a paper showing the disbursements made on account of the Port Augusta and Government Gums Railway. It then transpired that the amount paid to Barry, Brookes and Fraser was £549,511 0s 1¾d. But an additional sum of £22,207 15s 1d had been disbursed for extras such as reclaiming land for station buildings at Port Augusta, building sidings in streets, and restoring flood-damaged track at Mernmerna and Brachina. Thus the total payment had been £571,718 15s 2¾d.

There had been other costs, however. These included £119,388 for railway stations; £17,430 for goods and locomotive sheds; £30,000 for office buildings; and £100,000 for cranes, steam-pumps, tanks, and drilling-machines, and additional switches, crossings, and turntables.

The total amount paid or still to be paid for the line, including the cost of every particular of expenditure, was £1,012,331. The cash balance then standing to the credit of the railway was £34,500, a sum it was proposed to expend in flattening curves in the Pichi Richi Pass, in roofing reservoirs, and in building additional fencing.

On 5 January 1883, when clearing and grubbing gangs had begun to prepare the way northwards from Farina, Governor Jervois criticised the financial policy of the colony in a speech delivered at a farewell luncheon before his departure from Adelaide to take up a new appointment as Governor of New Zealand. He pointed out that £556,812 was being paid in interest on loans for works that were showing a net annual return of less than £180,000. If the colony continued to borrow so freely for a further seven years, the annual payment in interest would be about £800,000. "I still advocate progress," he said. "I still advocate railways, and I think the colony is thoroughly well able to pay for them. But I do not advocate such a system of finance as will not enable you to pay the interest on the money you borrow."

Later certain people who resented these comments drew attention to remarks the Earl of Roseberry made at an Adelaide dinner. Comparing the National Debt of Great Britain with colonial loans, the Earl said that while in Britain wealth had been dissipated in "gunpowder and glory", in Australia money had been spent to obtain practical assets like railways, bridges, roads, wharves, and harbours.

Opinion in other colonies was summed up by the *Australasian*. "The South Australians may well feel jubilant and complacent over the completion of their railway to Government Gums, which rather grotesque appellation is henceforth to give place to the more euphonius one of Farina. The event is of great importance in itself and of greater importance as a stage towards the larger developments of the future. South Australia, which was once the object of reproach for its lack of enterprise, has now the longest line of railway running from its Capital that is possessed by any of the colonies."

7

UPS AND DOWNS

Such were the facts of the building of the Port Augusta and Government Gums Railway. But behind the headlines—apt to be monopolised by the doings of the wheat-grower—a multitude of human happenings, all bearing on one or another angle of the great event, passed unnoticed in official records.

Reports from northern settlements made frequent reference to illness. Few of these places attracted a doctor, and so many settlers suffered anxiety for their families, particularly their young children. Government Gums found a solution to this problem.

Soon after the railhead entered the western plain, Hawker became a township of some importance and a doctor settled there, Dr Bruehl.

One day a resident of The Gums met Dr Bruehl and discussed the health problem with him. On returning home he proposed that a "doctor's fund" should be opened. To this fund single persons would be required to contribute five shillings quarterly, couples ten shillings. Dr Bruehl, said the promoter, was willing to visit the settlement once a month on an appointed day, when each contributor to the fund would be entitled to consult him free of further charge. If summoned urgently at any time other than on the appointed day, the doctor would attend, charging only travelling expenses.

A few settlers stood aloof from this proposal. These, if forced to seek medical help, paid a fee of £20 a visit. The yearly "fund" collection at The Gums started at about £100 and continued long after the settlement became Farina. Other places followed this lead and soon Dr Bruehl had a busy practice, travelling up-line as well as down-line out of Hawker.

One day the railway station at Hawker burned down. Alive to the risks of fire in country that often was tinder dry, the railway authorities had installed reservoirs, each of 5 million gallons capacity, at Beltana, Leigh Creek, Lyndhurst, and Farina, but not at Hawker. Instead, according to one semi-humorous newspaper account of the incident, they issued tin boxes to all employees, with instructions to use these for their matches. At the enquiry, held in Laidlaw's Hotel, witnesses were asked in turn whether or not they had obeyed orders in this regard.

The repetition of this question seems to have annoyed the station foreman. When asked about his tin box and the time of the fire, he answered shortly, "My matchbox was kept in front of my little clock. With hands the clock would go. As it was I could not tell the time of the fire. But I did have a look. So I know the matches were as they should be."

It appears that he also looked at his thermometer, for he was able to report that the temperature in his office had been 110° F. But he considered that the heat in the women's room had been greater. If the Board of Enquiry disliked the foreman's sarcasm, they accepted the lead he had given them. Unable to uncover a better explanation, they found that the women had been responsible, for they had failed to lower the blind so that the sun, shining through the glass, had ignited clean waste in an open locker.

At the time of the Hawker station fire the problem of women travellers masquerading as men happened to be particularly troublesome. A young woman dressed in trousers, coat, waistcoat, and bowler hat, and possessing a ticket to Farina was "detected" in the burned-out station. The account does not say how she was recognised as a woman. She was arrested and charged with "impersonation". However, there was no law under which this charge could be pressed and the case collapsed.

Whatever the purpose of their masquerade, the women who posed as men at least paid their fares. The rumpus that arose when the public learned that many well-known persons were travelling free of charge effectively diverted attention from women in men's clothing. The celebrity who did not pay was even better news value. And on him most editors went to town.

Described as "The Great Free Pass Debate", the scandal—as many people viewed the circumstances—consumed a vast quantity of printers' ink. It first became an "indignation topic", as such matters were then styled. A Clare correspondent wrote: "The Government seems determined to waste the public money. A short time ago, they spent about £5,000 in providing board and lodging and large quantities of champagne and other liquors for the guests they chose to invite to witness the opening of the Great Northern Railway." How was it, he demanded, that money could not be found for farming relief without first consulting Parliament, when funds could be poured out on free railway passes and food and drink for selected persons, without such consent?

This article was followed by strong reaction, sometimes outraged, sometimes ironical. From Beltana came a typical example of the latter: "A large party holding free railway passes to Farina arrived here safely, all in excellent spirits. Some of the passengers had amused themselves by frightening kangaroos along the line. Thank Heaven and Ernest Giles that the labours of the explorers are not in vain! — Free passes to travel from Adelaide to Farina by rail to frighten kangaroos! Would it not have been cheaper to send the marsupials to the Metropolis for the amusement of the people?"

An Adelaide journal noted in a snide aside: "We learn that several residents of Port Augusta received passes allowing them to travel gratis over the Northern Railway. We are glad to notice this extension of the privilege to one of the most deeply interested towns in the country."

Was this intended as salt in the wound caused by the omission of Port Augusta from the Quorn invitation list? It may well have been so for the rejoinder came promptly. A Port Augusta story that soon gained wide currency concerned a visitor from Adelaide. "He was one of the 'free pass' travellers, a man sent into the North to circulate a little wealth and spread good will amongst the people of the newly-opened districts. So when he got out of the train he asked a lumper standing by to carry his luggage to the hotel. The man, nothing doubting, did so. Arrived at the house of entertainment, the traveller, placing his hand in his pocket and then withdrawing it empty, observed casually, 'Ah, that'll do, my man. I have no change on me now, but I'll remember you when I come again to Port Augusta.' "

Many letter writers appear to have resented especially the permission granted to the holders of free passes to break their journeys at intermediate stations. But there were many angles for dissatisfaction.

That free passes caused overcrowding was the complaint of one woman with a wry sense of humour. Writing of a trip from Farina to Quorn, she remarked: "I had to nurse a fully developed male because there was insufficient room for him to sit down save in my lap. During the journey two persons fell from the train. I cannot name the immediate causes of the falls, which, fortunately, ended without damage, and I do not know whether it is the guard's duty to report such simple occurrences to headquarters."

The lady's irony was not without basis. "Simple occurrences" of this kind appear not to have been at all unusual. Another passenger wrote: "A traveller fell off the train in the act of uncorking a bottle. He was seen to pick himself up and run after the train. But when the driver stopped, and then backed up, he turned about and ran away, perhaps thinking that there would be some penalty for stopping the train."

Perhaps the Government felt that when such mishaps as these came to be linked with free passes the breeze of protest could well develop into a gale. Be this as it may, the Commissioner of Public Works decided that a public explanation was desirable. He justified free passes with the argument that there were times when even small countries should indulge in a little lavish expenditure. It was fit and proper that South Australia should let the world, within and without, know what she was doing. In any case, said he, the facts were not as stated.

Promptly the Press capitalised upon the Government admission. One paper, in a column headed "Adelaide Gossip", observed: "The vials of indignation that were to be poured on the heads of the Ministry for the Northern Railway outing are likely to come short of making much stir. The little bill turns out to be for £2,000 only." Readers were left to judge whether or not the colony, hard up following a railway spree, could afford such a sum as this for free passes with wining and dining.

The popular view was that if the Government wished to publicise the new railway, it should issue an unlimited number of excursion tickets at a token cost of, say, £1 for the return trip. Then everyone would be placed upon the same footing. Any suggestion of favouritism rankled. And there the matter dropped out of the news in diminishing rumbles of public disgust.

Grievance was voiced as loudly by the railway employee as by the passenger. A typical instance was the letter of a fettler, signing himself "Navvy", who wrote to the editor of the *Dispatch* shortly after traffic opened to Farina. "Your columns are always free to the interests of the working man," began this complainant. He then proceeded to bewail the fact that railway maintenance workers were to be charged rent for Government cottages, over and above a deduction from pay already made for wood and water. "Prior to what would certainly be a great injustice being done us, I would like to point out a few facts in support, NOT of an increased burden but in favour of an increase in wages and a removal of all charges. We have to pay nearly double as much for food as those working nearer towns, and what we get is by no means any too fresh. Then we are compelled to remain nine hours a day at work in a blazing sun with no shelter . . . I can only say that if the Commissioner was in our place for one day he would, instead of suggesting an increase of expenses, favour an increase of two shillings a day to place us on something approaching a footing of equality with our more fortunate bretheren down south who, in a cooler country and nearer town, receive sixpence a day more than we do."

Another and better-founded complaint followed soon afterwards. "The principles of justice and common sense are so far ignored by those in authority in the Railway Department that men who have served the Government and public satisfactorily for many years have had to give place to young men, without any special qualifications, who have recently arrived in the colony as immigrants and for whom the Government is obliged to find employment . . . One case is that of a man who has been employed on the line almost since the day building began — first as a cleaner, then as a fireman, and for the last year-and-a-half as a driver. During all that time no fault has been charged to him, although on many occasions his duty has extended over the 24 hours without an hour for sleep. And while the traffic was gradually organized his work time was generally from thirteen to sixteen hours without a spell. When the immigrants were sent up here a month ago this man was virtually disrated and a person who, I am informed, had only a fireman's certificate, put in his place."

This writer's statement was supported in an article, "Our Railways", published in the *South Australian Register. Inter alia* this said: "It is rumoured that there has been great waste in the laying out of some of the lines because proper attention has not been paid to the exigencies of traffic. It is rumoured that the rolling-stock is insufficient for working the lines. It is rumoured that many hands have been dismissed from Government workshops to make room for new arrivals. Other rumours are afloat that we need not indicate."

Some of the unspecified rumours related to rivalries between railway townships; between, for example, Farina and Beltana, Wilson and Kanyaka, Port Augusta and Port Pirie. Said one report: "Much of the *jalousie de métier* is amusing." And, indeed, this was so. The case of Terowie and Petersburg, for instance!

Here the cause of rivalry — which came to a peak some months after the northern line had reached Farina — was a see-saw struggle over the choice of a junction on the main trunk railway for the Barrier Range branch line. Silverton was at the root of this particular contention. The purpose of the prospective extension was to tap the New South Wales boundary country in the neighbourhood of the mines. In those times, settlements had a way of springing up suddenly, almost as though Aladdin had rubbed his lamp. So Silverton!

There was a new Government in South Australia just then and the Premier announced in Assembly that orders had been given for the survey of a line based on Terowie, because it was the meeting-place of the gauges—the metropolitan broad-gauge system and the northern narrow-gauge line—and because it had a supply of fresh water, a necessity at major steam-engine terminals.

Instantly smouldering township feeling flared in burning rivalry between Petersburg, Orroroo, Carrieton, and Hawker, while in the background the ports seethed contentiously. "Are we asleep?" demanded one angry correspondent. "Port Augusta is the natural seaport for the Northern Territory and the western parts of Queensland and New South Wales. But Port Pirie is in the field. It has held a public meeting to press its claims to be the terminus of the Silverton line. Shall we lag behind and allow our superior advantages to lie hid? Is there no leading townsman who will call a public meeting to demonstrate our incontestably superior claims?"

Probably, the Premier secretly anathematised the disputatious townsfolk. But he ordered a flying survey to be made from each of the claimant townships. Surveys were to converge upon Glenmore, a station on the New South Wales side of the border some sixty miles north of Silverton.

When all was done, Petersburg remained the sole alternative to Terowie. At the time these townships had populations of 400 and 700 respectively.

The *Terowie Enterprise* described what followed. "The feeling in Terowie has alternated during the week from grave to gay, from lively to severe. The triumphant passage of the Bill for a line via Petersburg last week caused wailing and gnashing of teeth here, while in Petersburg there was general rejoicing and festivity and bands playing 'Happy are we tonight, boys'. Wednesday a change came o'er the spirit of our dream with the news that the Upper House had rejected the measure. Terowie jubilant; champagne flowing, flags flying, and Petersburg bands playing 'I'd mourn the hopes that leave me'. Telegrams of condolence from Terowie. Thursday reversed matters again. Bill via Petersburg re-introduced and passed. Telegrams came back to roost. Bonfires and beer at Petersburg. Terowie band playing 'Oh! Chide not my heart for its sadness'. Toiling, rejoicing, sorrowing! Such is life!"

Ups and downs, indeed! They were many in the days following the completion of the line. People seem to have been far freer with complaint than praise. Many who once had regarded a railway as the peak of hope now whinged at its performance, and all demanded that their local need should receive priority—for example, the Port Augustans and their railway station.

A leading article in the *Dispatch* said: "The railway station of Port Augusta, the terminus of the Great Northern line, is an insult to the town. There is not a wayside station at any mud gully in any of the more advanced sister colonies which does not afford better accommodation to passengers. Platform there is none, and ladies and children have to fall out down the step as best they can. There is no verandah overhead and the footwalk is a penance. The whole affair is the most contemptible thing in railway stations we have ever beheld . . . If the ground were only asphalted! The rocky road to Dublin is a fool to our railway station footwalk."

Shades of the goats that made every street corner stink! Once the cry had been that when a railway was built the Government would hear no more murmurs from the North.

8
ON TO HERGOTT SPRINGS

Moorhouse, Robinson and Jesser got away to a flying start. "The countryside being so level, they are able to make very rapid progress with the earthworks of the line," said a report from Farina. Yet three months later only eleven miles of rail had been laid.

The plate-layers had been halted by shortage of sleepers, a large consignment of which was somewhere on the road from the Big Tree country in the south-west of Western Australia. It was said that a railway smash had taken place, though just where this had happened is not clear today. But the accident—if indeed one occurred—can have been only a contributory factor, for the holdup was of more than four months' duration.

It was during this pause in construction that an event occurred that caused much exasperation in Adelaide. Perhaps with some reason, Ministers felt that the people of the Far North were indeed hard to satisfy.

At the end of May 1883 Port Augusta began to argue a new and highly controversial issue.

A letter had just appeared which, in all probability, the writer had itched to publish since an announcement made in March by the Commissioner of Public Works at a dinner to mark the opening of the Adelaide and Nairne Railway. The Commissioner had said: "It is on the programme of the Ministry to introduce next season a Bill to carry a line of railway—or rather to extend the present line advancing to Hergott—to Strangways Springs, a distance of one hundred and forty-four miles."

One might suppose that this was exactly what everybody had anticipated, whether or not they happened to know of the Engineer-in-Chief's announcement that a preliminary survey had been made. However, the Commissioner's remark sparked off what seems today to be quite unreasonable indignation in the minds of a number of influential men in Port Augusta and district, and thus triggered an astonishing situation.

Today it appears that the proper time to raise the matter that these people now determined to put forward would have been in 1877 or earlier; at any rate, before the construction of the Port Augusta and Government Gums Railway began. Of course at that time the Terowie extension, that had the effect of by-passing Port Augusta, had not been built, and the Quorn junction had not risen from the bush. But the virtual certainty that a main trunk line to link Adelaide directly with the north would be completed must have been foreseen by the Port Augustans.

It seems that this would have been the more reasonable time to press for a route that, in addition to being more direct, would have ensured to Port Augusta the position of chief southern port of the future transcontinental railway.

At that time thought had been in terms of a through railway, not just a local line to serve the needs of the Flinders region. It may be that the wheat-farmers' agitation obscured the issue, causing the Flinders corridor to be seen as the only possible route for the railway. Perhaps the farmers were so noisy that theirs were the only voices to which Government and public gave heed. But if the Port Augusta dissidents did in fact first make their proposal at what would appear to have been the proper time there is no record of this. In the circumstances, one must conclude that they did not do so.

The controversy that arose is of particular interest today, because now we have come full-circle, returning, in the national interest, to an 1883 counter-move which then would appear to have been motivated entirely by local politics. For shortly a railway is to be built from Tarcoola to Alice Springs, following a route running as nearly north and south as is practicable. The proposal put forward by the Port Augustans in 1883 visualised a standard-gauge line from Port Augusta West to Strangways and so north. Insofar as it was to run in the west and to be a standard-gauge line, it may be thought to have provided the germ of an idea that now, at last, is to be given effect.

Today the project is rational. But then, in view of the immense labour just completed, it was hopelessly ill-timed.

However, the letter which now sparked off a situation that appeared to set aside lightly all that had been achieved began by praising the feat of the builders of the Overland Telegraph Line and stressing that the proper starting point of a transcontinental railway, "the twin sister of the telegraph", was Port Augusta, now relegated to a position at the foot of what amounted to a mere extension line.

"Look at the map showing the one-horse railway which at present exists from Terowie to the Government Gums," continued the writer acidly. "Then consider that this railway, which is allowed to be a blunder, is to be further perpetrated by cutting across country from Hergott Springs to the Strangways. And this, says Mr Commissioner Ramsay, is to be the nucleus of our Transcontinental Railway. I can understand the reason for continuing the present line as started, and that is the selfish one—centralisation. All our legislation, in the railway line, seems to be with one idea—carrying everything direct to Adelaide and Port Adelaide."

Here, it seems, was the true source of the writer's spleen. The railway had developed into a Darwin-to-Port Adelaide line via Quorn and Terowie, by-passing Port Augusta. The writer proposed to substitute another line to the west—Darwin to Port Augusta direct, with an extension by sea to the south of the colony. He added that if "a steamer like the *Investigator*" were held in readiness, cattle from Strangways could be delivered on the wharf at Port Adelaide within forty-five hours of being entrained.

He concluded on a note of surprising bitterness and, in the circumstances, outrageously poor taste. "I trust, for the credit of our colony, that this narrow-gauge abortion will not be further continued."

This letter produced an immediate reaction among the writer's fellow townsmen. It seems probable that the subject had been well discussed and future plans laid before publication had been sought. Perhaps, indeed, the sole spontaneous response came from a correspondent who signed himself "Diamantina" and who urged an extension to the east rather than to the west, an extension into Queensland, for this, he said, would transform vast areas "from cattle to sheep runs and bring a large traffic to the railway".

Eight days later, on a Friday evening, a public meeting was held in the Council Chamber. The advertised purpose was to oppose the extension of the existing railway to Strangways, and to decide whether or not it would be in the best interests of the colony to adopt an entirely new route for the transcontinental line.

As Chairman, the Mayor opened the proceedings. The gist of his brief address was to the effect that it was the business of the citizens to make their town one of the great ports of the world.

A Councillor then proposed the first resolution: "That this meeting approves of a railway being made from Port Augusta in a north-westerly direction."

Conceding that the line to Hergott would be useful to open up the north-east of South Australia and to tap the Queensland trade, he said that it should be abandoned as part of a transcontinental railway, and a line to Phillips Ponds substituted. The Ministry that initiated the existing line had run into the project hurriedly and without formulating any plan as to where the line should go on its way to the Northern Territory. The result was that, having by some means reached Farina and laid plans to Hergott, they had been brought up short by Lake Eyre. Now they found themselves compelled to branch off in an almost due westerly direction, thus losing fully 100 miles of northerly progress at a cost of some £300,000—all money wasted. This fresh outlay would be better spent in building a standard-gauge line to Phillips Ponds, the first instalment of a new western transcontinental line.

Next a grazier, the owner of Wirraminna Station, said that millions upon millions of sheep could be carried in the north-west country, and that the colony should develop its own land before showing interest in that of the eastern colonies. (It is interesting that Wirraminna, 157 miles north-west of Port Augusta, is now a halt on the East-West Line, and exactly 100 miles from Tarcoola.)

Speaker after speaker supported the resolution. One claimed that Governor Jervois had expressed the view that the railway now proposed would have to be built one day, and that the Chief Secretary had supported this opinion. He added that the meeting might judge the time that would be required to reach Darwin by narrow gauge, since sixteen hours were needed to travel from Port Augusta to Farina, a distance of less than 200 miles. Why, with no food available on the train, they would starve on the way!

Another speaker remarked sarcastically that when the line was built in the wrong place few people who knew the country supposed that the projectors were sane men. The line had been sent anywhere because the Parliament of the day evidently considered that a railway was not needed at all and that a wheelbarrow would carry the traffic. The scheme had been laughed at by the Adelaide Press.

Yet another, slightly less biased, said that though the north-east railway might suffice for a time, it would prove to be inadequate to meet future needs. The narrow gauge was a mistake. So why perpetuate it? Better to build anew. The money being spent on cartage to and from the north-west would go far towards paying for the railway.

Clearly all this had been discussed again and again by the townspeople since the start of work on the Terowie extension, for it appears that no one in that packed meeting felt surprise at a proposal that must have astonished the colony as a whole. Everyone, it seems, had forgotten the satisfaction with which Port Augusta had viewed the coming of Barry, Brookes and Fraser, and the loud cheers with which they had greeted the turning of the first sod of the narrow-gauge line by Governor Jervois. For when the motion was put to the meeting it was carried unanimously.

Next, the citizen whose letter had brought the matter into the open proposed the second resolution: "That a memorial be drawn up, and forwarded to the Government through the Members for the district, asking for an immediate survey to be made from Port Augusta to Phillips Ponds as the first section of the future Transcontinental Railway, thence to Strangways Springs, the Peake and Charlotte Waters." This motion, too, was carried unanimously.

Had those who signed the memorial that was now prepared known all that was going on behind the scenes in Adelaide, they would have realised that they were wasting their time. The Government was sick of memorials. It was beset by them.

For example, a report dated 29 August from the temporary terminus of Farina spoke of "our Queensland neighbours who swarm down with fat cattle and sheep to supply our markets". The drovers apparently were cracking wry jokes about the prospective railway extension to Strangways, pointing out that it was Queensland traffic that caused "our P.A. and G.G. Railway to pay such handsome returns". They estimated that for every ton of goods that might go to Strangways, at least ten were already going to Queensland. So Farina petitioned for a railway to the Queensland border. "The route via Innamincka is considered the most desirable."

But the hopes of the people of Port Augusta and Farina alike must have drooped on 26 September, when Act No. 281 of 1883 was assented to by Governor Sir William Robinson, who had succeeded Sir William Jervois: "Whereas it is expedient to provide for the construction of a line of Railway from Hergott Springs to Primrose Springs; And whereas plans of the proposed railway, showing the line thereof, together with the book of reference thereto, have been duly prepared and deposited in the offices of the Surveyor-General at Adelaide and signed 'R.C. Patterson, Deputy Engineer-in-Chief'; Be it therefore enacted by the Governor of the Province of South Australia, with the advice and consent of the Legislative Council and House of Assembly of the said Province in the present Parliament assembled, as follows . . . " The provisions were as before with the sole difference that steel rails now were to weigh not less than fifty-one pounds a yard.

It was at this time that an estimate was tabled in the Legislative Assembly for a three-foot-six-inch gauge railway to extend between Port Darwin and Pine Creek, a mining settlement. This railway, 146 miles long, was proposed as part of the prospective transcontinental railway, the southern and northern sections of which were to meet somewhere in the Centre. Here, iron sleepers were to be used and rails were to weigh forty-one pounds a yard. The cost was estimated at £1,011,000, a figure that included the outlay for a jetty at Port Darwin.

Thus a month after the further extension of the Great Northern Railway had been sanctioned, Act No. 284 provided for the formation of a line of railway from Palmerston to Pine Creek.

Meanwhile, sleepers from Western Australia had reached construction headquarters ten miles north of Farina, and plate-laying began afresh on the last day of October. Once more building advanced rapidly in flat country.

Far away at Hergott, surveyors were camped. Their job was to lay out the township now officially proclaimed as Marree. The Aboriginal name for the springs was Mari, meaning "the place of many possums".

Sidings would not be built until after the arrival of the railhead, but a store and warehouse, two shops, and two eating houses had been erected in preparation for the arrival of the gangs. Already camel drivers from the first tented camp near the springs were moving their goods the short distance across country to stake claims near the track of the approaching railway. It was then that the district to be known as Ghan Town began.

A contemporary report speaks of an excellent supply of spring water in the early township. An old-timer, born in Marree, explained this. Pipes were laid over the plain from the springs and water was pumped to the settlement by means of a steam donkey-engine. The water was not disagreeable to the taste. A police camp was established at this time, but a post office did not come until later, some time after the building of the railway siding.

Despite the Government decision to name the new township Marree, the name Hergott was transferred from the springs with the camel drivers. It continued in use until the time of the first World War, when all German names were removed from the map or altered to their English equivalents.

Although the Department of Lands has no information on the population of the district at the time the railhead arrived, the probability is that it was considerable, even though the number fluctuated. For, despite Hergott's importance as an outback communications centre, the first settlement consisted of tents and a few huts built of wattle and daub. The number of tents must have waxed and waned with the arrival and departure of the camel strings.

One day in November people looking southwards across the plain from the new dirt street saw, far away, the figures of the men in the construction gangs, toiling in the summer heat. After that, the railhead itself was not long in arriving. And on the evening of Saturday 8 December the contractors' engine stopped running to Hergott.

By this time a second store and three more boarding-houses were in business, all hastily-erected wood-and-iron structures, the corrugated-iron sheets obtained from stores brought on the construction train.

On 6 January 1884 the first train carrying Government supplies steamed into Hergott during a raging dust storm. It is recorded that on that day the heat in railway tents was 120° F. The Queensland Road was closed to bullockies, for there were stages of over seventy miles that were waterless. Consequently several teams were in camp in the neighbourhood of the springs. But camel strings continued in business. The *Dispatch* reported: "A great deal of sickness prevails, probably on account of the heat. The wind has been high for the past three days accompanied by clouds of dust."

Shortly now, farm selectors were to be permitted to convert credit purchases into long-term leases. Once more the country became divided broadly into agricultural and pastoral zones. It was understood that the Act which had carried the farming frontier to the border of the Northern Territory had been no more than a nonsense. So the grazier, recovering confidence, again invested in his land.

Now, with the first mobs being entrained at Hergott, the *Dispatch*, which six years previously had said, "Our children may see the present narrow belt of cultivation extended far into the interior and thousands of thriving homesteads and busy towns where now not even sheep can live except in winter time", had second thoughts. "It is sincerely to be hoped that sanguine views with regard to the future will not be extensively indulged in," wrote the editor. "It may now be regarded as an established fact that wheat cultivation by itself, except in very favourable seasons, is not a remunerative pursuit in the dry areas of the north." Which, of course, was very much what George Woodroffe Goyder had said in the beginning.

At this time South Australia had 2,886,000 sheep and 123,900 cattle depastured on 219,000 square miles of land held under pastoral lease from the Crown. But the people of the colony were consuming some 900,000 sheep annually. Of these about 300,000 were imported, and an even higher proportion of the beef eaten was drawn from outside sources. Indeed, it was estimated that about £500,000 was paid annually to sister colonies for meat. A situation now arose which brought the railway authorities into bad odour with the public.

Adelaide was very largely dependent upon the railways for its meat supply, and so whenever (from whatever cause) railway deliveries were delayed, the effect was felt at once. A time came when—entirely through the ineptitude of railway management, said the public—scarcity was such that best quality beef sold at the scandalous price of 10d a pound.

Most of the cattle reaching Adelaide came from Queensland, and it was claimed that drought prevented stock from travelling the tracks from the border to the railhead. However, cattle from the Farina district could be trucked south. Many felt that the railway was failing to justify its high cost.

Then two facts leaked out. First it was learned that a deputation of station owners had waited on the Commissioner of Public Works to ask for a reduction in the charges for the carriage of livestock, and to propose a sliding scale based on rates levied in other colonies. Their request had been refused. Next it transpired that only twenty-four sheep and cattle trucks were available on narrow-gauge lines.

The praise that had been accorded the railway authorities for their achievement in constructing a railway to Hergott faded into abuse. People drew unflattering comparisons with the railways of New South Wales and Victoria where, after paying working expenses, managements contributed to State revenues sums sufficient to pay the interest on the cost of construction, reckoned at four per cent. They pointed out that South Australian railways, though costing less, returned only two-and-a-half per cent on the capital invested. They demanded to know why this was the case when the rates charged for the carriage of livestock were up to twelve per cent higher than those levied in the sister colonies.

"Give us cheaper meat," people said, "and the increase in traffic will counterbalance a lower return per truck." They also demanded that more trucks should be built.

In point of fact, twenty-four new cattle trucks were ready to leave the builders' yards. But an irate public was not appeased when this was made known. Much of the glamour of the early rail days was thus dissipated in a flurry of vexation.

A traveller of the time has left a brief description of a train journey from Wonoka to Hergott, through country north of the failed wheat-lands. "Hour after hour, the train jogs steadily along over plains as stony as a badly-mended country road. Not a blade of grass is to be seen. The vegetation consists of salt-bush and other salsolaceous bushes, with scrub and perhaps a line of gum-trees marking the course of a distant creek, the shingly bed of which is usually dry."

9

THE HARD ROAD TO OODNA

Late one afternoon our brakevan jolted under a heavy impact. The Slow Mixed had arrived and our journey from Marree to Oodnadatta was about to begin. A station assistant fastened the couplings and walked away.

We ran to climb aboard and found that a rocky outcrop, hitherto convenient as a step in the absence of a platform, was convenient no longer. The jolt had shunted the van some feet out of position. The porter was out of sight and no ladder was handy. The door-sill, at head height, was something of a haul for Sally who, though slim, required a boost.

Somehow, she stuck midway. "Hooshta!" I urged. My position being strategically sound, I had no fear of retaliatory backward kicks.

Just then a yell came from down-line. "Hang on, mate, hang on!" And then a willing, if hilariously cheerful, citizen reeled up. Who he was I have no idea. But he was well oiled and quite resolved to be of service in what he clearly conceived to be an emergency.

To have declined assistance with the assurance that help was not needed would have availed me nothing in the stranger's condition. As we heaved jointly and successfully, he looked sideways and grinned. "All gentlemen here, mate—I hope!" He hiccupped and staggered away in quest of the next beer. Ten minutes later we moved off into the glory of a Lake Eyre sunset.

A sweep of desert sprawled towards a horizon resembling the curving rim of a vast ball silhouetted against crimson splendour. The broad shadow of the train was like a sliding black ribbon on the surface of the plain, golden in the last of the sunlight.

Leaning back in V.I.P. comfort we watched the lonely track where, some ninety years previously, construction navvies had toiled and sweated, and strings of camels roped nose to tail had padded silently on their way to Oodnadatta and the Centre.

In the main those navvies were very different from the men who built the line from Port Augusta to Government Gums, and then carried through to Hergott. For that matter, the whole manner of construction was different, for on the present stretch the Government controlled operations instead of contractors.

Times had changed. During the period when the line was built between Farina and Hergott many stations on the camel communications network were being abandoned. The great drought that had halted the advance of the wheat-farmers had ruined many graziers, and apparently the country west of Lake Eyre was the region most seriously affected.

But depression was general. Unemployment spread throughout Australia. Mass meetings of jobless were held in Sydney and Melbourne—angry meetings. In Adelaide the Trades and Labour Council assembled many long lists containing the names of hundreds of men who lacked all means of support. These lists lengthened daily. They included tradesmen as well as labourers—bricklayers, plasterers, masons, painters, and so on.

Storekeepers and merchants were forced to give long credit, and so many shop assistants were dismissed. Jewellers and watchmakers lost their livelihood and joined the queues of unemployed.

Three poor harvests in succession obliged even southern farmers to borrow and so pile up debt.

Soon the banks restricted loans. Then farmers could no longer employ the labour they were accustomed to use. Even the wealthier graziers suspended work on fencing, dam-building, and well-sinking.

Eventually road boards ran out of funds. Then the ranks of the unemployed were swelled by road contractors and their men.

In these serious conditions the Government issued free rail passes to men out of work so that they might travel to look for jobs. Seldom was the search successful. Gangs of unemployed were sent to the forests to fell timber and cut railway sleepers. But expedients such as this were palliatives only. The emergency compelled the Government to resume railway construction in the north after a pause of about five months, instead of the three-year interlude that had been planned for financial recovery. Work had to be found quickly and the transcontinental railway, though insufficient in itself to meet the need, was an obvious starting point.

But to use railway construction to provide work for the unemployed meant that the Government must turn builder.

Although the extension to Strangways had been announced publicly, there was talk now of the recommendation of the 1875 Railway Commission to build a railway link with Queensland. Probably the discussion originated with a few Members who wished to vary the Government's decision at the last moment and route the line to the Northern Territory by way of Birdsville and Camooweal in order to gather Queensland trade on the way.

Long afterwards, the then Assistant Engineer for Railway Construction in South Australia, giving evidence before the Commonwealth Parliamentary Standing Committee on Public Works, referred to this effort to change the route of the railway from Hergott, to turn it to the north-east instead of the north-west. "The survey was made, I believe, because . . . the question of running the line to Birdsville was considered in State circles. But a lot of propositions like that do not come to anything." Evidently, however, the dissident members obtained a hearing.

But there is no doubt that the wish of the majority was to keep the railway throughout its length within the borders of South Australia and its huge dependency. Probably some hot argument occurred, but the proposal was rejected, though consideration was given to the suggestion that a branch line should be built to the Queensland border as a tributary to a direct north-south trunk line. This is made clear in the Public Works Report for 1884. "An examination of the country between Farina (via Strzelecki Creek and the Cullamurra Waterhole on the Cooper) and the Queensland border was made between June and August."

It appears that this suggestion was even adopted—briefly. A leader in the *Dispatch* said: "It may now be taken as a settled thing that a railway is to be constructed to connect our northern line with the Queensland border. The question which remains to be settled is the route. From Hergott to Birdsville—a town which has lately sprung into existence on the Diamantina Creek—a direct line would make the connection in about 280 miles . . . The other route proposed is via Innamincka from Farina, a distance of 230 miles . . . The question of engineering difficulties must, of course, be decided by professional authority, but on other points the weight of evidence is in favour of the direct line to Birdsville."

Though nothing happened after all, the proposal remained a lively probability for long afterwards. In 1887 when the railhead was far away to the west of Lake Eyre, Surveyor Bagot was sent to examine a railway route from Hergott in a north-north-easterly direction to reach the Queensland border thirty-odd miles to the east of Birdsville.

However, early in 1884, the Government announced abruptly that it intended to abandon the projected railway to the Queensland border and push on with the transcontinental line. Perhaps the deciding factor was inter-colonial jealousy.

Rivalries were keen in those days. Just how keen is suggested by sharp comments made at this time by the Engineer-in-Chief. "Invidious comparisions have been drawn in the last Queensland railway report between the cost of maintenance of the railways in that colony and the cost of maintenance in South Australia. In that report the cost of maintenance on [our] broad gauge lines was given as the actual cost on all lines. The figures which were given respecting the narrow gauge lines were disregarded. It is obvious that any fair comparison (if any comparison should be made at all) should be between lines of the same gauge. All the lines in Queensland are of the 3'6" gauge, and if the cost of maintenance of these lines is compared with that which obtains on our lines of equal gauge it will be found that the Queensland lines have cost double as much to maintain as the South Australian lines. These remarks are due to the officers of the Engineer-in-Chief's Department whose work will stand comparison with work of a similar nature in any of the other colonies."

Feeling was just as sensitive in Ministry circles as in railway departments. A newspaper leader had this to say: "The Territory is at present a failure. Though a part of South Australia, its trade belongs almost entirely to Queensland and New South Wales. But this colony is responsible for the cost of its government and for the construction of the public works necessary to develop the resources of the country."

In the light of such comments, one must suppose that an important factor in the decision to continue the line by way of Oodnadatta had been a keen sense of rivalry. The South Australians' chief concern was to unite the Territory and the main portion of the colony by means of a direct railway link in which other colonies had no share or say. In those days the interests of each individual colony came first, those of Australia second. In fairness, however, it should be said that to the South Australian who had recently built a telegraph line, partly at least to establish close touch with his huge dependency, it must have seemed logical that the railway should follow the same route which, furthermore, was the most direct.

However, geographical considerations probably had a place in the decision. Charles Fenner (for twenty-three years Superintendent of Technical Education in South Australia) considered that the resolve to take the railway to Oodnadatta was greatly influenced by the presence of mound springs along the south-western border of the Great Artesian Basin. He pointed out that the distribution of pastoral population and the location of stock routes were related to the artesian bores, said to rise from great depth through fissures in a fault that occurs where the floor of the Lake Eyre basin meets ancient rock to the west. Thus, Blanche Cup, the Bubbler, and other free-flowing springs providing completely reliable supplies probably influenced the advice that the railway engineers gave the Government in the matter of the route to be followed by the railway.

Construction began on 16 July 1884, "for the purpose of finding work for the unemployed". Because the Government was now a builder, no tenders were invited from contracting firms.

The Department of the Engineer-in-Chief was placed in control of the operation and as a beginning 250 unemployed labourers were drafted up-country from Adelaide.

By this time the permanent staff of Moorhouse, Robinson and Jesser, the late contractors, had been withdrawn. Furthermore many of the navvies employed on the workings between Farina and Hergott, wearying of the lonely places, had returned south despite warnings respecting the state of the labour market. Nevertheless a large number of old hands remained to form the experienced nucleus of the new work force.

Simultaneously, with the arrival of the newcomers, 21,000 jarrah sleepers from Western Australia were landed at Port Augusta, where a special siding had been built at a cost of £1,042 to receive these and other materials for the Strangways extension.

At the time when clearing and grubbing gangs left Hergott, a report of the Public Works Department announced a change in the railway plan. The line was to be taken round "the western side of the Mount Margaret Range, instead of going to Primrose Springs, in order to give better facilities to local traffic and to avoid some rough country". This carefully worded statement covered an official blunder. Parliament had passed a Bill to take a railway to a place where later it had been found impossible to build one. For some time afterwards the railway authorities were sensitive to any reference to Primrose Springs.

So they moved out of Hergott into the eye of the sunset for, to begin with, the workings advanced only slightly north of west. They were hard on the heels of the surveyors, who did not complete their task until November.

The permanent way entered and left Hergott lightly ballasted and unfenced. It was unchanged in the days of the first World War when Edwin Brady described it and spoke of his train running down a camel on the common outside town.

One pictures the scene as the construction workers moved out of the settlement. Soon they were breaking ground in pursuit of the Overland Telegraph Line. Slender poles, each with its insulator-carrying steel cross-bar, beckoned them on. A seemingly endless string of white-capped guides pointing the way to the north!

On either side of the marching posts ran a strip of cleared land, a chain wide. This was maintained by a patrolling line party.

For the greater part the going was flat. But building advanced slowly because of the inexperience of an increasingly large part of the labour force. It appears that, to begin with, a fresh draft of unemployed men arrived each week from Adelaide. These clerks, drapers' assistants, waiters, watch repairers, and hotel porters, many of them no longer young, were unable to compete with the seasoned, professional navvy. Some flaked out on the job, and frequent rest periods were allowed to newly-arrived men.

Understandably in the circumstances, work on the extension lacked the enthusiasm of the initial track-laying out of Port Augusta; but gradually the earthworks pushed out on to the virgin and reluctant plain.

The feelings of the newly-enlisted navvies must have been mixed indeed. However, the popular attitude towards the Territory being what it was, the sight of the telegraph line must have brought them inspiration. So they swung their unaccustomed picks and "banjos" with whatever vigour heat and overstrained muscles allowed. Many hearts were willing. No doubt of that!

But those who had read even a little history must have wondered about the country that lay ahead. Charles Sturt had written of scurvy, of heat so intense that the ink dried on his pen before he could put it to paper, of finger nails that cracked like glass, of provisions that lost weight and value. What would their experience be?

The sight of the telegraph poles marching ahead, prim and correct, must have restored their waning confidence. Then, of course, their pay was assured and regular. This must have done much to reconcile them to their lot. Navvies were paid well for those times. For example, a good ballast worker earned between £3 and £4 weekly, and this wage enabled him to provide for a family. On the workings meat was cheaper than in Adelaide or Port Augusta, and bread was the same price. Tents and wood were provided by the Government.

At this period trains ran from Hergott to Port Augusta thrice weekly—on Mondays, Wednesdays, and Fridays, departing at 6 a.m. and arriving at 9.06 p.m. Already the population of the township had grown to about 600, a figure that included the personnel of the railway base camp, for Hergott was construction headquarters.

Now the long, straggling main street included "several black-smiths and wheelwrights, three saddlers, and some considerable stores and forwarding agencies". And, added the report, "One firm has contracted with Jemedahr Faiz Mahomed for sixty camels to take fifteen tons of loading to Birdsville". Mahomed, one of the early drivers of the camel communications network, and others who had transferred from the old tented camp, often worked also for the Department, transporting sleepers and rails from the railhead to the forward plate-laying parties.

Already the Town and Country Bank had a branch in Hergott—a wood-and-iron building only, but superior to the quarters afforded the police. The *Dispatch* described the conditions under which the police worked: "The Police Camp, so called, is on the east side of the railway and is the most miserable apology for quarters conceivable. One tent, about 10 feet by 12 feet, is used by the troopers as a living room and for keeping their arms and darbies. Another tent, very much the worse for wear, is used for forage, while a third is the 'lock-up'. There is a log, not a very large one, to which prisoners are chained. Three or four prisoners would have no difficulty in carrying away chains, log, handcuffs and all, if the trooper on guard should be called away to help his colleague. The railway line runs between the township and the camp and taking a refractory prisoner across is a matter of some difficulty."

No paddock had been fenced for the police horses. So whenever they were turned loose, next day the Aboriginal boys spent hours trying to catch them and bring them into camp. The animals strayed far, for the surrounding country was "all bare and stony—as if it had been raining stones—the grazing capacity about one bandicoot to the acre and not calculated to fatten him at that".

Eventually a properly fenced paddock was allotted to the police. It was situated between the township and the old tented camp, and close to the pipe track so that water-troughs might be kept full.

According to contemporary reports, the post and telegraph office at the new railway depot was "a structure to be seen and admired. The tent in which the business of the Department is conducted is 12 feet square. One half is used for sleeping. In the other half the table is open to all and, in the case of a rush—as on a Saturday afternoon—liable to be overset."

But a few substantial buildings were being erected. Chief among these was the railway hotel, the Great Northern. This occupied a site eighty-three feet by forty-six feet in area. The bar, nineteen feet by twenty-two feet, was larger than the dining-room, seventeen feet by sixteen feet. Upstairs were fourteen bedrooms and a bathroom, and an annexe contained eight extra bedrooms. "Each room had one or more air-brick openings to draw off heated air." There was a large billiard room, and a wide balcony served the upper rooms.

This was a very modern hotel for its day. It had stone stables comprising eight stalls and a loose-box, and an underground tank with a capacity of 20,000 gallons.

Six months after the arrival of the railway the Education Department opened a school, renting as a schoolroom the Wesleyan Chapel, a small, wooden-frame building with galvanised-iron roof that had been put up at a cost of £165. Most of the twenty-seven pupils were the children of railway employees.

In October the railway station was finished. It included a running-shed large enough for an engine and tender and two carriages; a goods shed, sixty feet by forty-five feet; staff offices; and a large water-tank for the supply of locomotives.

Until this time, locomotive water had been obtained from a pipe leading across country from the springs. Now an artesian bore, 340 feet deep and five-and-a-half inches in diameter, was sunk for railway use. This bore was situated within the railway enclosure and, since, under its own pressure, water rose in the piping to a height of sixty-four feet, the tank, some 200 yards distant, could be supplied without the use of a pump.

Bore water was of better quality than spring water, and it freed engine boiler-tubes from spring-water crust. The low ground about the springs was described as being "white with the soda and magnesia deposited by overflowing water". An interesting point is that Mr Allan Crombie, born in Hergott at the turn of the century, recalls that when he was a boy, waste water from the bore ran for over a mile across the plain and supplied both mosques.

After the bore had been sunk, a coaling stage was built close to the water-tank. The practice was to carry coal in large baskets from a bulk store in the yard. When full, a basket weighed eighty-four pounds. Raised to the platform by means of a hand-operated hoist, it was emptied by hand into the waiting tender. One hundred and thirty baskets were needed to fill a small tender. To man-handle this quantity of coal required two hours of hard, sweating toil.

Along the length of the line it became the custom for train crews to pay Aborigines to do this work. The practice was popular with station staffs who were supposed to assist in coaling. Apparently it was popular with the Aborigines, too, for they delighted in working the hoist. Usually they were paid in food and tobacco.

For a time after work began on the Strangways extension, all materials were stored at Port Augusta and sent up-line as needed. But the engineers on the spot pointed out so many disadvantages in this arrangement that two sidings were laid down parallel to the line at Hergott, which thus became the main supply depot as well as the base camp.

Placed in convenient stacks, sleepers, rails, and iron work were handily situated for the provision of the service gangs that travelled backwards and forwards along the extension each work-day until the railhead receded to a distance at which this method of supply was no longer economic. When this happened a work train was put into use.

The new arrangement inconvenienced local storekeepers and forwarding agents, who complained to the railway authorities that their business was obstructed. Indeed at this period complaint appears to have been the rule throughout the length of the railway. Goods were said to have been mislaid, railway servants to have been inconsiderate, and so on.

Often the complaints were well-founded. The fact was that construction materials received priority everywhere. But this apart, the hauling power available was insufficient to handle the traffic. A train might leave Quorn with twenty-six loaded trucks, two passenger coaches, and a brakevan. If the weight proved too great on steep gradients, several trucks would be shunted at a convenient siding and there abandoned until such time as a lighter train arrived to take them forward.

Graziers had their peculiar complaint. Cattle trucks, they said, were poorly designed.

The cattle wagon was narrow. It accommodated six, or at the most seven, beasts, and the animals travelled with their heads outside, for the unslatted walls stood breast-high. Occasionally horns were snapped off; and when animals slipped, they injured others in their frantic efforts to recover themselves. Sometimes they trampled down and mutilated their weaker fellows. Cases occurred in which unfortunate beasts hooked their horns in low roof timbers and strangled themselves, and at times steers even broke out when trains stopped.

Losses became so heavy that some owners preferred to continue droving all the way to Adelaide. These spoke of "the cruel risk of the cattle truck".

To the travelling public the lack of third-class coaches was an especially sore point. An angry member of the Farmers' Mutual Association pressed the matter. "The most miserable railway ride I ever had was from Quorn northward," he wrote. "The second-class carriage was crowded with drunken navvies. This, I hear, is not an unusual occurrence. It is too bad that respectable people, whose means prohibit paying first-class fares, should be subjected to annoyance more easily imagined than described."

Newspapers made scathing reference to "railway inefficiency" and the inconvenience this caused the public. "A striking instance of the way in which things are done in the Railway Department is the arranging of the time table," remarked one editor. "This little pamphlet is certainly an unique work of art and would command the highest admiration and esteem if its object were the same as that of the Chinese puzzle — i.e. to exercise the patience and ingenuity of the person who undertakes to unravel its mysteries." And, elsewhere, "The ridiculously complex arrangement of the railway timetable — popularly known as 'Pendleton's Puzzle' — which astonishes and perplexes visitors from other colonies as much as it irritates South Australians is, year after year, adhered to with a dogged tenacity which would do credit to an early Christian martyr at the stake."

The post office, too, was vigorously attacked. One day, a protest meeting gathered in a store at Hergott. It decided unanimously to call "the attention of the authorities to the urgent need for a suitable post and telegraph office, the present accommodation affording no security to letters".

Two days later boisterous weather, with high wind-velocity, flattened the police camp, and the post and telegraph office scarcely avoided disaster. Then the meeting's resolution was pursued down the line by a sackful of indignant letters.

That was in August, when between 500 and 600 of the Adelaide unemployed were strung out along the finger of railway pointing in a north-westerly direction and now extending some ten miles into the desert.

So far the works consisted of cuttings and embankments. Again the line was being constructed cheaply. Ballast was used as sparingly as was consistent with safety in boxing up, and the smallest quantity practicable was placed under the sleepers.

Wherever possible, creeks and depressions were crossed on the surface. This procedure recognised in advance situations, certain to arise from time to time, when floods would halt traffic and cause inconvenient delays. However, wherever it was decided to build culverts or bridges, deviations were arranged to avoid traffic interruption during construction.

Navvies were quartered in four camps, sited according to the men's duties — earthwork gangs, plate-laying crews, and so on. As the workings advanced these camps were moved forward, their relative positions being maintained.

By this time many of the men belonging to the early drafts of unemployed workers had hardened physically, learned the routine, and developed into useful labourers. But others had failed to adjust mentally. Dissatisfied with the new way of life, some of these were leaving the camps in search of shearing jobs or other station employment, and, of course, higher pay.

Lacking knowledge of the country, a few men of this type ventured on to the Queensland Road and lost their lives.

A considerable number appear to have turned out to be no-hopers. These just knocked off work entirely, said manual labour was too much for them, and looked to the authorities to provide for them elsewhere. What action the Department took in such cases is not recorded. Presumably the men were sent back to Adelaide.

Meanwhile the importance of Hergott as a trucking centre began to build up. During that year 1,946 steers and 1,180 sheep were entrained there. Notably, the comparable numbers for Farina were 6,132 and 13,884.

Though much of the Farina trade derived from neighbouring stations, it seems clear that then drovers were using the Strzelecki Track more than the Queensland Road.

Eventually the situation was to be reversed. And perhaps the process had begun already, for in June an item in the *Dispatch* had noted: "The Queensland Track from Hergott which, till lately, was deserted, is now alive with teams and travellers, and a number of mobs of travelling cattle going down to market. There are at present ten mobs between the border and the above township."

Eight years later the swing was complete. In 1892 Hergott entrained 15,651 steers and 20,093 sheep and Farina 1,501 steers and 11,645 sheep.

Perhaps one reason for the change in the fortunes of the townships was a marked increase in the risks encountered on the shifting and dangerous Cobbler sandhills at the southern end of the Strzelecki Track. (A "cobbler" is the last and always the most difficult sheep to be shorn. So shearers, travelling southwards, applied this term to the sandhills—the last and most difficult on the route.) Another factor was the much-needed improvement in yarding facilities at Hergott.

Once, Queensland mobs travelled to Adelaide via Broken Hill and a route known as Peg Track that led to the Burra, the railhead of the 1870s. Or else they followed the Warrego, Darling, and Murray rivers. But when the Great Northern Railway was built much of this traffic was diverted to the new railside townships.

At first Hergott had afforded primitive trucking conditions. Old records give a disastrous picture. Not only were the yards cramped, but they were also unpaved; and after rain the ground became badly cut up so that beasts stood up to their knees in mud. When this situation was remedied, business improved rapidly.

While the northern railway workings advanced unimpressively towards Stuart Creek, the situation in the south worsened. Railway traffic declined as the depression that followed the failure of the wheat drive deepened. The Public Works Report dwelt at some length on the subject of loans because "the South Australian debt has now attained very large proportions".

Other public works were put in hand in an attempt to absorb the mounting numbers of unemployed. Thus arrangements were made to complete Largs Bay Fort, to add to the fort at Glanville, and to make a beginning on a military road from Largs to Glenelg. Gangs of unemployed were used more extensively in cutting sleepers and cross timbers in the Wirrabara Forest. The materials produced here were used largely on the New South Wales Border Railway—authorised on 14 November 1884—but some of the sleepers were sent to Hergott for use on the Strangways extension.

Today it is difficult to decide the cost on the northern construction site of these and Western Australian sleepers, for no record remains. However, in those days, prices seem not to have fluctuated a great deal and at about the turn of the century the cost of a sleeper delivered at Port Augusta was between 6s and 6s 6d. An assistant engineer, reporting from Oodnadatta, remarked: "If we add 2/6 to 3/- for the trip from Port Augusta the price per sleeper is 8/- or 9/-." These were sleepers imported from Western Australia. Probably those cut locally cost considerably less.

The end of the year was a time of gloom in Port Augusta. Not that the general depression had affected the town importantly, for it appears to have escaped the more serious effects of the prevailing unemployment. Moreover the cost of living there must have been astonishingly low, to judge from the prices of food and housing. For instance board and lodging was being advertised in Gibson Street, "the best part of town", for £1 weekly. The fact was that the authorisation of the Border Railway made the rejection of the Phillips Ponds Railway Bill doubly hard to accept. (The events took place in the same week.) It was no consolation to learn that the Memorial had caused a great storm in the Legislature, opponents denouncing it as a brazen attempt to obtain the expenditure of a large sum of public money for the benefit of eight squatters. The Port Augustans were furious, and many citizens swore that more would be heard of the matter.

On 23 June of the following year, the longest work-train so far seen in the north steamed slowly into Hergott. It consisted of forty-five trucks loaded with sleepers and rails for the extension still described officially as the Primrose Springs Railway. Despite sensitive feelings on the matter of the change in route, the inaccuracy was perpetuated, presumably because this had been the title of the 1883 Act. The weight of the train was 450 tons, or 70 tons greater than the previous record haul.

At this time the *Cambrian Princess* landed ironwork for use in the construction of the crossing at Boorloo Flat, the first bridge on the extension. Ahead lay many creeks where bridges or culverts would be essential—Callanna, Welcome Springs, Flathill Crossing, Wangianna, Pole, Davenport, Finniss, and so on. And here was the first causing serious delay, because the materials needed were late in arriving.

Why plate-laying gangs did not make use of the diversion, half-a-mile long, that had been built for the benefit of the earthwork parties is difficult to understand. But it appears that plate-laying had halted at the spot where the future bridge was to begin.

Meanwhile clearing and grubbing gangs, followed by those building banks and shaping cuttings, had reached Pole Creek, twenty-six miles from Hergott. The disadvantage attached to letting the bridge contract outside the colony was now apparent.

Contemporary reports described the conditions encountered by the earthworks navvies. "With the exception of two or three miles past the sandhill at ten miles, the line is a constant succession of banks and cuttings, varying from a few hundred to ten or eleven thousand yards. Generally, the banks average six to seven feet and the excavations eight to ten feet. The heaviest cuttings in the first twenty-five miles are those at the twenty-third mile where the bank is fifteen feet high. The bank at Pole Creek is over twelve feet high."

Soon, however, the earthworks ran into an additional difficulty. Rock was struck and explosives were needed to cut the track.

A main ballast pit was opened at the 18-Mile Camp. The deposit at this spot turned out to be an important discovery. A ballast train continued to run backwards and forwards between the railhead and the 18-Mile even when the line reached Strangways. Other important shingle deposits were found in the watercourse of Flathill Creek. One of these supplied over fifty thousand cubic yards of ballast. These and similar discoveries saved the colony many thousands of pounds sterling.

Additional ballast was obtained from stone scattered on the surface of the plain. Indeed, during the weeks immediately prior to the start of construction, Afghans had been employed to gather this into piles. So to begin with, as the earthwork gangs moved on, they constantly came upon small stones raked into high heaps on either side of the surveyed route.

Stone suited to bridge-building was not found in the region, however, so culverts were made of concrete. Lime was brought up-country from Windy Creek—the spot where Barry, Brookes and Fraser had obtained their supplies for the Port Augusta and Government Gums line, for no longer was timber with which to burn limestone to be had near by in sufficient quantity. The concrete was hand-mixed on boards, turned over three times, mixed with water, and then placed by hand.

Base camp remained at Hergott for many months and it appears that throughout this period the township was as noisy as it was busy. A correspondent described what appears to have been a typical week-end: "Hergott should have been called Hades because the Hergottites do not keep the Christian Sabbath, but do more business on that day than on any other of the week." (The work of unloading a construction train had continued throughout Saturday and Sunday.) "The clanking of the rails as they were thrown from the trucks was heard distinctly in the village." Then, the men of the gangs came down-line to base camp for time off. There was drinking and much shouting and horseplay.

Nevertheless, a Church of England service, with Sunday School to follow, was held each Sunday in the Assembly Room, where there was seating space for sixty persons and where a cabinet-organ was kept.

Of the small camps, Pole Creek was the most important. Here was a store, a baker's shop, and a butcher's shop, all large tents. These were branches of establishments in Hergott. Two were owned by an enterprising firm of Chinese merchants, a circumstance that was to lead to trouble later on. Everywhere up-line, prices were identical with those at base camp. Thus one cause of complaint, usual in railway building operations, was absent.

A year after the railhead had moved on from Hergott, the Commissioner commented on what had been accomplished. His remarks were scarecely enthusiastic. "The construction of the Hergott Springs and Strangways line has afforded employment on the average to between five hundred and six hundred men. The work has been carried out satisfactorily and economically by the Engineer-in-Chief's Department, but has not progressed so rapidly as I could have wished."

One feels sympathy for the Engineer-in-Chief. He had many difficulties to meet, among them inefficiency in the delivery of ironwork—partly caused by Government delay—and inexperienced labour. Nevertheless, it seems probable that the change in management accounted in large part for disappointing results. The drive that had attended contractor construction was no longer present.

As though wishing to speed tardy procedures, one day the Chairman of Committees asked the House to commit itself by formal resolution to an early completion of the transcontinental railway. He moved that a permanent survey should be undertaken for a narrow-gauge line from Strangways to Pine Creek, and that plans and estimates should be laid on the table of the House. The cost of such a survey had been estimated at £50,000. But the Chairman of Committees was not daunted by this figure. He pictured vast expanses of well-watered, richly-grassed country, all lying idle. He prophesied rich mineral discoveries, anticipated flourishing tea, rice, and sugar plantations; he enlarged on the likelihood of an expanded Indian horse trade; and ended by proposing Port Darwin as Australia's European gateway. A speedy link-up between Adelaide and Darwin was, he said, an absolute need.

But on this enthusiastic speech the Member for Stanley poured derision. Indeed, he condemned the whole transcontinental railway project. Central Australia was a desert; tropical rainfall in the Territory a delusion. Sheep would neither breed nor grow wool even where there was water and grass, and the Territory would never become a horse-breeding country.

The debate followed a divided, unconvincing course, sanguine expectation more or less balanced by chilling pessimism.

Eventually the Premier followed a middle course: a preliminary survey would be sufficient for the time being. And there the matter was dropped.

As often happened, the editor of the *Dispatch* struck the dispassionate, commonsense note. "With regard to the ultimate construction of the Transcontinental Railway there can hardly be two opinions. But as to the necessity of rushing it through at the earliest possible date, that is quite a different matter. If the railway were actually completed now, there can be no doubt as to the financial result for many years to come—a heavy annual loss to the already heavily burdened revenue of the colony . . . Such development works should be gradual, and keep pace with settlement and population, instead of rushing far beyond them."

Meanwhile, at the construction camps, camels were being employed more than ever before. Horses, of course, had always been in use—fine beasts that did a magnificent job in earth-clearance by dragging heavy iron scoops. For a long time hired teams were employed. But now the Government was replacing these almost entirely with others purchased by the Department, which had also bought a number of camels overseas.

At about this time the Resident Engineer accepted delivery of two batches of camels. The first was landed at Port Adelaide and Afghan drivers travelled the beasts up-country in twenty-one days. The camels were spelled for a month on the common at Hergott and then divided among the camps up-line. The second batch, this time landed at Port Augusta, was handled similarly. All the animals came from the Bikanier district of Rajputana, where the climate resembles that of the Lake Eyre district.

Most surprisingly, one of these camels was entered for an event at the first meeting of the Hergott Springs Racing Club, held on 2 December. The card included seven races. A camel would scarcely have competed in the Handicap Hurdles, so probably the event concerned was the Hergott Springs Handicap—one-and-a-half miles. Unfortunately, no record of what happened now remains: all we know is that large numbers of navvies, released from duty, came down-line for the day. But that the experiment should have been made at all is astonishing in view of the fear in which the horse held the camel. Strings and teams were kept apart as far as was possible.

The newspapers of the day constantly printed accounts of disasters following surprise encounters between camels and horses. One described the arrival of camels at a spot where teamsters had camped. "A team, which had been unyoked and turned into the stockyard, became so excited that the horses jumped the rails and one got staked." Elsewhere, a drover wrote: "As I was travelling along the main road nine camels passed in a string when a valuable mare, belonging to one of my men, looked at them, suddenly reared up, and fell dead."

In Adelaide a week later a deputation of the unemployed waited on members of Parliament. The discussion that took place was inconclusive and that evening a mass meeting was held in the Central Market to demand that additional public works should be started immediately.

At the time when clearing and grubbing for the formation of earthworks began at the Darwin end of the transcontinental railway, nation-wide depression had established so firm a hold that, in Adelaide, the price of wool had fallen below a paying figure.

Returns on a scanty wheat crop had been meagre. The market for copper had shrunk to so great an extent that mining the metal was no longer a worthwhile venture. Everywhere business stagnated. The insolvency courts were overworked. Direct taxation, hitherto resisted, had been imposed. Fires were causing the loss of property valued at many hundreds of thousands of pounds. And, of course, unemployment figures continued to rise.

Provision for a line of railway from Palmerston to Pine Creek had been made in Act No. 284 of 1883, twenty-five years after the first proposal to build in the Territory. The Act had authorised the formation of a railway with tolls and charges identical with those levied on the Port Augusta and Government Gums line. But no action had been taken until the completion of the Farina to Hergott Springs extension, when funds had been borrowed to implement the Act. Then no time was lost, for the survey began before the loan was finalised.

The first surveyors to reach Palmerston went direct to the fortieth mile mark on the track of the future railway, while the second party began work at the eighty-first mile. The third party surveyed the harbour before starting work on the northernmost section. Advancing

Sketches of two railway towns in the 1880s: TOP: Hergott Springs (Marree). BOTTOM: Farina (*Archives of the State Library of South Australia*)

simultaneously, the parties completed the survey in September 1884.

Subsequently a Public Works Report stated: "The permanent survey of this line has been completed, and the contract plan and section issued for the purpose of assisting intending tenderers when visiting the Territory to go over the line. Working drawings are being rapidly prepared so that tenders may be invited as early as possible. In connection with this undertaking a contract has been entered into for the erection of a jetty at Port Darwin, which, when completed, will enable the largest vessels to go alongside and discharge. The jetty will form part of the railway system . . . Arrangements have been made to prepare a stacking-ground upon which to store Government materials."

The firm awarded the contract to build the jetty was C. and E. Millar of Melbourne, who agreed to finish the job in time to receive the first shipments of sleepers and rails, due to arrive in 1886.

As soon as this work was in hand, clearing and grubbing began. But these preliminaries were hurried on entirely as an unemployment relief measure, for building was still far in the future.

On 17 December 1885 tenders were advertised.

Construction work was to be the responsibility of the successful tenderer, but the Government undertook to supply all permanent way and fencing materials, and to install weighbridges and signals. There was an unusual point, however. Firms interested in submitting tenders were asked to prepare two distinct schedules—one visualising the employment of European labour only; the other using coolie labour working under European supervisors.

Four firms submitted tenders in the form desired. But as the lowest proposal was in excess of the provision that had been allowed, the Government re-advertised.

The second call resulted in five offers. The one found acceptable was advanced by the firm that already held contracts for the Palmerston jetty and the Border Railway. On Wednesday 12 May 1886 the *Dispatch* said: "Millar Brothers, the successful tenderers for the construction of the Palmerston and Pine Creek Railway, signed their contract yesterday. The price is £605,424 and the contractors are not restricted to the employment of European labour."

With European labour only, the price quoted had been £713,854.

The matter of the Government's preference was taken up in a Public Works Report. "In the letting of this contract covenants of a special nature have been entered into by the contractors, who have undertaken to employ European labour as far as possible, and to procure from South Australia proper all materials required for the construction of the line. I believe the effect of the arrangements thus made will be to give some stimulus to the trade and manufactures of South Australia, and to

TOP: The Ghan goes north—a scene from the very early days (*R. D. Kempe*). BOTTOM: Quorn railway station and yards in the early 1880s (*Archives of the State Library of South Australia*)

check excessive competition with white labour in the Northern Territory for such work as Europeans could carry out in a sub-tropical climate."

While undertaking to pay an entry tax on each coolie imported, the contractors obtained a promise that this money would be refunded when the man left the country on the completion of the work.

Building began in August 1886. By the end of December five ships had discharged cargo at the new jetty, and the stack-yard was full. The materials included 3,000 tons of steel sleepers and fasteners, 20,000 tons of rails, 180 tons of fishplates, and eighty tons of bolts. The last vessel to arrive, the *Ardmore*, docked with a cargo of sleepers in the following June. By this time a reservoir with a capacity of 2,500,000 gallons had been built close to the locomotive workshops.

The Report for the year 1886–87 stated: "The European force now on the line consists of 39 gangers, 40 mechanics and strikers, 20 horse-drivers, and 54 labourers." This made a total of 153 Europeans. The non-European workforce, however, appears to have comprised 3,000 Chinese and Indian labourers. But about a year later rather more than 300 Europeans were distributed along the length of the workings. The Report continued: "There are 72 horses and mules and 34 wagons in use on the works. Labourers are spread all over the first division of the line between Palmerston and Rum Jungle, and the earthworks are well in hand to 33 miles. The concrete works are being pushed on with energy on both divisions—A and B. Platelaying has been commenced; four and a half miles have been laid, all of which are fully ballasted."

Throughout the operation, the Chinese appear to have been the plate-layers, setting an average of half-a-mile of line a day, though at some bridges they were held up for considerable periods. The Indians and Singhalese formed the earthworks.

Two locomotives—South Australian Railways W-class and Y-class engines the *Port Darwin* and the *Silverton*—hauled all materials from the port depot to the railhead. A diminutive shunting engine with an oil headlight and a wide timber cab, pre-dated both of them, but Millars appear not to have regarded this as a locomotive at all, perhaps because it was used only between the wharf and the depot in Palmerston. It was called the *Sandfly* and was destined to become more famous than either of its rivals.

The Wet brought great hardships to the gangs. Not only did it stop progress, but in many places it seriously damaged the work already completed. At one period 300 coolies were occupied in repair work alone.

In all, between Port Darwin and Pine Creek no fewer than 300 bridges and flood-crossings were built. The work was completed some months ahead of the contract date, and on 15 June 1889 the Permanent Way Inspector screwed on the nuts which bolted the final fishplate in position.

However, the line was not taken over officially until 1 October. The occasion appears to have been sufficiently brusque to satisfy contractors thankful to be through with a difficult and wearying task. But not everyone was pleased. A newspaper correspondent has left his dissatisfaction on record: "The railway was duly taken over by the Government on Monday without any fuss or flow of champagne, and there was not even a free excursion."

During the early days of construction, Millar Brothers had become involved in a banquet which had cost them £500. Perhaps, not without reason, they felt that this had been flow of champagne enough.

The railhead was situated about halfway between Finniss Camp and Stuart Creek when the trouble began.

Indignation with the Railways Department exploded first in Adelaide. A leader published in the *South Australian Register* on 10 February 1886 caused many readers to suppose that the unemployed were exploited on the northern workings. It discussed two letters recently received. These "directly charge the Government of this colony with wilfully misleading and cruelly ill-treating men sent to Hergott Springs. If what their authors say is true, the unemployed in Adelaide have been dealt with in a most shameful manner. They have been told that there was work for them to do on this line; they have been given passes up to the present terminus; and then, when they arrived ready for work, and naturally expecting to get it, they have been told by Government officials to look for it in a warmer place even than Hergott. It was cruel—nay, even inhuman—to induce men whose only crime was that they had no work to do to travel so far from their families and then to leave them destitute in an inhospitable country."

A column of such forceful rhetoric reached a somewhat one-sided conclusion: "If the men had refused to go to Hergott they would not have deserved sympathy, but having shown themselves ready to take what offered for the sake of gaining an honest livelihood, the public are bound on the score of duty and of common humanity to see that they are not made the victims of heartless neglect and official insolence." The Department's angle seems not to have been ascertained.

The more important of the letters which occasioned this outburst had been signed by no fewer than fifty navvies. If verbose, it was outspoken. It began by saying that the true state of affairs had never been placed before the people of South Australia. "The treatment which has been meted out to us is cruel; words cannot paint too strongly the treatment we have received."

Then the writer (for on the face of it the letter had been written by one man) let his pen loose: " . . . at that point all responsibility on the part of the authorities seems to have ceased. In plain language we were told to shift for ourselves, and one of the officials, on being applied to civilly for information as to what we were to do, told us, in language more forcible than polite, to 'Go to ——, and look for work up the line.' Only fancy, Mr Editor, to be told this in a country devoid of any place where we could get a bite to eat or a roof to shelter us! We started to walk, intending to get to the next camp, but one of our party fell exhausted on the track and died shortly after. When we reached the camp there was no food to be had. Our only resource was to start for the next camp where matters were no better. All along the line the state of affairs was the same—no work, no food, no one to tell us where to go or what to do, and we were forced to lay down that night hungry and weary on the stony ground with no roof to shelter . . . Even as I write men are lying about in all directions on the plain. Some of us have not lain under a roof of any kind during the last week."

Some readers may have paused here to wonder a little about that statement. The time was high summer. Surely the hardship of being without a tent might have been borne with equanimity where many people would prefer to sleep in the open air!

However, this aspect of the matter appears not to have occurred to the writer, who continued bitterly: "The works from one end to the other seem to be in a state of confusion. There are no tools nor tents, nor no means for employing the crowds of men which are constantly arriving, or providing for them. We want to lay the true state of affairs before the unemployed of Adelaide, particularly those married men who intend coming up here. There is no work at present here, only stone raking at 1s 3d per yard, and that is only offered to a few. And it is almost impossible to make a fair wage at that even by working eighteen hours a day. We can assure those persons who intend coming up here that they will have to work the first month or six weeks for their tools and for the debts they will incur before they get a chance to start work. And as for those married men who have allowed a pound a week to their families, heaven knows where it will come from, for at present they do not get a chance to earn it. It would require the pen of Dickens or Thackeray to describe the condition of those men who left Adelaide for this place last week. The supply of provisions along the line is totally insufficient and we are at the mercy of a Chinaman for stores whose attendance is uncertain. There is need for an alteration in the management of this line, or the lives of some of our brave fellows will be sacrificed to the blundering of the pack of incapables who at present govern this unfortunate country. We appeal to you, Sir, to lay these facts before the public, and we can safely assert that on enquiry they will be found substantially true. The Government, or the official who manages the Labour Bureau, must have been aware that there was no provision made for the numbers of men who were sent here last week, and whoever is responsible for sending men to starve in a wild country like this ought to suffer. The men who have signed their names to this letter can vouch for its truth."

As might be expected, the publication of this letter caused considerable activity in Government quarters. Clearly, the public would demand an enquiry. The Commissioner of Public Works called for reports from the Resident Engineer and the Resident Medical Officer. A few days later these reports were published with a further leader in the *Register*.

But it was the *Dispatch*—showing its usual direct if portentously expressed good sense—that summed up the situation most dispassionately. "About a fortnight ago, the senior Adelaide daily, which has of late shown an incautious readiness to accept as gospel the communications of its correspondents, indulged in an hysterical article on the conditions of the Hergott railway camps, on the strength of a letter of piteous complaint, professedly written and signed by men employed on the railway works."

The Government action was then outlined. The leader went on: "The result, as we anticipated, is that the complaints have proved to be mainly false, and grossly exaggerated where there was any foundation of fact to exaggerate. That the works were glutted during the first week of January and that temporary inconvenience followed is plainly stated by Mr Mann in his report, but the responsibility for that rests not upon him, but upon the Government, for sending up to Hergott large batches of unemployed without having taken the precaution of ascertaining whether work could be found or accommodation provided for them all without notice. With regard to the authenticity of the letter of complaint, it appears that a number of the men whose names are attached never saw it, and are prepared to deny the truth of the statements it contains."

In his report, Mann had stated that he had good reason to believe that the letter, or at any rate the greater part of it, had been written by a minister at Quorn at the dictation of a navvy he had paid off at a lower rate of wage than the man had expected.

The leader continued: "During December the Government sent 350 unemployeds to Hergott, though the Resident Engineer had only work for 150 . . . In the latter part of December the gangers and the most experienced workmen on the line applied for and obtained a fortnight's leave. This naturally disarranged the regular routine of work, and on

January 2nd the Government sent up 65 more men. They were duly fed and lodged at Hergott, and were sent on next morning by rail to the ballast pit at the 18 mile camp. As many as possible were to be taken on at the ballast pit, and the rest were to go on to successive camps, being taken on where practicable until the 50 mile camp was reached, and all arriving there were to be set to work at stone raking. Some 30 reached the 50 mile camp where there were tools enough and sufficient tent accommodation for more than that number, and also a boarding-house."

It appears that it was the practice in stone raking for the men to be formed into squads, with one shovel, two rakes, and a barrow being issued to each party of three. Nobody worked by himself and the labour cannot have been unreasonably hard. Yet some complained that it was too much for them.

Arrangements seem to have been made in advance to put all of the expected men to work, but then the Government sent a further batch of forty. These were sent to the only work available—stone raking. Meanwhile, the men left at the ballast pit had decided that the work there was too hard, and had taken upon themselves the responsibility of going up-line. Because of this the number at the 50-Mile camp had increased to over one hundred, and then tents and tools had run short for a few days. This situation was rectified by drafting thirty of the strongest men back to the gravel pit.

The editor of the *Dispatch*, who clearly had made extensive enquiries on his own account, appears to have had little sympathy with the letter-writers. "The entire work, tool and tent complaint thus resolves itself into an overcrowding of one camp for two or three days caused in the first place by want of forethought on the part of the Government, and in the second place by the men abandoning work at one camp to seek lighter labour at another. As to the food supply on the road, the men had at the most to walk 32 miles, with several railway camps intervening. There was a store at the 18 mile, and another at the 41 mile camp, and a boarding-house at the terminus. If the storekeepers en route were cautious about giving credit the fact that many of the relief work men are in the habit of giving procuration orders in false names accounts for the circumstance. At the boarding-house, while the rush was on, the supply of bread failed once or twice, but there was always plenty of meat."

Respecting the sensational statement that one man dropped on the road to the 50-Mile camp and died soon afterwards, "Mr Mann simply reports that not only did no such death take place, but not one of the men was reported ill or knocked up". In fact, the Medical Officer expressed satisfaction with the health of the camps, saying that only six out of the 750 employed were laid aside by illness, notwithstanding the climate, the character of the work, and the weak constitutions of some of the men.

There was no truth in the complaint that men were charged for their tools. And as to the alleged hardship suffered by the families of married men, enquiries showed that the weekly amounts for which they signed procuration orders had regularly gone down to Adelaide.

The editor dismissed the matter tersely. "The whole complaint is evidently a tissue of fabrications and exaggerations founded on the fact that there was a sudden rush of men to the works in the first few days of January; and the responsibility for this rests with the Commissioner of Public Works whose zeal to provide for the unemployed was not, for once, tempered by due forethought and discretion."

So a ten days' sensation fizzled out in a sputter of editorial sparks. But scarcely had the effects worn off in Adelaide than a new cause for anxiety arose. An epidemic of typhoid fever broke out on the line.

Later the infection was traced to a lad who, having somehow contracted the disease at Willunga, walked into Hergott, spending three days on the journey. He slept by the roadside and afterwards stayed for two days in the township before his condition was discovered.

Alarm spread in the district and on up the line. But the situation was taken in hand very promptly and for once navvies spoke highly of the manner in which an emergency was handled. The small tented hospital at Hergott was enlarged, and trained nurses were sent from Adelaide. Soon the outbreak was controlled, but it gave rise to further complaint, this time on the part of the public. Should typhoid fever cases be sent south to hospital by train? Controversy quickly built up.

The Medical Officer at Hergott was instructed to report on the practice. He wrote: "The character of our hospital—it being a movable casualty hospital composed of tents—and its small size make it impossible to retain anything like the number of patients coming from a wide tract of country, right up into Queensland, and also from the railway works. On the first week of my arrival here, I obtained a large new tent especially for fever cases, but this can only compass cases of emergency."

In normal times a flapping, noisy tent cannot have been a likely place in which to treat patients requiring a cool, genial climate and quiet. During an epidemic it was hopelessly inadequate, and overflow patients had to be sent south. The only means of quick transport was the train.

Explaining the situation in which he was placed, the doctor defended his action by saying that the risk involved in using railway carriages was exaggerated. "It has yet to be proved that enteric fever is ever communicated except by actual inception of the poisonous germs into the alimentary system, and thus a person travelling with an enteric fever patient, who is ordinarily clean, is—so far as we know—not much more liable to contract enteric fever than he who travels with a dog is likely to catch hydatid disease."

The doctor claimed that he had treated 800 cases of typhoid fever and that therefore his knowledge of the disease was fairly extensive. But it is doubtful if people who used the railway were satisfied.

However, local hospital facilities were improved and the emergency passed.

The railhead reached Stuart Creek late in June. Two years to build a trifle more than sixty miles of line in flat country! Scarcely an epic in railway construction!

At the time, the advanced earthworks camp was pitched at Hewson's Springs, twenty miles south of Strangways. Now the staff of the telegraph station, and the owners of the tavern-cum-eating-house that stood beside the north-south camel pad, came out each morning to stare southwards for the first sight of navvies raking stones on the gibber plain and shaping the railbed.

Probably they wondered at the slow progress of the gangs. They knew nothing of the trials of the Resident Engineer, who just then must have felt that he had a fight on his hands every time he requisitioned so much as half-a-dozen new wheelbarrows. For of late the Department had grown niggardly.

The colony was now £1 million in the red, and many heads in the Ministry were being scratched perplexedly. For though the South Australian potential was enormous, the fact remained that times were bad, the situation serious. During January the Railway Department had earned £47,899 compared with £61,852 in the same month of the previous year. And, breaking down these figures the Great Northern was shown to have earned £5,171 as against £7,371. Here was small encouragement for men who wished to be persuaded of the economic sense of the great undertaking to which they were committed.

The most determined optimist had to agree that the railway situation was unsatisfactory and that (especially in view of the current depression) heroic measures should be taken. So the Railway Commissioners Bill was not seriously opposed. This sought to transfer railway management to an independent, non-political Board removable only on address to the Governor from both Houses, or address from one House in two successive sessions.

Now came a period when the remarkable record of northern construction for safe working took a sudden plunge. Hitherto the camps had been singularly free of serious accident. But one day a disaster occurred at the 38-Mile post. This involved a ballast train and a mob of cattle: the train was derailed, and a number of navvies were killed. The smash at the 38-Mile was followed by several deaths caused by falls from moving work-trains.

Then a new occasion for anxiety developed and with it a possible explanation for the sudden spate of accidents. The body of a navvy, dressed in ragged trousers and a tattered shirt, was found lying about fifty yards from a spring, which the man appeared to have been struggling to reach when he collapsed and died. The doctor who examined the corpse found no sign of violence. But he said that, probably, the man had been suffering from delirium tremens following an extended period of heavy drinking.

More accidents followed, but in no case was there proof that drink had been the cause. Then came the discovery that alcohol was being smuggled up-line in large quantities and that there was much drunkenness in the lonelier camps.

The practice of illicit grog-selling was difficult to trace to the culprits, even when the authorities became positive of their identities. A typical case was that of a man described as Thomas, though the name was an alias. Thomas was arrested in Hergott and charged with selling liquor in the camps on the line. But the navvies called to give evidence against him had been his customers, and so all were reluctant to testify. Some made inconclusive statements, valueless to the police; others doubtless, perjured themselves. The case collapsed. Thereupon charges against three other suspected grog-peddlers were withdrawn.

Police, dressed as navvies, tried to lay traps for men known to sell liquor. But there were few of them, and always somebody recognised the copper carrying the banjo. Then the word went round, and of course no offer was made to the policeman in disguise. Little could be done, save in rare cases when the vendor happened to be caught in the act by someone in authority. But such cases were rare indeed.

To add to the troubles of this period, a vast army of rats swarmed out of Queensland and spread across northern South Australia. Railway stores suffered. For instance, at Hergott 100 bags of oats and twenty tons of chaff were consumed in a few days.

Once when a teamster drew up to unload his dray outside the main store, myroos (the Aboriginal name for rats) leaped from among the loading. They were fine, plump myroos, said a report, for they had fed on Government flour all the way from Priscilla Creek, a journey of about fifty miles.

In addition to raiding food stores the rats attacked stables, gnawing harness, canvas, and boots. Bold, they rarely troubled to move far away when disturbed. They were too numerous to deal with effectively, a circumstance which they appear to have understood. So for months supplies throughout the construction area were periodically depleted as the swarms moved here and there about the country.

At last in July base camp moved to Stuart Creek, where a telegraph station was opened. At once Chinese traders from Hergott moved up-line, opening a store and bakehouse at the 102-Mile post, just south of Strangways. They did this partly because they knew that, in due course, the settlement would become construction headquarters; partly because a Government well had just been sunk there.

Government well-sinking parties put down several railway bores at this time. The most important was situated just off the line ten miles from the shore of Lake Eyre South. This site, seventy feet above sea-level, was chosen jointly by the Resident Engineer and the Conservator of Water. The diameter of the bore was six-and-three-quarter inches. At a depth of 308 feet, the diamond drill struck an artesian spring of such volume that the first rush of water drove the workmen back. When the fine sand that partially choked this bore washed out, the gush attained the then phenomenal flow of 1 million gallons daily. The water poured into a deep, prepared trench 200 yards long. An official report said that this well was the finest in Australia: "Now the problem of what becomes of the western drainage of the Dividing Range of Queensland is in a fair way to be settled."

Chinese merchants on the camps frequently caused jealousy because of their enterprise, often successful. But at this period in particular there was much feeling among rival traders, some of whom wrote to the newspapers alleging favouritism on the part of the railway authorities. But out of much correspondence, in the course of which charges and counter-charges were made, one fact emerged—all traders, whether European or Asiatic, were cheated consistently by many navvies who appear to have regarded them, along with boarding-house keepers, as fair game. An example was an occasion at the 50-Mile camp when five cases of dishonesty were brought to the notice of the Resident Engineer. In each case a navvy, whose name appeared correctly in the pay-sheets, had given procuration orders under many false names to storekeepers and lodging-house proprietors at numerous camps along the line. The defrauded traders, who could not know all their customers by sight, had no means of protecting themselves.

One day soon after base camp moved up-line, the Government unexpectedly invited tenders for the supply of 8,000 tons of steel rails for use on a further extension to the Peake. Though a decision to build this section may have been made late in 1884, the present move appears to have been the first public intimation that construction would continue without pause. It was a logical step, of course. Men and equipment were on the spot. But the estimated cost was heavy—£505,000. And there was a little bill for £43,000 for new rolling-stock that had to be included in the reckoning.

However, the notice in the *Gazette* was timely, for rough sheds were being built by the springs at Strangways for the use of the clerks of the Department when base camp advanced once more, and large numbers of tents were shortly to be pitched against the arrival of the earthwork gangs. It was at this time that a butcher, a blacksmith, and a saddler opened shops by the track close to the tavern, soon now to become a hotel.

A Strangways record notes that the season was very dry. Teamsters experienced difficulty in travelling the north-south track, not, oddly enough, through lack of water, but through scarcity of feed. "Camels do much better than horses or cattle, and large caravans pass here every week to and from Hergott."

In September an inevitable event took place. Strangways might be a very small settlement, but it could muster sufficient nags to open a racing club. A meeting that seems to have included the entire district decided that the principal race — the Transcontinental Railway Stakes, one-and-a-half miles — should be for thirty-five sovereigns.

And they were impatient, those punters. The first meeting was arranged to take place a fortnight later, during the second week of October, by which time, it was most optimistically anticipated, the railhead would have arrived. In this respect the meeting was disappointed. The earthworks navvies attended in force, but the plate-layers, always belated, arrived on 1 March in the following year.

Later at a time when locomotives were running to the 86-Mile post — a spot about sixteen miles south of Strangways — the earthwork gangs came upon trouble. The obstruction was a broad belt of sandhills immediately to the north of the settlement.

To begin with, in this sandhill country, the gangs drew on a water-hole known to them as The Old Yellow. But this dried up. Then the Department was forced to incur heavy additional expense, for water had to be carted either from Strangways or from Emily Springs.

Fighting sand, the workings had reached the 9-Mile post on the new extension, when the navvies — some 700 of them — stacked picks and "banjos" along the length of the line and went south for Christmas.

Now the works were at a standstill. Between Hergott and Strangways perhaps seventy men remained on duty as locomotive and equipment caretakers. Doubtless many of these unfortunates (chosen, one gathers, by lot) considered their chore needless in that lonely region. Who would want to make off with a steam engine?

They did not fail to point out that the Resident Engineer was among the holiday-makers, but neglected to recall that his leave followed two years of uninterrupted duty.

However, their chagrin is understandable in view of the special nature of the occasion that had brought about so complete a shut-down. On 28 December Adelaide was to celebrate the Jubilee of the colony.

Perhaps, though, the activities of those who remained on the line were more in character with the occasion remembered than the festivities of the men who returned to the towns. Fifty years before, the pioneers had used tents and wattle-and-daub huts. They named their camp Port Misery; the caretakers on the railway did likewise. There is an early story of six settlers who, having one dress-coat between them, took turns to shrug this on before stepping into the reed shack where Governor Hindmarsh held his first levee. So men left on the line who felt so disposed were justified in feeling themselves more in tune with the anniversary than those who let off fireworks in Adelaide parks.

No account records that extra leave was granted to the holiday-making navvies in recognition of the Jubilee. But it appears that this must have happened because a fatal accident aboard a leave train returning northwards took place near the Ballast Camp on 18 January.

About a hundred navvies were travelling that day, and one gathers that many of the men, if not technically drunk, were under the influence of liquor.

Suddenly someone yelled that a man had fallen off the train. Confusion and shouting followed. The only means of alerting the guard was to shuffle along running-boards to his van, and few of the men were in a state to accomplish this feat safely, let alone rapidly. When at last a search was made, the unfortunate casualty was found caught between buffers. He had been dragged for a long distance, and his legs were almost severed from his body. He died in Coward Springs hospital.

Early in February, plate-laying reached a spot within three miles of the Strangways bore. Here work came to a halt for want of rails, deliveries from Hergott having failed. In an attempt to keep construction moving, disused sidings and deviations were taken up, but supplies obtained in this way were insufficient to meet the need.

It was during this pause that an unhappy incident involving a newly-appointed medical officer led to the exposure of a shabby graft that exploited railway arrangements for the unemployed.

When Stuart Creek became base camp in the previous October, a doctor had been posted there. Newspaper reports pictured him in a poor light. He seems to have been a hasty man, given to ill-advised retorts, and, perhaps, to keeping his own council on occasions when it would have been better to give an explanation.

One day a navvy belonging to a Strangways plate-laying gang reported sick. He was put aboard a returning work-train and travelled the twenty-three miles to Coward Springs, where the doctor was known to be that day.

The hospital at Coward Springs was merely a small marquee, and when the sick man arrived the doctor refused to admit him, saying that no bed was available. Eventually, however, a place was made under the fly. That night the newcomer slept in a draught, more or less in the open.

Next day he was sent on to Hergott. The doctor, who himself needed to go down-line, accompanied him. On arrival—for a reason that only appeared later—the sick man was taken to the goods shed, where he was told to lie down.

The astonishing account that follows is taken direct from a contemporary newspaper report.

The Justice of the Peace at Hergott learned of the arrival and something in the story must have struck him as unusual, for he went to investigate. He found the doctor, who was smoking and looking down at the patient. When he asked why a sick man had been brought to the goods shed and what could be done for him there, he was told curtly that questions prompted purely by curiosity would not be answered. Half an hour later the patient died.

The doctor wrote a certificate testifying that the cause of death was exhaustion consequent upon an inability to take nourishment because of a debilitated constitution. Later he returned to Coward Springs.

An inquest was held. The jury was informed that a telegram had been sent to the doctor requesting him to attend the Court and that he had refused to comply, saying that he could not leave serious fever cases he then had on his hands. No time remained in which to issue a subpoena.

At first the jury refused to accept the doctor's certificate. However, they were obliged to give way because the Attorney-General declined to order a doctor to be sent up-country from Adelaide when a legally qualified medical practitioner was available on the spot. Nevertheless they added a rider to their finding: "We wish to call the attention of the proper authorities to the heartless conduct and neglect shown to the deceased."

Learning of the censure that had been passed on him, the doctor sent a report to the Commissioner of Public Works. He told the facts from the time of the sick man's arrival at the hospital, and stated his diagnosis. "All that was the matter with him was a pain in the back and slight oedema of the legs—a common complaint easily relieved up here." He continued by saying that the patient had decided to return to Adelaide on the next train, but on arrival at Stuart Creek he had appeared to be dying. So at Hergott it had seemed best that he should be taken off the train. He was removed to the goods shed "as the nearest and best place". The report ended by elaborating the statement in the death certificate: "The poor man must have left town with great constitutional debility as he was so short a time on the works, and I could detect no specific disease to account for death. The immediate cause of death was pure exhaustion on a broken-down constitution."

Clearly, the doctor's opinion was that the man should not have been accepted for work on the railway. The Commissioner of Public Works decided to order an enquiry.

During the subsequent investigation an irregular practice was uncovered. It was found out that sometimes unemployed men, having been accepted as navvies and issued with passes to the railhead, would change their minds and sell their tickets to others who often were old men, unfitted to navvies' work, and who would not have been accepted by the selection board. In certain cases payment was extorted— "consideration money"—on account of the jobs surrendered.

It appears that this was the means by which the dead man had found his way to the works. Needless to say, steps were taken to stop the underground traffic in passes.

Apparently the delay caused by the failure in the supply of rails continued for about four weeks, for the plate-layers brought the permanent way into Strangways on Tuesday 1 March 1887, a month after Coward Springs was opened to traffic.

"Teetulpa will save the colony yet" was a popular catch-phrase in those days of depression. For gold had been found and many people, hopeful of renewed prosperity, pinned their faith to Strawbridge's and Brady's, two gullies on the diggings that had shown particularly promising returns. Strawbridge's, especially, was discussed on the line. A correspondent wrote: "A large number of men have taken the gold fever and left the works to try their luck at Teetulpa."

Generally speaking, perhaps, navvies drawn from the unemployed were not of the type, when settled in what they supposed to be secure positions, to buy sieve and panning dish and try their luck with the diggers. But life had been rough to them, thrown them out of their comfortable niches, and offered them the chance to flex their muscles, mental as well as physical, among tough mates. So viewpoints had changed and now they were disposed to take risks that a couple of years previously they would not have faced.

Indeed, perhaps predictably, they in particular were susceptible to the restless pull of gold. The professional navvy might listen to the latest rumour, then shrug, spit on his hands, and turn to again. After all, this was his job. He might go at last, but he needed more than first rumours to shift him. The newcomer to pick-drill, on the other hand, would listen avidly. This time, he had no roots to pull up. According to the record, he would "hearken to the latest buzz, then stand staring into distance, perhaps for minutes on end". This, presumably, if no ganger were near by. Then, suddenly one day, two mates would straighten their backs, toss down their "banjos" and leave camp on the long road to the diggings. It is said that one-third of the labour force walked out in this way.

Before long—certainly by March 1887—the fame of Teetulpa as an alluvial field faded. Then, even the discovery of a nugget weighing twenty-one ounces failed to restore the first eager enthusiasm. However, indications that high profit might be had from the working of gold-bearing reefs maintained interest, and extensive pegging took place. But usually the owners of these claims were professional miners, not amateurs at shaft-sinking, and gradually the drain from the workings eased. Nevertheless, the restlessness caused by the thought of gold persisted.

Meanwhile the normal tax on manpower continued—men who proved to be physically incapable of sustaining the navvy's way of life, and those others who, wearying of the outback, determined to return south, whether or not they found work on arrival.

In all, between 350 and 400 replacements had to be found. Not that this was difficult in the circumstances then prevailing in Adelaide. Unemployment still mounted. When the Commissioner of Public Works offered emergency jobs—tents, tools, and 4s 6d a day—men had flocked forward. Later the Premier had said that the Ministry would put 370 men and seventy teams to work cutting sleepers in the Mount Remarkable forests on similar terms, and within hours the vacancies had been filled.

It was therefore a simple task to recruit labour for the construction gangs at pay now fifty per cent greater than that offered in the south. From the angle of the Department, the rub came in the need to allow time for each fresh draft to become acclimatised to new conditions and the use of pick and shovel.

However, in due course fully 800 men again worked on the line. Said one report: "Nearly all nationalities are represented—from the Englishman to the Ethiopian—and almost every trade under the sun."

The head of the line was a camel depot as well as a railway depot. Here camel strings came to serve the needs of travellers, who now were allotted special trucks attached to every work-train. Camel buggies accommodated the women and children; riding camels or horses carried most of the men. Pack camels—or sometimes donkeys—moved the heavy goods, whether personal baggage or station supplies. The travellers went to Alice Springs and beyond, or to intermediate telegraph and cattle stations.

Three days after rails were laid into Strangways, a large company of navvies newly arrived from Adelaide passed through on their way to the advanced workings, then situated a mile beyond William Creek bore.

Clearing and grubbing gangs were, at this time, over twenty miles ahead of the plate-laying parties. The gap between the two construction groups varied: sometimes it was as much as thirty miles. But recently the earthworks had been delayed in the sandhill country, and several parties had been left behind to finish sections of track that had been prepared only in the rough.

During the plate-laying hold-up south of Strangways, some of the idle workers had been employed in building a telephone line between the recently-erected railway office-sheds and the Overland Telegraph station, a mile and a quarter distant. This line was half-finished when, on 24 March, an inquest was held at Strangways that resulted in further adverse criticism of the medical officer whose behaviour had been censured by a Hergott jury only three weeks previously.

This case concerned the death of a railway guard who fell from a train on the Strangways line. No one was present at the moment of the accident, but two passengers, looking out a window, saw a man lying at the side of the track holding one thigh while signalling with his free hand. One of these men tried, unsuccessfully, to attract the engine driver's attention; the other jumped off the train, which was travelling at about fiften miles per hour, and ran back to the injured man.

A few moments later a youth clambered along the running-boards from coach to coach, yelling, "Man overboard!" But the train ran on for about two miles. Then the driver backed up to the place where the hurt man lay.

The guard was laid in a van and the train returned to Hergott where it was learned that the doctor was at Strangways. A telegram was sent asking him to come, since the Hergott chemist considered that the case was urgent. A tourniquet had been properly applied beside the line, so the chemist did not touch the injury, but he suggested that the guard should be taken to meet the doctor half-way. So a second wire was sent asking the medical officer to meet the down-train at Stuart Creek. But when the party arrived there the doctor had not come.

In the event, the doctor met the train at Strangways. The patient was taken to the hospital and died shortly afterwards, the cause of death being haemorrhage and shock.

TOP: The result of a derailment near Port Augusta in the early days—date not known (*Archives of the State Library of South Australia*). BOTTOM: Around the turn of the century at Woolshed Flat. Notice the "cow-catcher" on the front of the engine (*R. D. Kempe*)

1060

NM 32

At the inquest a railway engineer said that on receipt of the telegrams he had arranged to send an engine. However, the doctor had declined to travel, saying that the chemist was competent to care for the injured man and he would have everything in readiness for the arrival of the train.

In his evidence the doctor said that on noting the guard's condition and the extent of the operation that would be needed, he had decided that to operate would be hopeless. When questioned, he continued that his reasons for the course he had followed were sound. Had he gone down-line, he could not have operated on the train, since afterwards the patient could not have been moved to hospital. In any case the shaking of the engine would have unfitted him to perform an operation. Moreover, he had no skilled assistant to leave at Strangways.

Recalling the recent case at Hergott, the jury were not satisfied. Having found that the guard "met his death accidentally by falling off the train whilst in the execution of his duty", they added a rider: "We think that the doctor would have shown more humanity than he has done had he gone down to see the patient on the road when telegraphed for, and we hope that, in future, whatever the case, whether it is 50 or 100 miles away, he will at once attend."

Contemporary accounts afford occasional picturesque glimpses into life on the line at this period. If some navvies spent their free time in gambling, in bawdy sing-songs, and in sly-grog carousels, others found relaxation in sport—particularly cricket—and in reading. A few were interested in serious music, and occasionally opportunities occurred for these to indulge their preference. For instance, there was a gathering at Strangways: "An entertainment consisting of vocal and instrumental music was given at the telegraph station here on Monday by lady and gentlemen amateurs. The attendance of visitors was not very large, but the audience was sympathetic and applausive."

During the previous year only 3.17 inches of rain had fallen, so the face of the land was cracked and dry. But in April a little rain fell and at once the country was on the move again. Soon cattle streamed past the railhead, the drovers exchanging rough banter with the navvies. Five mobs were listed as passing through Strangways that month, a total of 800 beasts. In each case the boss drover was mentioned by name, also the station from which he came—Barrow's Creek, Bond Springs, Dalhousie, Cootanooria, Abminga. The way-sheets directed entrainment at Hergott or Farina, for the practice of trucking cattle further north did not begin as soon as the line arrived, a circumstance that caused concern to the Railways Department. Droving was cheaper and it was also the established custom, which counted for much.

Horses, however, did travel by rail—provided they were aristocrats

An old "steam wagon" at Edwards Creek. George Stirling is standing beside the engine (*G. L. Stirling*)

of the equine kingdom. "Three stallions of the Suffolk Punch breed, imported from England by Sir Thomas Elder, arrived on the way to Mount Burrell Station." No droving for such as these! They travelled in specially-padded trucks.

Early that month, as soon as the rain came, Graham Stewart, Superintending Surveyor of the Engineer-in-Chief's Department, left Strangways for Alice Springs with a string of fourteen camels. "He is going to examine the country from the Peake to about a hundred miles beyond Alice with the view of ascertaining the most suitable route for the continuation of the Transcontinental line," said a report. "Mr Stewart expects to be absent about seven months."

Stewart seems to have travelled light. The average survey party took thirty camels and consisted of six or seven men including a couple of Afghans.

Immediately following Stewart's departure came news that the Yellow Waterhole Creek was running and that the waterhole itself had filled—"an immense benefit to pastoralists in this district, and a great saving to the Government as water-carting on the railway will now be abandoned for some time".

But, as so often happened, disadvantage attached to a benefit. Running creeks washed away lines laid in streambeds where deviations skirted the sites of future bridges.

Rain, full waterholes, and washaways dropped out of the news, however, when accidents became frequent once more. A typical case was that of a train loaded with bridge materials that came to disaster at Pole Creek. Ropes slipped in a truck loaded with seven tons of iron trestles, each about ten feet high. Near a crossing at the foot of a steep grade the trestles overbalanced and tipped the truck, which threatened to derail adjacent coaches. An alert driver stopped the train just in time to avoid a wreck. The passengers, of whom there were many, congratulated each other on escaping disaster.

Accidents to individuals happened frequently, and sly-grog continued to be a worrying problem. Then yet another inquest involved the unpopular medical officer.

This time the body was that of a woman, one of the people who had watched for the first glimpse of approaching railway gangs. The wife of the tavern-keeper, she had been bending over an open hearth, preparing tea, when her clothes caught fire. Her husband beat out the flames with his hands, but the burns were extensive, and the doctor was not available to give prompt help.

Perhaps as a result of the criticisms passed upon him, he had left that morning to attend a distant case. So the woman was not professionally treated until the following day, and this proved to be too late.

When the advanced workings reached a point fifty miles north of Strangways, the railhead lay on the far side of the sandhills. One day the Commissioner of Public Works arrived to inspect the job that had been made of building the line through this formidable obstacle. He appears to have been well satisfied with all he saw, but the only interest that now attaches to his journey is that he travelled in the first passenger coach to run on the Hergott–Strangways line.

Shortly after this, a Royal Commission, appointed in January to enquire into the best method of completing the transcontinental railway, submitted its report. The Commission included such respected men as Simpson Newland (later to play an important part in railway development), David Murray, and Allan Campbell.

The report came appropriately, for two weeks previously on 19 July the first locomotive to run on the Palmerston and Pine Creek Railway had been named the *Port Darwin* amid much festivity. (The contractors saw fit to disregard the miniature *Sandfly*.) It recommended that the remainder of the railway should be built on the land-grant system, the line to permit uninterrupted traffic between Quorn and Palmerston. The limits of deviation were fixed at sixty miles on either side of a direct line from Angle Pole to Pine Creek. This recommendation, at the time perhaps thought to be of little importance, was to have great significance in later years.

Conditions recommended were that the land-grant syndicate should be obliged within seven years to complete the work to the satisfaction of an engineer appointed by the Governor; that not more than one-third of the total railway frontage should be assigned, and that no block of land should be more than twenty miles long, or lie directly opposite a neighbouring block. Thus, the grant was to be planned in chessboard style.

Should Parliament decline all land-grant approaches, then it was recommended that districts lying north of the 30th parallel of south latitude (this cut the railway near Farina) should be set aside for sale. The proceeds from all such sales were to be allocated to a special account to be drawn on, as opportunity served, to defray the costs of future extensions.

The Commission condemned proposals to borrow more money for further construction. But two members dissociated themselves emphatically from this negative recommendation. They considered that, should an acceptable land-grant offer not be forthcoming speedily, the Government should borrow the necessary funds and continue to build in sections as hitherto.

Unquestionably, the Committee had been influenced by a realistic assessment of the colony's record in railway construction to 30 June

1887, or a few weeks before the submission of the recommendations.

The colony then had 1,420 miles of line open to traffic, and 350 in process of construction. The railways in use had cost £9,083,093 — an average of £6,397 per mile. Including equipment, the total expenditure had been £9,676,131. Of this sum only £429,000 had been found out of revenue. The difference had been provided by loans, on which no less than £3,558,525 had been paid out in interest. And the railways had earned, over and above working expenses, £1,809,611. Thus the colony faced a net loss on interest of £1,748,914. No capital had been repaid. The refusal of the majority of the members to recommend fresh loans is therefore understandable.

By this time many people who had opposed the alienation of land in grants to capitalists had changed their minds. The public understood at last that a transcontinental railway, though valuable as a work of development, would not for many years pay both working expenses and interest on cost, let alone refund capital. Thus for an indefinite period huge sums would have to be found by taxation and this, of course, was another kettle of fish.

The alternatives facing the Government were to halt the work; to accumulate gradually the necessary cash by means of land sales; or to adopt the land-grant system, should a syndicate of sufficient standing be found.

Generally speaking, the public agreed with the Commission's recommendations, and the popular feeling was strengthened by events then taking place in Western Australia.

It happened that a land-grant scheme had been put up to the Government in Perth by a London syndicate whose representative, J.R. Browne, had visited Adelaide in the hope of negotiating a South Australian line to meet the railway it was proposed to build in the west. In short, an east-west line was in prospect.

For much of the distance this planned interstate line was to follow the coast of the Great Australian Bight. The proposal made to Western Australia envisaged a line from York to Eucla; that to South Australia an extension of this railway from Eucla to Port Augusta. In each case, the grant of land was to be at the rate of 12,000 acres for every mile of railway built.

So the subject of land-grant railways was much in the news, and the *Dispatch* pointed out the advantage that might be anticipated from doing business with Browne's syndicate. "It does not require to be demonstrated that when an individual is hard up, has borrowed as much as he can pay interest on, has a property which he is unable to utilize, and wants money to carry on his business, the wisest thing he can do is to sell a portion of his land to redeem the rest or to enable him to utilize it. And what is true of the individual is also true of the community. The principle is perfectly sound, for it is a matter of indifference whether railways are paid for in land, or in cash obtained by land sales. The vital question is the price. Of course, railway syndicates which take payment in land that cannot find purchasers until it is made accessible by means of a railway, expect to make a profit out of their bargain, and it would be simply idiotic in them to take works in hand at an unremunerative price. The difference between them and the ordinary railway contractors is that the latter demand hard cash for their work and have no more interest in it, while the former take in payment property which is practically unsaleable, improve it, stand the loss of interest until the investment becomes remunerative, and provide traffic for the railway they have constructed."

Such straight-from-the-shoulder talk was calculated to impress people who were going through hard times. After a good deal more in the same vein, the editor drove home his point. "If we take the average cost of the line at £2,000 per mile—and certainly the South Australian Government have never built a railway at so low a cost—the State would receive £100 worth of work for a square mile of country which they cannot now get anyone to take at 2s 6d a square mile rental. Even if this computation be reduced by one half, the direct advantage the State would derive is obvious, while the indirect advantages would be still greater."

While public attention was temporarily distracted to the west, platelayers in the north reached Anna Creek, and base camp was moved up from the William bore.

It was at this time, when east-west links were in the news, that Randall Knuckey, later to become well known as Officer-in-Charge of construction on the South Australian section of the east-west telegraph line, nearly lost his life outside Strangways. Knuckey was supervising the distribution of poles (they were some of the iron rails condemned ten years before and since stored at Port Augusta) for a telegraph line the Government had decided to build between Strangways and Anna Creek. The construction train was moving at seven or eight miles an hour and navvies were engaged in unloading the rails. Suddenly the train jolted and Knuckey, who was directing the intervals between deliveries, overbalanced and dropped between two trucks. Because of the slow speed at which the train was travelling, he just saved himself from the wheels.

Despite hard times, money was always available for betting, and railway builders and settlers by the line went in for horse-racing in a big way. Even Anna Creek announced "A monster programme including horse-racing, athletics, and a baby show to be followed by a concert and a ball in the evening."

Because of restlessness among the men on the workings, and because constant turnover in the workforce decreased efficiency, the Resident Engineer made use of such occasions to provide a little variety in the lives of the navvies, running special trains for the benefit of railway personnel stationed within a reasonable distance of each meeting.

But restlessness persisted, and just as men had left the line on the rumour of gold, so others downed tools and went south when news broke that rubies had been found between Mount Freeling and Blanchewater. But the ruby field did not develop.

At this period the topic of land-grant railways was never rested for long at a time and now it was nudged into fresh prominence by John Forrest, Surveyor-General and Commissioner of Crown Lands for Western Australia.

Forrest, whose interstate outback journeys had made him a colourful personality, arrived in Adelaide full of enthusiasm for the Eucla railway project. And his views carried weight. So when, in an interview with the *Register*, he remarked, "I think this is a work we may expect to see done", people took notice. "The greatest difficulty will be to get South Australia to agree to the proposal," he added. "If the South Australian Government is prepared to give a grant of land for every mile made, I believe there are capitalists in Melbourne who could induce English capitalists to undertake the work."

Just then it was common knowledge that large sums of English capital awaited investment and that financiers were interested in Australia. Meanwhile the hard times and impatience with constant interest payments on railway capital added to the revulsion of feeling that was taking place. So, remembering the recommendations of the Royal Commission, public opinion moved firmly in favour of land-grant building. A dog-in-the-mangerish attitude over land was short-sighted: the thing was to get the job done. There was land enough and to spare—land that would never be worth anything unless someone got moving!

On 9 December assent was given to Act No. 413 of 1887: "Whereas it is expedient to provide for the extension of the Great Northern Railway to Angle Pole . . . "

Oddly enough, the Act was the outcome neither of freshly-negotiated loan nor of land-grant offer. Astonishingly, the Government had built the railway from Hergott to Strangways for £177,000 less than the amount of the estimate. It is said that this satisfactory outcome was due partly to the circumstance that fair seasons had afforded better supplies of surface water than had been anticipated.

The decision had been taken to spend the "saving" on yet another extension.

In introducing the Bill, the Commissioner of Public Works had drawn a dramatic word-picture of the rise of large towns in the interior, of Darwin as "the Brindisi of Australia", and of trains steaming busily northwards and southwards across the continent. Such was the inception of the line to Oodnadatta.

The Act of 1887 officially established the name of the railway. Hitherto the line had been known by many descriptions, section names sometimes serving for the whole. Now no doubt was left about the correct title.

Following the usual wordy preamble, the opening clause decided the matter. "In the construction of this Act, the words 'the Great Northern Railway' shall mean the main line of railway from Port Augusta, via Government Gums, Farina Town, Hergott Springs, and the Peake, duly authorized by Parliament and shall include any future extension."

The Act then proceeded to legalise the irregularity that had arisen when a later decision had varied the route originally laid down by Parliament. The Act of 1883 had opened: "Whereas it is expedient to provide for the construction of a line of Railway from Hergott Springs to Primrose Springs . . ." Now this provision was amended. The new Act stated: "The extension of the Great Northern Railway from Hergott Springs to the Peake, as already constructed, is hereby authorized, and the making and maintaining thereof shall be deemed to have been and to be duly authorized by the 'Hergott Springs to Primrose Springs Railway Act of 1883' as if the same had been expressly mentioned and referred to therein, instead of the railway from Hergott Springs to Primrose Springs."

Certainly the Government lawyers left no loophole for misunderstanding. Not until the situation had been clarified beyond a peradventure—the archaic legal term seems suitable here—was the purpose of the new Act developed. Clause 3 laid down: "The Commissioner of Railways may make and maintain a further extension of the Great Northern Railway from the Peake to Angle Pole, together will all proper works and conveniences connected therewith and may take possession of the lands delineated in the said plan deposited in the offices of the Surveyor-General for the purposes of this Act."

Then, finally to button up the situation, Clause 4 added: "The Hergott Springs and Primrose Springs Railway Act, 1883, and this Act shall be incorporated and read as one Act."

Perhaps the words "any future extension", so specifically added to the opening clause of the Act, and duly publicised through the Press and the Overland Telegraph, put fresh heart into those railway navvies who, not deluded by rumours of rubies, feared the sack should railway construction come to an end. Ten days later a report described exuberant workers starting their Christmas leave. "The four hundred Peake navvies who came down the Great Northern line on Monday for the holidays on the whole behaved well. They were the best lot of boys ever under the paternal supervision of a northern railway guard. True, not all were blue ribbon men, and the cup that cheers but also inebriates was too much for a few. But nine arrests out of four hundred railway navvies on holiday is a low percentage."

However, the New Year appeared to give the lie to Christmas optimism. In mid-January, a Strangways correspondent reported despondently: "Platelaying operations between here and the Peake are entirely suspended for the present. Rails are laid to the 148th mile post, and five hundred men are employed on the works. But a notice is posted at the Head Office stating that the Government will not employ any more men in addition to the present number on the line."

The mile post mentioned lay almost exactly half-way between Anna Creek and Box Creek. But the fact that the rails had reached this spot did not mean that the line was yet open so far north. In fact opening day at Coward Springs, sixty miles to the south, had been fixed for 7 February. For "a great deal of work remains to be done before the Traffic Department will take over the line. Several gangs are employed in raising and ballasting between Hergott and Coward."

While the railhead remained in the region of the 148-Mile, navvies must often have looked westward, perhaps still thinking of rubies. For there, seventy miles distant, low opal-tinted hills gave dramatic displays of changing colours at sunrise and sunset. A quarter of a century later, Coober Pedy—"White fellows' hole in the ground"—would grow up in those hills. Could they have known of this, the navvies would have envied the future cave and dug-out dwellers their escape from great heat and, according to the whim of the seasons, bitter, searching winds.

Of this stage in the construction, records—often scanty—are largely lacking. Perhaps the delay that now occurred was due to a hold-up in bridge building. Ten weeks later, the *Dispatch* reported: "The Government are erecting an engine shed at William bore, 124 miles north. A railway platform and station, also cattle yards, have been built. The Camp will be opened there in a couple of months, as soon as the William and Warrina bridges are erected."

Though the camp was probably moved forward in July, William Creek was not opened for traffic for more than a year. So just when work was resumed in earnest is uncertain.

In this doubtful period, one may date the advance with some assurance from accident reports. For instance: "Yesterday, another fatal accident near 160 mile camp! Mounted Constable Davey, stationed at Anna Creek, reported that James Cole, a railway guard, had been run over and killed. The body of the man had been reduced to pulp, but his head was uninjured. The dead man, a ballast train guard, about forty years of age, fell from a loaded truck while applying the brake." Published on 10 August, this grim little account shows that, on this date, the permanent way had reached a point at least half-way between Box Creek and Edwards Creek.

Incidentally, here no fault attached to the railway authorities for employing an inexperienced member of the unemployed in a responsible post. It appears that, apart from eighteen months on the Hergott–Strangways line, Cole had worked as a guard on the London and North-Western Railway for many years.

Exactly five weeks after this accident a navvy was killed at Edwards Creek, "at the end of the laid line where a bridge was being built". This fatality pinpoints the position of the plate-laying gangs in mid-September.

In the February following, a further report on the progress of the line is headed "Sly Grog at the Peake". A navvy had been charged by a constable stationed at "the Head Railway Camp". Six months later an earthworks labourer, one Patrick Ellegate, was "carting water at the 231 mile camp; his dray tipped backwards throwing him onto the tank receiving the water, and, at the same time, one of the casks from the dray fell on his thigh".

So in mid-August 1889 the head of earthworks had passed Mount Dutton and was nearing Oodnadatta.

A report dated two weeks later described the death of a stoker who jumped from a water-tank to the toolbox of his engine and fell on the rail near the ballast pit at Warrina. At the time, the train, consisting of twenty loaded ballast trucks, was leaving for the railhead. So it seems clear that in early September plate-laying—lagging behind by the usual twenty miles or so—was proceeding north of Warrina, probably in the neighbourhood of Algebuckina Bridge, then in course of construction.

Base camp was now situated something more than 200 miles north of Hergott. The line was opened for traffic to Warrina in November 1889.

The Board of Commissioners to whom the management of the railways had been entrusted consisted of a Chairman and two members. They appear to have introduced few changes, and there had been criticism of their failure to produce spectacular results.

Conscious of some public disapproval, the Chairman decided to acquaint himself at first hand with what was happening in the north. He visited the workings by special train in company with the Engineer-in-Chief, the Traffic Manager, and the Locomotive Superintendent. It may be that he reached useful conclusions: if so, these have gone unrecorded. What has been recorded is that he shared in a particularly shocking fatality.

At about nine o'clock on a dark evening the "special" came to a jolting, grinding stop as the driver applied the brakes violently. The guard, followed by members of the party, jumped down and ran back along the line. They came to a place where wreckage littered the track. The dim light of the guard's lantern lit a ghastly scene. Amid the remains of a ganger's tricycle lay the bodies of two men, literally cut in pieces.

Later the engine-driver said that the tricycle had shown no lights, though railway regulations required their use after dark. But the men had not been warned that a "special" was expected and it seems that the rattle of the tricycle must have covered the sound of the approaching train. During the enquiry the pitiful fact was uncovered that the elder victim had been the father of nine children. His companion, twenty-seven years of age, was unmarried.

Tragedy seems to have beset the railway camps at this period. At the head of the line, a Chinaman was found with his skull fractured as a result of what must have been a furious attack. The body, partly buried and then covered with boughs, lay near Algebuckina railway camp. A drag-track led back to a small hut in the bush. Traces of blood were found on the door-posts and on the floor bags. Enquiries, made in the camp and on a small goldfield then operating near by, were inconclusive. The verdict reached at the inquest held at Peake was that the deceased man was murdered by some person or persons unknown, though suspicion attached to a fellow-countryman known as Charlie the Cook.

Eventually, the suspected man was traced to Crown Point, where he was arrested and sent to Adelaide for trial. And there the record ends.

At about the time of this murder, when plate-laying still lagged in the Algebuckina region, land-grant railways again became a topic of immediate importance.

The Board of Commissioners were called upon to deal with a surprise proposal made by a Monsieur Violette, a French engineer representing an Anglo-French syndicate which had conceived the idea of building a railway from Roebuck Bay to Angle Pole, a distance of over a thousand miles.

Violette pressed his terms energetically. These were that the completed line—of five-foot-three-inch gauge—should remain the property of the syndicate, which would engage to work it to the satisfaction of the Governments of both South Australia and Western Australia; and that a grant of 35,000 acres should be made for each mile of railway built.

Apparently Violette informed the Press that Bills for the authorisation of his proposal were to be introduced to the Parliaments of both colonies. This the South Australian Premier promptly denied, remarking sardonically that he had no intention of assisting a proposal to divert the Transcontinental Railway to Western Australia. He added that his Parliament objected to land-grant schemes. This was a surprising statement in view of the recommendations of the Royal Commission.

Parliament might object, but now increasing numbers of people became demanding. They had come to feel that the colony could not support the strain of more loans. They recalled the words of Governor Jervois. How, then, save through a land-grant scheme, might the Adelaide–Darwin link be completed? But some, including those members of the Royal Commission who had supported loans, wished to press on regardless of mounting debt. A little tremulously, it seems today, they whistled for a wind. With what passed for confidence they assured the colony: "The Government will have the good sense to wait till the promised land of plenty, far beyond, is opened up by the iron horse before expecting payable results."

But could the Government stand the pace if it refused to consider land-grant offers? Clearly, Melbourne thought not. The *Evening Standard* wrote at this time: "It is rumoured that the giant enterprise of South Australia—the construction of a transcontinental line of railway through the very heart of the Australian continent—is about to be discontinued. If this is true it will be one of the most lamentable events, and the other three great states of Australia should devise joint means for the expedition of intercolonial travelling facilities."

Then the editor proceeded to anticipate proposals that were to be put forward thirty years later. He wrote: "If the line were continued from Port Darwin to the Queensland boundary, with a branch to Brisbane; to the New South Wales border, with a branch to Sydney; from thence along the western district of Victoria, with a branch to Adelaide, and finding its terminus in Melbourne, a work of immense importance would be carried out at the joint expense of the four great states of Australia . . . The scheme is one with solid grit in it and rises above the parochialism of party politics."

But a proposal to divert the northern portion of their great linking railway to Queensland, New South Wales, and Victoria, leaving the middle and southern sections stranded in mid-continent, did not suit any of the factions into which South Australia was now divided. This was worse even than the ridiculous proposal to tap the Great Northern Railway at Angle Pole for the advantage of Western Australia.

Moves by sister colonies to employ their wealth to secure a part in the great enterprise and so deprive South Australia of much of the fruits of enterprise might be handled with a blunt refusal. But how to handle weakness within? By this time, the South Australian man-in-the-street had begun to suspect that his Government might halt construction at Angle Pole indefinitely. On 25 October 1889 the *Dispatch* warned of the likely reaction among construction workers if work on the railway were stopped. The Government should consider well before dispersing the railway gangs. "Take these men from navvying and make idlers of them; they will not work for farmers."

However, the probability is that the Government planned to continue the railway after a short pause only at Angle Pole, the early name of Oodnadatta.

When Graham Stewart had moved north from Strangways his orders were to make a preliminary survey "bearing in mind a Government intention to advance the railway in stages, at more or less regular intervals, ultimately to meet the line moving southwards from Palmerston". This instruction had resulted in a careful assessment of the country between Angle Pole and Burt's Creek, some twenty-five miles north of the MacDonnell Ranges. Stewart had submitted three progress reports dated respectively July, September, and November 1887.

His final report, submitted in June 1888, concluded: "I would respectfully urge the advisability of having the route of the transcontinental railway between Angle Pole and Pine Creek definitely fixed by trial survey. The advantages of such a course would be—(i) That the line could be constructed in sections as required with the absolute certainty that the best route had been selected; (ii) that the water supplies could be provided along the route in advance of the construction. Before the trial survey could be extended north of the MacDonnell Ranges it would be necessary to make an examination of the country between those ranges and Pine Creek, similar to that recently completed from the Angle Pole northwards, which forms the basis of this report."

Thus over an extended period, Government attention had been directed constantly to a far northern survey. On receipt of Stewart's final report the Commissioner of Public Works requested the Railway Commissioners to have a trial survey prepared in readiness for the extension of the Great Northern line from Oodnadatta to the MacDonnell Ranges.

On 6 June 1890, shortly before Stewart's report was printed by order of the House of Assembly, the *Dispatch* reported: "The preliminary arrangements have been completed by the Engineer-in-Chief. All the necessary staff has been appointed, and the first party leaves as soon as the equipment can be completed. The length of the survey will be about 280 miles at the end of which it will join on with a survey previously made through the MacDonnell Ranges thus giving the Department a permanent survey for a distance of 1,000 miles from Adelaide."

This seems conclusive evidence that the Government still fully intended to continue the transcontinental railway.

That public confidence had been restored in large measure is suggested by moves now made by private interests to press individual needs. Otherwise, surely, the firms concerned would have felt their efforts wasted. For example, "A deputation waited on the Commissioner of Public Works to ask that a route via Blinman and Wilpena to the Queensland border be followed—as forty-two mines would be served thereby." It was the old story again—mine railways: and this application seems to have received no more serious attention than earlier requests.

In the same month—an unusually cold September when snowstorms occurred in hills 200 miles north of Adelaide, and an epidemic of "Russian" influenza plagued the colony—the Premier, "Honest Tom" Playford, announced that the Government would spend £3,500,000 on public works, including a railway to the Queensland border (though not by the route the miners desired). He did not say where the money was to be found—unless, hopefully, it was from a tax increase of twopence in the pound on incomes from property. But, to demonstrate the new Government's genuine concern with railway progress, he witnessed successful trials of the Westinghouse brake on the Great Northern line.

At about this time the first locomotive built in the colony was driven from Gawler to Adelaide, a preliminary delivery under a contract for fifty-two engines that had been placed by the Government.

Meanwhile the bridging of the Neales River progressed slowly. The Neales, named after an early Adelaide auctioneer and Member of Parliament, rises in two branches in the Stuart Range to the west of Oodnadatta. In places the bed of the dry stream spreads over three miles of plain. The bridge was being built wide enough to accommodate the broad gauge, despite the fact that throughout its length the railway had been built to the narrow gauge. "We thought it advisable to build such a bridge" is the explanation offered by the record.

Eventually the line was opened to Angle Pole on 7 January 1891, six-and-a-half years after it had left Hergott Springs. A hard road indeed!

Within a fortnight of opening day there began the verbal beating that was to become an accepted part of railway life. A leading journal opened the attack on 16 January. "For real uncommon unpunctuality we would recommend the North where the proper time for the arrival of trains has been almost universally forgotten."

Not that complaint was limited to time-keeping! Departments responsible for maintenance came equally under fire. And, sometimes, editorial wit degenerated into sarcasm. "Some time ago, we referred in rather uncomplimentary terms to the antiquity of the jarrah sleepers in the Great Northern line in the neighbourhood of Saltia. The Commissioners, we see, have awakened to the fact that something more substantial between northern passengers and eternity is desirable. We beg to offer the Commissioners a little further humble advice, viz., not to send the displaced sections of timber to the Adelaide Museum. If they do, the railway revenue will most assuredly suffer next year."

Though usually employed in the spirit of banter, the pattern of stricture thus set was to continue down the years.

10

SILVERSKIN IN A DESERT MOON

Switching off lights, Sally and I stood in the brakevan door, looking out across desert. We were stationary once more, and that night a full moon dimmed the splendour even of Orion, the constellation that cattlemen call "The Stockyard" because it includes some hundred stars.

Space and moonlight! Then, space and moonlight and a waxing gleam glittering in the corner of one eye. We looked northwards.

Rising at the edge of the plain, a white light blazed. I thought of the bright eye of Kuddimuckra, the legendary serpent of Lake Eyre. Usually, though, Kuddimuckra appeared in the Stuart Springs region. Perhaps it was Jeedara, the moaner, up from the Nullarbor? Each great plain has its especial terror for the Aboriginal.

Suddenly the glaring eye sank from sight. Well, a trick of Jeedara was to dive down blowholes. But here were no blowholes. Then it blazed again, rising from a depression in the plain.

The goods train did not arrive for twenty minutes, and another five passed while it moved by. We counted forty-five bogie vehicles. Then the guard shouted a greeting that was lost in the diminishing clatter. Afterwards, space and moonlight and a red eye, slowly dwindling as the "goods" travelled southwards.

Once more the prospect was two-dimensional. Within sight, no shed or tree gave depth to the vast expanse. Here and there was a low bush, a shadow in moonlight, no more. Otherwise there were only gibbers—hundreds of square miles carpeted with stones that we knew to be dark red or yellow in colour and usually from one to six inches long. Surely, it was the rim of the world!

Gibbers—formed by the erosion of sandstone rock—may be boulder-sized, but here all were of the small variety. In some areas they fitted into each other like pieces in a Roman pavement, though this we did not discover till next day.

Polished by the sand-blast of the winds of ages, gibbers may reflect light like fragments of bottle-glass. We might have been watching the reflection of moonbeams splintering on water instead of on stone. The "Dead Heart" can be enchanting in both moods—arid and flowering. After all, the Arab calls the desert "The Garden of Allah".

Standing there, we might have been in a vast planetarium, so near seemed the stars. In such situations, one wonders how the Soviet scientist argues Communist theory. Dispatching his probe to Mars or Venus, he must act in the belief that the laws upon which he has based his calculations will be maintained. As a reasonable man he cannot argue that law is the outcome of chance. So, what? Surely, the answer is that in claiming atheism, the thinking Communist intends that he is a deist as opposed to a theist—that is, he acknowledges a creating, guiding Power, but not a god sustaining a personal relation to his creatures.

So we argued—till Sally marched off to the kitchen. "We," she called, "are talking moonshine." And, perhaps, she was right.

It had been a fascinating experience, travelling by night with the Slow Mixed, staying awake all the time out of interest in the places where once the construction gangs laboured.

At one spot the train had halted apparently in the middle of nowhere. No platform! No station building! Just a narrow, stony track beside the line. To the west, gibbers, wilderness, and silence; to the east, gibbers, Lake Eyre South, and silence. From this place the Lake was not visible. But I thought of spots where fragments of old fences run out from shore, reminding the traveller of the banks of Lake George. As at Lake George, these fences wade into water, with the difference that, normally, their water is mirage.

At this point the train was bow-shaped, following a curve in the line. Some forty trucks in all, they seemed to stretch for ever in that deceptive light. The bulky figure of the guard climbed down to the track, his lantern bobbing as he walked. He passed beneath us. "How's she comin', mate? Can't yer sleep, then?"

On being told that too much of interest was forward to waste time in the sack, he grunted and stopped short. "Break it down!" he said, staring up.

Sally laughed. "Dinkum oil!" He guffawed at that and, I suppose, at the ways of galahs. Then he went on to open the refrigerated van.

Clang of iron! Squeal of hinge! Then parcels were dragged out and set down at the side of the track.

Now two dots of light appeared in the distance, and soon three men arrived, one pushing a wheelbarrow. They did not hurry. The train would wait. "Wotcher, mate! Bloody Ghan late per usual?"

The guard snorted. "Break it down!" His favourite apostrophe.

Just then a man jumped down from the sit-up coach. He reached back through the door for his luggage. Then, a suitcase in either hand, he tramped away without a word to anyone. Alone into desert, so far as we could see. I thought of a Chaplin film recently fished up from a Hollywood limbo and shown to young audiences, all as delighted as their grandfathers long ago. Charlie had signed off in this piece by shuffling away into the distance, lunch-box in one hand, absurd twirling cane in the other, following the toes of tattered, turned-out boots. This stranger shuffled, too, and appeared to have no clearer notion of his destination than Charlie had.

Soon the stooped figure merged with the night. "Where's he off?" I called. The guard paused, a parcel in each hand. "Who? Old Sam? To Bill's place, I reckon." Just that. Nothing more of Sam. Nothing of Bill. Or of his place—somewhere in the loneliness. It was all too everyday a matter for comment.

Presently the deep barrow was loaded. Parcels had been tossed in without checking. Then the men sat down, lit cigarettes. The guard's voice growled from within. "That's the lot by my book." Even then, nothing was examined. "She'll be right, mate." "Maybe we'll be lucky."

Barrow and escort disappeared into the night. An unseen homestead had been supplied—Bill's place, perhaps—a homestead already standing when earthwork, plate-laying, and bridge-building gangs had passed this way, or so the guard said.

The lantern waved. The diesel's horn wailed, and the train moved on, at walking pace until the guard was abreast of his van and had swung up through the doorway.

Then we were away again, trundling across the moonlit plain for thirty miles before the next stop. Or perhaps it was only twenty miles. We did not study maps that night, and when a train saunters, distance is hard to judge. Anyway there was time for three coffees, sipped at ease in our V.I.P. kitchen.

At last, another platformless halt! But this time there was a homestead near by, stark and lonely under the moon. The old house and its quiet drew me. But then Sally calls me a solitary. A hermit's life, she says, would have suited me well.

Somewhere a small engine put-putted busily. The sound explained the bright, welcoming lights in windows and doorway.

Two men came down a dirt track, one pushing a small handcart.

Surprisingly, they trotted. On this occasion many packages were off-loaded and the little cart shuttled backwards and forwards in the moonlight.

A woman stood just inside the house doorway. She appeared to examine each item and then to give instructions to someone out of sight. This time nothing went unchecked. It was like watching a dumb charade. The scene was brightly lit, but voices did not carry the distance in competition with the sound of the generator.

Presently the woman raised an arm and then disappeared inside. The guard waved his lantern shoulder-high. The horn answered mournfully, and the starting jolt travelled down the length of the train. "Wotcher, George!" "Good luck, cobber!" And, a little unexpectedly from the man pushing the handcart, "Adios, amigo."

Once more we were off, trundling purposefully northward under the eye of the moon.

Sunrise came at Edwards Creek, eighty-two miles from Marree. Now a four-house fettlers' camp, this halt was an important watering point for locomotives in the days of steam, supplies coming from a freshwater well in the creek.

Brakevanning by day is as fascinating as by night. Mistakenly, I said as much to the guard. His double-chin trembled. "Good on yer, mate." Then he added as an afterthought, "Reckon the old saying's all wrong. Should be two every minute." And, chuckling softly, he tramped away.

Though traversing country popularly described as desert, the strip of line we had just covered in darkness is strewn with spots of railway interest. Its stories are less familiar than the tales told of the southern sections.

Callanna is about mid-way between Marree and the site of the Ballast Camp of the 1880s. It may be said that the legends of the Lake Eyre region begin here. Near by are two hills, the Minakuka. The whitish appearance of these hills stirred the imaginations of the Aborigines, who held them to be the eyes of a Mura-Mura warrior named Warrumandina.

Tradition says that the Mura-Mura, legendary predecessors of the Aborigines, became enraged very easily. One day Warrumandina fell into so great a fury that he tore out his own eyes and flung them from him. The cause of his passion is not stated. Should you doubt the tale, there stand the eye-like hills to prove its truth.

Mura-Mura chiefs appear to have specialised in tearing themselves apart in emergencies. To the north-west, in the area of the Look-Out—the cape overlooking Lake Eyre South, where Edward John Eyre supposed that he had reached the coast of a continuation of Lake Torrens—are liver-coloured hills to which a parallel legend attaches. Aborigines believed that here another warrior, when attacked by dingoes, plucked out his liver and hurled it far away so that it, at least, might not be eaten.

Here is desert that proves the truth of the old text, for the country may blossom like the rose, though few who have not seen this happen would believe it possible. In this area it happens perhaps ten times in a century; so it is a change that the navvies probably witnessed, since the Strangways section took many years to construct. Mr G.L. Stirling spent forty-six years in the service of the Commonwealth Railways, and so travelled the line many hundreds of times. His brother-in-law owned Callanna Station and in February 1972 he arrived there for a three months' visit. Then the country was little more than sand-drift. In scorching temperatures, scarcely a trace of green appeared, and the only water available came from wells and bores. One day an Aboriginal stockman, pointing here and there in the sky, made what seemed like an unlikely prediction. A good general rain was coming, he said. "See!" he exclaimed. "Storm birds!"

Soon clouds gathered. Then rain fell, and for the first time in ten years the flat lands became carpeted in a hundred varieties of flowers—*Dodonaea*, Sturt's Desert Pea, Button Bush, and so on. The seeds had lain dormant, and then in propitious conditions had sprouted and burgeoned in kaleidoscopic colours—green, red, and purple predominating. Birds came then—wild turkey, black swan, duck, and many other species.

Unfortunately desert gardens fade quickly. The mass of vegetation consists of annuals, as transient as the wiry, dark-green grass. The colour soon blows away, leaving the sandhills bare once more.

In the Bopeechee region, near the site of Finniss Camp, the 38-Mile post of rail-building days, mirage seems to be especially notable. Sugarloaf Hill must have afforded the navvies many an odd display. Along with the country about its base, this hill can give the illusion of being entirely airborne, with clouds floating beneath.

An old story of the railway tells of the time when base camp lay at Stuart Creek, twenty-five miles to the north-west. One evening three Irish navvies came white-faced into camp, swearing that they had been pursued by a monster snake. In those days when sly-grog was prepared, copper coins were tossed into the boiler to add strength to the brew. This practice must sometimes have produced odd effects in superstitious minds stirred by tales of the Lake Eyre monsters. It seems the most likely explanation of the incident.

The legend of the monsters appears to have had two parts, which were sometimes confused. The first concerned a giant serpent, Kuddimuckra, said to search ceaselessly for human victims with whom it writhed away into fathomless mud. Aborigines avoided travelling along the shores of the Lake, just as they avoided advancing deep on to the Nullarbor Plain, where Jeedara was thought to drag the unwary along underground waterways to the Bight. Serpent beliefs had so strong a hold on the minds of tribesmen that they fled on seeing a train for the first time.

Closely interwoven with the first, the second legend, the myth of the Kadimakara, or Kadimerkera, seems to have some slender basis in fact. A tribal recollection of the Dieri people of the Cooper Creek district, it spread throughout the Lake Eyre region.

Once upon a time, the Kadimakara climbed down great gum trees from a green land that roofed the country. They came to graze on rich lands beneath. But one day when many monsters were below, lightning destroyed the strongest gums. The trees that remained could not support a Kadimakara, so the creatures were trapped on the ground, where they remained a perpetual terror to men.

Gradually, the holes formed in the green land above spread, until, joining, they became one. This gave rise to the Dieri name for the sky—"Puri Wilpanina" or "The Great Hole".

Some ethnologists suggest that the second legend may be a shadowy racial memory of an infinitely remote period when Lake Eyre was many times its present size. At this time an inland sea occupied the great basin of Central Australia and rain forests filled the land.

At the time when the railway arrived, dinosaur remains were found in various places about Lake Eyre. And when the bore was sunk at Hergott, huge fossil bones were unearthed. Later, when H.Y.L. Brown, the Government geologist, examined phosphate deposits in the country between the Birdsville Track and the Lake many more fossils came to light. All the remains were those of *Diprotodon australis*, a huge wombat-like creature with teeth some eight inches long, that appeared perhaps 100 million years ago and died out, according to the radiocarbon test, about 12,000 years ago.

In any case, when your train stops at Curdimurka and you recall the story of the great beasts said to have climbed down from heaven thereabouts you are justified in supposing that there is as much foundation for the legend of the Kadimakara as for the folk tale of Jack and the Beanstalk.

Curdimurka is the nearest approach that the railway makes to Lake Eyre, which at this point is the lowest land in the continent—thirty-nine feet below sea-level. Here in 1963 Donald Campbell planned his attempt on the world land speed record. At Stuart Creek—still sometimes called Chambers Creek because Stuart himself gave it that name after one of his patrons—explorers, prospectors, surveyors, and early graziers camped to recruit their expeditions before venturing upon the most desolate part of the route between Port Augusta and the Centre. The creek reaches the Lake between tall cliffs containing quantities of fossil shells.

At Coward Springs the railway follows the edge of the artesian basin. The springs—named after Corporal Tom Coward, who shared the journeys of Major Peter Egerton Warburton, explorer and Commissioner of Police—form part of the string that made possible a stock route about the south-western corner of Lake Eyre.

A railwayman once remarked to me, "Whenever I go north, Strangways is where I begin to gibber." A weak grin matched the feebleness of the joke, but until the coming of the railway, the gibber country of the region was hard on all travellers—horsemen, cameleers, and drovers alike. It is said that camel strings slowed from a steady four miles an hour to a shaky two-and-a-half.

Here, on top of a knoll to the west of the line, are the remains of a staging camp used during the construction of the Overland Telegraph. The site was chosen primarily for the sake of the water that flows from springs on the summit. But security may have had a part in the choice.

A story is told of a party of men, women, and children speared to death by Aborigines in the Strangways district. The massacre took place shortly before the arrival of the telegraph builders, and some say that the victims were a pioneer grazier, and his family and servants. That is as maybe, for most of the pioneers were young men, and none would have been likely to take children with them into the unsettled north. However, the railway halt inherited the name of the telegraph station, called after H.B.T. Strangways—"the St George of the Land Reformers"—who in large measure was responsible for the decision to build the Overland Telegraph Line.

When the railway construction-workers arrived, they found six men stationed at Strangways—the stationmaster, an assistant operator, and four linesmen. The lonely little settlement was supplied with twelve horses and a bullock team, and provisioned for a year. It is easy to understand the change that the coming of the line made in the lives of these men.

Warburton spoke of Lake Eyre when dry (the normal state of the northern and larger section) as terrible in its death-like stillness and sterility. Perhaps a similar feeling prompted John McDouall Stuart to name a spot near Box Creek the Spring of Hope. This discovery followed a long period of disappointment and it put new heart into him, less perhaps for its immediate importance than for the future opportunity it opened. For the newly-found water assured the explorer a line of retreat in yet another of his northward thrusts. Thirty years later, the spring was put to good use by the railway navvies.

At Edwards Creek the guard paused beside the brakevan before we left. He liked, it seemed, to pull a leg. "You like yer butcher of beer, I reckon?" he asked, grinning. I nodded. "Well, so they did in the old days, seemingly." And chuckling, he signalled the train on, his manner that of one who thinks, "Now work that one out, cobber."

His context was obscure, but it happened that I had the clue and so did not need to ask the question that perhaps he expected. I have heard parts of the Eyre Highway described as "Bottle Route" because of the many unsolicited offerings that are made to the roadside. Well, for a similar reason, it seems that this part of the line might well be nicknamed "Bottle Track".

One wonders if the general sterility alleged by Warburton causes this district, say between Strangways and Warrina, to be especially marked by the old bottle parade. Here lie countless mute witnesses to the thirst of travellers over three-quarters of a century. I have been told that careful scrutiny discovers small differences in size and shape marking, presumably changes in brewers' styles through the years.

Similarly, though more obviously scattered, lie remnants of the first permanent way. Most of the old sleepers—they seem to be particularly numerous in the immediate region of Lake Eyre—remain where they were pitched down by the navvies who discarded them. But some lie far away on the plain where dropped by floodwaters.

West of Warrina lies Mount Barry Station which is owned by Mr Bob Kempe. His father worked as a young man for an uncle, E.C. Kempe, who then held the Peake Station in partnership with Sir Sidney Kidman. When Bob Kempe went to Mount Barry in 1947 cattle were walked to Warrina siding. But today road transport has taken over and beasts go by road to the rail at Oodnadatta.

When the construction gangs first arrived, copper was known to exist east of Warrina. A mine was opened and ore was carted to the railhead by horse and donkey teams.

Warrina, ninety miles from Strangways, became an important trucking centre soon after the arrival of the railway. Shortly after the turn of the century, J.W. Gregory made it the termination of his expedition round the northern end of Lake Eyre from a base at Killalpanninna, the mission station on Cooper Creek. Towards the end of the journey the party made forced marches in order to reach Warrina in time to catch the fortnightly train to the south.

From early days, grasshoppers seem to have been particularly troublesome in the Mount Dutton district. Slippery rails have stopped many a train. The stories began with an account of the trials of the driver of a work-train that ran into a grasshopper swarm. His load consisted of sleepers and rails—heavy to move in ordinary conditions, impossible to shift when the driving wheels lost traction. He and his mate laid cloths on the rails to get the train moving, but when the cloths had been crossed the wheels spun afresh. The plate-laying gangs lost a day's work on account of that grasshopper plague, or so it is said.

Of course this nuisance is met on other sections. At intervals, jumping and chirping insects of various species used to invade the line between Port Augusta and Quorn, when this was still open to general traffic, and occasionally it became necessary to divide trains and take the parts through separately because the wheels of engines climbing the Pass lost grip on the metals. However, it appears that for many years Mount Dutton held the record for delay. An elderly fettler stationed at the halt told me of an occasion when the Slow Mixed ran into a " 'hopper" swarm near by. "And did those jokers curse!" he exclaimed, grinning. "There was no holdin' them." That day the Mixed had been running on time, but it was four hours late on reaching Oodnadatta, twenty-five miles away.

George Stirling confirmed the nuisance that " 'hoppers" represent. But oddly enough ants seem to have caused him more difficulty in the Mount Dutton region. Using a broom to sweep the metals ahead of an engine seldom proved effective, for by the time a fresh start was made other ants were swarming on the rails.

Similarly, rushing an engine at an invading horde of insects did not ensure unhindered passage. If the area affected happened to be large the wheels soon whirled round uselessly and the train came to a halt. On such occasions the smell of hot metal combining with the odour of roasted insects caused a terrific stench. George Stirling said that a driver might empty his sandbox on the rails in an attempt to give traction. But even sand was not always effective.

On the East-West railway, particularly in the Pimba district, trains may be held up by woodbugs crawling on the steel.

Now, in the brakevan kitchen, we made coffee, afterwards sitting by the open window to obtain the full benefit of the breeze created by a fan above the door.

Perhaps the whirr of the blades, the only stir in the night, was the cause, but we talked of the "Desert Sound", wondering if we might have the fortune to hear it.

As in the case of the Min-Min Light of northern Queensland, many have listened to tales of the phenomenon, but few have experienced it. Those who claim to have heard the "Sound" describe it as a booming resonance that ends as abruptly as it begins. One infers, however, that it is felt more than heard.

And the explanation? Some say that from time to time movement occurs in fissures in the fracture line of the "Shatter Belt", a series of faults that begin to the east of the Eyre Peninsula, continue northwards beneath the western plain, and end in the mound springs country south and west of Lake Eyre.

Now that the roof hid the full brightness of the desert moon, the stars appeared as sparkling drops. We were sitting just absorbing silence, when suddenly my eye was caught by a sparkle from the trackside. I peered down. The night gleam reflected from the base of a discarded beer bottle!

The sight returned us to earth with a bump that seemed physical. Loud laughter appeared to be unseemly in the hush. We laughed all the same, and presently turned in.

11
THE LONG PAUSE

When a stationmaster's house was built at Oodnadatta the dwelling was lonely indeed. The tented camp of the camel drivers was near by. But save for a few widely-scattered stations on the Overland Telegraph Line, no solidly constructed building stood between it and the northern railhead at Pine Creek, more than a thousand miles distant.

In those days, the region consisted of a few cattle and horse runs of up to 6,000 square miles. Years later the then owner of Erldunda Station, giving evidence before the Commonwealth Parliamentary Standing Committee on Public Works, remarked: "Before the line went up to Oodnadatta there were no small men at all."

Graziers took up huge blocks, not because they wanted so much land, but because they could not afford to put in water improvements. They had to occupy vast areas in order to obtain enough water.

When the railway reached Oodnadatta no bores existed in the region. The first was put down near the line in 1893, the preliminary gush throwing sand to a height of eighty feet. Previously, in times of drought, all water had to be carted from a distance to the camel camp.

One newly-arrived grazier decided to bore. His practice was to sink a shaft from twenty-five to thirty feet, and then bore to 100 feet. If he struck blue shale, he knew he was in sub-artesian country and stopped that particular bore. In all, he sank 2,000 feet at £2 a foot. In return for his work and outlay, he obtained two successes only, water in wells at twenty-four feet and eighteen feet respectively.

This was a heavy expense, and a couple of bores was not an adequate answer to the water problem. For the grazier with a bore could feed stock within a circumference of ten miles in soft country, but of five miles only in hard country. Cattle will not willingly travel far across stony land in summertime, though they make little trouble on sandy surfaces. Thus a station owner might have—in a good season—many hundreds of square miles of feed country, yet be unable to use it because he had insufficient water.

Owners of large stations therefore considered that the Government should provide water before planning to extend the railway farther north.

However, this was not necessarily the view of the small man, who was now beginning to strike out on his own. For when the railway arrived at Oodnadatta, many employees of the large stations, men who had saved a little money and collected a few horses, decided to start in business for themselves. These bought a few cattle and—having the advantage of a thorough knowledge of the country—took up small blocks from the Government, usually on some waterhole they had found. They were to make the best settlers. For each man lived on his property, making it a home. The big owners, on the other hand, usually lived in Adelaide, Melbourne, or Sydney, seldom visiting their properties, but taking all they could squeeze out of them through managers.

Whenever possible the small man chose his waterhole within easy reach of the railway. It might be merely a little limestone pot-hole going down some fifteen feet, scarcely sufficient to water saddle and pack-horses. But gradually the settler would develop his find to meet his growing needs. Cases are recorded of small holes being slowly enlarged until they could supply 1,000 head of stock all the year round.

Once the railhead was established at Oodnadatta, the number of small owners grew year by year. To the north, many stations were settled by men who had been head stockmen on big runs, men who had worked for, say, 35s to £2 a week; or by bullock drivers earning from 25s to 30s weekly. Relying on their courage, knowledge, and enterprise, these struck out for themselves, and often succeeded.

Apart from its over-riding purpose of linking Adelaide and Darwin by rail, the Government would have liked to build promptly in support of such men, but money was tight.

The railway from Port Augusta to Angle Pole had cost £2,318,242—all borrowed funds. In 1891 the colony's total bonded debt—including £1,756,400 incurred in respect of the Northern Territory—was £21,657,300.

These figures were much discussed, and now there was contention between the Government and its supporters—those who styled themselves "the prudent", and the build-at-any-price faction which was quite large enough to be noisy and a nuisance.

For the time being, said the prudent, sufficient had been spent on communications. A great stride had been taken towards the construction of a transcontinental railway. Now time should be allowed for financial recuperation before consideration was given to an extension to Alice Springs. Had not the Royal Commission advised against building farther on borrowed money? However, they qualified this view by saying that should a responsible syndicate make an offer to complete the line on acceptable land-grant terms the situation would be changed. But the impatient and perhaps imprudent rated this assurance as little more than a sop to their insistence. They pointed out that the Commission's findings had not been unanimous, and that two prominent and distinguished members had dissociated themselves from the negative recommendation, stating their opinion that the colony should borrow all necessary funds unless a syndicate willing to build in return for land-grants were found—"speedily".

The prudent then recalled the criticisms of the colony's financial policies made by Sir William Jervois on the occasion of the farewell luncheon prior to his departure to New Zealand at the end of his term of office. They pointed out that seven years had passed and that the colony was in danger of relapsing into just such a risky situation as that Sir William had foreseen. Had not the depression of the Jubilee period been warning enough? To bridge the continent with a railway that would bind together the two great sections of the colony was a grand conception that must eventually be realised. But politicians in other and wealthier colonies were staggered at South Australian improvidence. *Festina lente* was an adage that was always up to date. Certainly, they said, haste must be made, but slowly and with circumspection.

This was the sort of talk that caused the enterprising to explode. They retorted that the net revenue from railways had increased materially since ex-Governor Jervois made his controversial and ill-advised speech, and that the north-south railway must be completed if the great scheme of public works to open up the Territory and the Centre was to become effective. There had been no question of halting the Overland Telegraph Line half-way. To have done so would have been thought insane. Yet now the irony of a situation that held the railhead marooned in the most arid tract of country between Port Augusta and Port Darwin went unperceived.

It was ridiculous, they said, to regard South Australia as an impoverished state! Did she not comprise territory approximately equal to the combined areas of New South Wales, Victoria, New Zealand, France, and Germany? As for the financial position, this was sound as anyone in his senses might understand. Deducting Northern Territory costs, the debt of South Australia proper was £19,900,900. For this liability there was abundant security in the colony's 243,244,800 acres. Some 7,026,000 acres had been sold for the fee simple of £9,022,745. But 236,218,278 acres remained unalienated. This represented great wealth. Moreover, on sold and leased lands over 7,000,000 sheep, 359,000 cattle, and 187,000 horses were depastured. With security such as this, why fear loans for sound economic development?

The cautious answered that much of this argument was specious. Most of the land available was not only unproved, but also unknown. The warnings of George Fife Angas should be remembered. Much had been accomplished. Now the time for caution had come.

And caution won!

A series of bad seasons, similar to the cycle that occurred at the time when construction began, followed the opening of the line to Oodnadatta. This disaster, following upon depression and widespread unemployment, alarmed the Government. The economy showed no signs of the anticipated recovery.

Fearing to move further into debt in such circumstances, the Government quietly dropped outstanding proposals to authorise extensions to the transcontinental line, though discreet enquiries respecting land-grant possibilities appear to have been made. Probably at first the public did not understand what had taken place, for the Government's resolve was not publicised, and the results of railway enquiries opened in recent months continued to be published. Railways thus remained news.

For instance in July—six months after the line to Oodnadatta was opened—a Queensland Border Railway Commission submitted its report. This stirred the simmering pot, causing the *Dispatch* to make scathing comment. "After reading this most people will agree that it would have been better for the country if the opinion of the members had never been taken at all. It is notable chiefly for its apologetic, personally explanatory, and dissentient tone. The whole of the report is so ambiguous and suggestively 'opposite' that it requires more than one reading to grasp the meaning intended by the Commissioners."

The editor of the *Dispatch* was right. The principal recommendation—that a railway should be built from Hergott to Goyder Lagoon—was supported wholeheartedly by only three of the nine members. Five members signed with dissents, set out in minute detail, and one member withheld his signature altogether, noting scornfully: "As two-thirds of the members are opposed to the recommendation it appears to me a manifest absurdity to have it embodied in the report."

The report was, of course, shelved. But, a year later, the topic of a railway branching from the Great Northern in a north-easterly direction was still a matter of hot argument.

Some time before, the Government had introduced a stock tax, and a depressed market had followed. Now, many station owners said that cattle breeding was no longer worth while. Indeed, a number of stations were being abandoned. A notable exception was Clifton Hills, however. A report of the day, pressing for a railway, remarked: "It is estimated that Clifton Hills will carry 150,000 sheep in addition to its cattle. Let the railway be made and people will be surprized at the north-east corner of South Australia . . . Give this country facilities to reach the seaboard, and let Hergott Springs be the junction, and the shipping at Port Augusta will be worth looking at."

Despite the abandonment of many properties in the north-east, the Great Northern Railway appears to have been doing well, at least as far as Hergott. A reporter wrote at this time: "It is proved beyond doubt that the railway pays handsomely from Hergott down. Since February (a four month period) the amount of railage for the carriage of cattle reached nearly £30,000 . . . The station-master is working from Sunday morning to Saturday night. The guards are scarcely missed ere wheeled back, and the engines, to use a bushman's opinion, are worked 'dog poor'. That Hergott is neglected so much by the various departments of Government is a crying shame. There is no common to spell a day or two on. The Railway Department has not sufficient rolling stock, and drovers are kept in a state of suspense. If they come too near the township and cannot get trucks they are in a fix, for they cannot go back as they are liable to a fine for trespassing. Through these causes owners and drovers, all along the Track, urge that the railway should be extended, if only as far as Kopperamanna. Here they would have plenty of feed and water, and stock would go into Adelaide in far better condition."

Lack of feed at Hergott was one, if minor, reason for the strong demand that a railway should be built beside the great droving route out of Queensland. In the droving season, a sheep train might leave Hergott at midday and the yards be crammed again by nightfall, while flocks and mobs of cattle camped in the vicinity without grazing.

An account remains of an 1892 occasion that was probably typical of the period: "Two mobs of cattle were trucked here to-day, but owing to a drizzling rain there was considerable difficulty in trucking the last mob. With the men in wet clothes, the yards sloppy, and the cattle running badly, it was not a very enviable job. At about 6.30 p.m. Mr Lawlor, being a lot over the time allowed for trucking and still having about sixty left in the yard, had to knock off. This tail end of his mob will have to remain here until Monday, and there being no reserve to speak of for drovers or teamsters it will be very awkward for Mr Lawlor."

Because drovers suffered great inconvenience in holding stock at

Hergott while waiting for trains, an experiment was made with a canvas sheep-yard. The canvas was put up one Sunday, but the first flock of sheep to arrive laid it in ruins. However, the idea was not discarded, and angle-irons were substituted for stanchions with reasonable success.

Though a decision had been quietly taken to allow a long pause at Angle Pole before building an extension to Alice Springs, there is no doubt that the Government had resolved to construct a branch "feeder" line to the Queensland border. In August 1894, in his speech at the opening of Parliament, the Governor stated categorically that the ministerial programme for the session included a railway from Hergott to Kopperamanna near Cooper Creek. This was rather less than half-way to Clifton Hills.

Though the line was not built, clearly the intention then was that it should form the first section of a railway to the border in the district of Birdsville.

Meanwhile Oodnadatta adapted to its new status as a railway terminus. Already a township had grown up—a store, a hotel, a telegraph office, a saddler's shop, and about two dozen houses; in all, enough buildings to form a short street which ran out into desert at either end. The Afghan tented camp, with its palm-surrounded mosque, was on the western fringe of the new settlement. The bore, 1,417 feet deep, had settled down to a daily flow of 260,000 gallons with a head four feet above the ground.

Trade in the region still turned on the camel. Without the strings that served the far outback, supplies brought by the train to "this dead-end in the middle of nowhere" could not have been distributed.

Oodnadatta was now the dispersion depot for Central Australia. Stations comparatively near by, such as Macumba and Todmorden—even a few as far afield as Dalhousie and Blood's Creek—collected their supplies from the railhead by packhorse or bullock wagon. But those more distant arranged for goods to be brought forward by the camel strings that followed the path blazed by the Overland Telegraph Line, branching off to east and west as necessary to make deliveries.

According to records, about 400 camels worked out of Oodnadatta at this time. They travelled as far north as Newcastle Waters, a little more than 700 miles. But no farther—for beyond that point grew the poison plant, *Gastrolobium*.

Camels were accustomed to reach out and snatch a mouthful of feed from plants and bushes that they passed. This habit, which the cameleer could not prevent, was fatal in poison-plant country. *Gastrolobium*, about three feet high, was an easy snatch. And once a beast had swallowed a mouthful nothing could be done to save it.

Strings required three weeks to cross the sandhills and gibber plains of the camel pad to Alice Springs, and five weeks more to follow the track across the spinifex downs to Newcastle Waters, where they turned about and returned southwards.

Because of the prevalence of *Gastrolobium* north of the 17th parallel of south latitude, an inconvenient gap, 300 miles wide, extended between the northernmost camel depot and the railhead at Pine Creek.

Advertisements of the day indicate the importance still placed on the camel string—so much more flexible than the railway as an instrument of delivery. One widely-publicised Hergott auction comprised "19 cows, some with calves at foot, nearly all others about to calve, and 20 bulls. These cow camels are fat, and fit to work hard. The bulls are wonderful animals for packing heavy weights. The late owner picked them during the past ten years so that all inferior sorts have been culled. About 9 yearlings will also be offered and a large quantity of tackling."

Years of bad and fair seasons passed and still the railhead remained at Oodnadatta. Very good seasons were rare indeed; 1895 was a wonderful season, but another like it did not occur until 1922. In such years as those the average rainfall of a little over three inches increased to ten inches and more. Then, even if there were not another drop for eighteen months, graziers need not lose stock.

There was no means of budgeting with certainty, however. So, during the "long pause", perhaps cattlemen showed more impatience over delay in the provision of Government bores than over procrastination in building a railway extension which, probably, was anticipated from year to year.

Trucking cattle at "Oodna"—the inevitable contraction had long been in use—gradually became usual practice; usual, that is, when Adelaide prices made it possible to carry the difference between freight and droving costs. In seasons of poor return it was customary for drovers to take mobs farther south—to Hergott or Farina, or sometimes even all the way to Terowie.

Despite all that was said to the disparagement of a tableland littered with fragments of ironstone resting on loam, some graziers considered the region about the railhead to be excellent mid-journey fattening country. A record speaks of one owner who sent cattle down-country in what he considered to be good condition—between 600 and 700 pounds—grazed them for four months on the tableland, and then railed them to Adelaide, where they turned the scale at 1,000 pounds and over.

Life at Oodnadatta settled down to a routine of trucking and handling the in and out flow of the camel traffic. The construction gangs had been forgotten long ago. The railhead, it seemed, had come to stay.

Then on an April day in 1897 the hope of a link-up with Pine Creek suddenly revived, though perhaps there was little enthusiasm in Oodna, for the position of the railhead meant prestige as well as material benefits. The Earl of Kilmorey had landed in Australia to "do the colonies". This explanation, it was generally understood, was mere "window-dressing". For the Earl travelled in the interests of certain English capitalists, members of a powerful Anglo-French syndicate that was thought to be on the point of making a proposal for the construction of the remaining portion of the transcontinental railway on a land-grant basis.

By this time, most people had grown impatient with the situation, for the pause at Oodnadatta had drawn out intolerably and a close link with the Northern Territory was needed urgently. If the Government still felt that the colony could not afford to complete the work, then let others, who were able and willing to make the necessary outlay, have their profit. Development at high cost was better than an insufferable stalemate! There is no doubt that this was now the opinion of the majority.

In the previous year, the syndicate had made a tentative proposal. This had been on the lines of the offer made a quarter of a century before, when the project had been violently opposed by a few Members and the House had allowed the matter to drop from sheer weariness of words.

On this occasion, however, the House had been entirely satisfied regarding the bona fides and capacity of the present syndicate, which on its part was said to be confident of obtaining a sound business return on the large investment. The Land-Grant Railway—the proposed title of the line—would be a commercial success. So had said the pundits.

Yet the Government had discouraged the syndicate's representatives, and now the public suspected that a renewed offer would be received just as coldly. The people wanted to know why. Was the Premier trying for better terms by playing hard to get?

This time public feeling appears to have been strong, and indignation at the Premier's attitude ran high. One influential editor spoke out. "If foreign capital is available for such work, why in the name of conscience should we deliberately shut it out? The railway extension would mean the development of the country beyond the 26th. parallel and the cultivation of sub-tropical products which should transform the White Elephant Territory into a possession of great wealth and importance. It would mean the influx of capital for purposes of mineral development. Without some vigorous effort made to put an end to annually accruing deficits we had better petition the Imperial Parliament to relieve South Australia of its responsibility in respect of the Northern

Territory. But our interest in the long-delayed railway extension is more particularly in the direction of developments which would follow in South Australia proper. Between Hergott and Oodnadatta we are losing in interest on construction a thousand pounds every week. The railway is left like a bridge constructed into mid-stream and then abandoned."

Evidently the position taken by the Government had become extremely unpopular. Talk of a "White Elephant Territory" and of the possible advisability of petitioning the Government in London to take it back again, was a volte-face indeed.

Just what went on behind the scenes at this time is not clear. However, it is recorded that "a certain popular member questioned the Premier in the Assembly with unsatisfactory results. Subsequently, he tabled a motion affirming the desirability of re-opening negotiations with British capitalists for the completion of the transcontinental railway on the land-grant principle." This member also "canvassed the House, securing the promise of a majority of members to help in pushing through the resolution without a prolonged debate". Unanimously, the Country Party pledged support and requested the Premier to afford an opportunity to take a vote. But all came to nothing.

Feeling against the Government grew. One newspaper, naming certain Members who supported the Premier, went so far as to remark bitterly, "They were mute as dumb dogs", and later referred to the Premier himself as "The South Australian Czar".

The Government may have been uncertain of its legal position. The London dispatch of 1863 had placed the Northern Territory in the "charge" of South Australia and had reserved powers to "revoke, alter, or amend the letters patent annexing the said Territory". So there were those who questioned the legal right of the South Australian Government to make grants of land in the Territory. However, even among the Premier's supporters probably there were some who experienced regretful second thoughts as the situation moved out of the period when a change of policy would still have been possible.

The Anglo-French syndicate had competitors. Several other powerful financial groups wished to complete the transcontinental railway in return for huge land-grants. All received the same answer—a very positive "no".

Now a matter of even greater importance temporarily monopolised the attention of the public. Federation had been an issue for many years. Anthony Trollope, writing in 1870, had described it as a current topic. Now it was at hand, and naturally was discussed to the exclusion of practically all else. The outcome was never in doubt. In the 1899 referendum South Australia voted: Yes, 65,900; No, 17,953.

When the last cheer had been cheered, people returned to the daily round perhaps a little disappointed to realise that, after all, nothing had changed in so far as current problems were concerned, and that the railway and "White Elephant Territory" still awaited their decisions. It was all very tiring.

Then one day a body called the National Association to Federalize the Northern Territory was formed in Melbourne. At once South Australian preoccupation with the transcontinental railway became intense once more. For the aims of the National Association went farther even than its title suggested. These included proposals for north-south railway routes other than a direct line through the centre of the continent. One pressed for a line from Pine Creek south-eastwards to Camooweal and Brisbane, and then southwards to Sydney. This was a revolutionary proposal from the angle of State-minded South Australians. It would entirely abort their fixed purpose to channel Territory trade through Port Augusta and Adelaide.

However, it soon became evident that the new Federal Government had far too much on its plate to take any immediate interest in the Territory and its railway. Presumably, the disappointment of N.A.F.N.T. members was the relief of most South Australians.

Nevertheless, the goad had been applied. It was up to the State, said the public, to take decisive action before the initiative was seized by others. A decade had passed and the railhead still dallied at Oodnadatta. The situation was intolerable. Tension built up, and indignation at the Government's rejection of each land-grant proposal mounted.

Probably, in part at least, the truth was that in Government circles the dreams of the 1880s had lost most of their glamour in the slow progress and frustrations of the years.

Meanwhile, far from the political stresses and strains of Adelaide, life on the line in the times of the "long pause" appears to have been pleasant and relaxed. Indeed, between Hergott and Oodnadatta, it was easy-going in the extreme! Tales told of those times all seem to turn upon a note of leisure. "She'll be right, mate" and "Mebbe we'll be lucky" are figures of speech—whether or not then current—that suitably depict the feelings of passenger and official alike. It is said that in those days the train travelling this section of line was known as "The Oodna Bumper", so casual was the manner of the service.

After rains it was customary for passengers to ask for their train to be stopped so that they might climb down to pick wildflowers. Or, perhaps, someone wished to brew tea and required hot water for the pot. Then a stroll along the track to the engine supplied the need, for when the driver pressed a knob scalding water flowed. The tales told are similar to those recounted of Irish railways shortly before the turn of the century. Nor, it seems, are they much exaggerated.

The Commonwealth of Australia was proclaimed by Lord Hopetoun, the first Governor-General, on 1 January 1901, and the first Parliament was convened by proclamation on 29 April, Sir Edmund Barton being the first Prime Minister.

It was in the following year that an abrupt change in the political wind took place in South Australia. Act No. 803 of 1902, the Trans-continental Railway Act, authorised the construction of a narrow-gauge railway between Oodnadatta and Pine Creek on the land-grant system.

So—with what regret in strongly conservative quarters may be surmised—tenders were advertised in the *South Australian Gazette* on 1 January 1903. Soon afterwards they were repeated elsewhere in Australia and also in Britain. The bonus offered to contractors able to show themselves capable of the tremendous task of building 1,063 miles of railway in Central Australian conditions was 79,725,000 acres of land in fee simple.

At last the Government acknowledged that this was the only way in which the State might obtain the railway that everyone wanted. Costs on the lines inherited from the early days were mounting fast. In 1900 working expenses had risen to £657,841, the highest figure ever. They were to continue to rise, and in 1907—the year that some State-centred people came to regard as "the time of the betrayal"—they climbed to £868,005.

The Government now announced that syndicates proposing to enter tenders must do so by 1 May 1904. It published the conditions that would be stipulated in any agreement. Briefly, tenderers were to be prepared to:

(a) Work in north and south simultaneously, building a narrow-gauge line with sixty-pound material to the satisfaction of the Engineer-in-Chief;

(b) Build a minimum of 100 miles a year and complete the work in eight years;

(c) Maintain a service for passengers and goods from each terminus at least once weekly and at an overall speed of not less than twenty miles per hour;

(d) Deposit a sum of £50,000 to be forfeited absolutely should default be made in any of the conditions of the contract;

(e) Transport all railway officers on duty and Parliamentarians and their baggage free of charge.

During the subsequent pause when contractors interested in the Government's project examined the country which the prospective railway must cross, the Chief Mechanical Engineer issued a report containing a section that underlined the tight budget upon which the railways were operated. He said: "I regret that money was not provided for lighting the three feet six inch carriage stock with a better illuminant than the present system of kerosene lamps. The introduction of Pintsch's gas on the five feet three inch gauge lines has intensified the need for improving the light on the narrow gauge stock as the change at break-of-gauge stations from a well illuminated five feet three inch gauge carriage to a badly lit three feet six inch gauge vehicle is a source of complaint by the travelling public. I strongly advocate the fitting of the narrow gauge stock with Stone's electric light which I saw in very successful operation on many of the leading railways in England. It is clean, economical and a beautiful light."

He was to get his wish. Nevertheless, kerosene lamps had been the sole means of lighting narrow-gauge coaches for a quarter of a century.

It was at this time that engines and passenger cars on the narrow-gauge system were fitted with the Westinghouse continuous brake. A beginning was made also in the work of altering passenger coaches to provide an internal passage, so that train staff might no longer have to shuffle their way along the footboards of moving trains.

The closing date for the submission of contractors' applications, 1 May, was a day of anticlimax. No offer was received! In view of earlier experience, this was a shock indeed.

Simpson Newland, who had served on the Royal Commission in 1887 and was an enthusiast for railway expansion, determined to stir the pot. He went to London with the object of arousing interest among British capitalists, and very shortly he made contact with the National Construction Company. One of the directors of this organisation was Deputy Chairman of the Great Eastern Railway and chairman of the Westinghouse Brake Company, a circumstance sufficient to guarantee the company's bona fides and capacity to perform the work required. The Board showed interest in the project.

When Newland had left home the Jenkins Government had been in office and it appears that Jenkins had authorised him to accept a deposit of £10,000. Now, in London, he obtained a cheque for this sum. But by the time he reached Adelaide again, South Australia's first Labor Government had taken over with Thomas Price as Premier.

Newland called with his deposit, but the Price administration refused to pay for overseas services with Australian land and declined to accept the money.

Various Australian syndicates now made offers. Why these had not come forward in 1903 is not clear. However, their proposals were considered. One in particular found favour. It seemed that the problem of the transcontinental line had been solved at last. A contract to construct the linking railway was discussed and brought to signing point. Then at the final moment negotiations broke down—not, this time, because of Government intransigence, but because of Federal restrictions on the employment of coloured labour.

Here was irony indeed! Coolie labour had been employed on sections of the Port Augusta to Government Gums line, and again on the Palmerston to Pine Creek Railway. Naturally there was bitter feeling in Adelaide.

So, still, the Northern Territory awaited development. Now the bright dreams of early years finally gave place to a dogged-does-it attitude. The views of George Fife Angas were recalled and argued afresh. Many said that he had been right, that to handle so vast a territory was indeed beyond the resource of a State of small population. It was at this time that one disillusioned northern settler wrote bitterly that Government House was "like a dirty barn with fowl houses jutting out around it", and that "South Australia and her rulers have decreed that her officials shall try and dwell in places where one would not put a horse".

Probably, most people believed that the Government had blundered in its choice of representatives, and that there had been much mismanagement. But equally they believed that a completed north-south railway would solve the Territory's difficulties. They must try again. Somehow the railway problem must be solved. It is certain, however, that only a minority agreed with the solution that a frustrated Government finally adopted.

12

TAKE-OVER

On 7 December 1907, the South Australian Government entered into an agreement with the Federal Government. This agreement provided for the surrender of the Northern Territory; the sale of the Great Northern Railway together with all railway property, except movable plant and rolling-stock; and the grant of rights to build and operate railways to the northern and western boundaries of South Australia from any points on the Great Northern Railway. The agreement was signed by Alfred Deakin on behalf of the Commonwealth and by Thomas Price on behalf of South Australia.

The Labor Government had decided to retreat from a position it considered to have become economically untenable. It was not interested in empire-building, and so in the previous February a memorandum outlining the conditions on which the State would surrender the Territory to the Commonwealth had been prepared and sent to the Federal Government.

News of this move had leaked. It came as shocking intelligence to the man-in-the-street, though it can have been no surprise to those in a position to know what had been the climate of Ministerial feeling, irrespective of political colour, for some years past.

Actually, less than four months after Federation, F.W. Holder, then the Premier, had written to Alfred Deakin in Melbourne to say that the South Australian Government was open to "offer" the Northern Territory to the Commonwealth.

Elections and a change of Government followed before the situation thus created had time to develop. But the next Premier, J.G. Jenkins, lost no time in pursuing his predecessor's move. In July 1901 he informed the Prime Minister that his Government, too, was willing to discuss the surrender of the Northern Territory. But no definite decision resulted from the subsequent correspondence.

In 1905 another approach was made to the Federal Government, this time by the House of Assembly. The House asked if the Commonwealth would agree to begin work to complete the transcontinental railway within twelve months of legislation handing over the Territory. The inference was that an undertaking to build the railway within a given period would be a condition of the surrender.

Very promptly the Prime Minister declined to consider the matter on these terms.

Taken all in all it could scarcely be said with justice that Thomas Price's action in 1907 came, as many claimed, "like a bolt from the blue". But this appears to have been its effect upon the general public.

Indignation meetings were held. Many speakers, whipping up popular feeling, insisted that the "betrayal" was being negotiated under wraps. All the old clichés were used. The Government was "selling the pass". The State's interests were being "sold down river". The Premier was prepared to sign without even obliging the Federal Government to complete the railway by a fixed date! Steps must be taken to prevent "this rape of South Australia".

These outbursts of feeling resulted in the formation of two bodies designed to oppose Government intentions. The first, and more important, was headed by Simpson Newland. It was called the Northern Territory Railway League. The second was named the Great Central State League.

A tremendous stir followed. Many fiery speeches were delivered at meetings attended by crowds of angry citizens. Booklets and leaflets condemning Government plans were distributed in the streets. All stated roundly that the Territory must remain a part of South Australia, and that the State, and no one else, must raise the funds to build the north-south line. At the same time, the newspapers received hundreds of letters from indignant readers.

But speeches, pamphlets, and letters all failed in their purpose. The agreement had a very rough passage, but it was approved by Parliament. The Northern Territory Surrender Act followed automatically.

This Act, No. 946 of 1907, was reserved on 21 December. The preamble opened with: "An Act to Surrender the Northern Territory of the State of South Australia to the Commonwealth of Australia and for other purposes." The other purposes primarily concerned railways. As arranged in the Agreement, the Commonwealth took over the Palmerston and Pine Creek Railway as part of the surrender; it acquired the Great Northern Railway, described in the Act as the Port Augusta to Oodnadatta Railway; it undertook to complete the transcontinental railway at an unspecified time in the future; it received permission to build the South Australian section of an east-west railway; it obtained the right to make railway surveys under the same conditions as the State Government.

With this Act hanging over their heads, South Australians passed a gloomy New Year. For in many, bitterness went deep. Fifteen years later, a grazier, when giving evidence before the Commonwealth Parliamentary Standing Committee then enquiring into alternative routes for a Great Northern Railway extension, remarked: "I regard the transfer as criminal, for the Northern Territory was our birthright . . . We would have been a State of importance and could have opened our mouths in the Commonwealth. At present, we are nobodies."

Another witness, who had been a Member of the State Parliament that entered into the Agreement, spoke caustically of "that craven-hearted House". He added: "We began in the Northern Territory with hope; but the South Australian population was small. We began the railway with hope; but it was a heart-breaking sort of thing to carry it to the border . . . While we started with these high hopes, we carried on with fear, and we ended in cowardice."

Yet another witness, a former Member of the Legislative Council, said: "The only thing that induced South Australia to transfer this attractive country was the true Federal spirit under which we went into the Union."

The Northern Territory Surrender Act was assented to on 14 May 1908. The Labor Government had now done its part in implementing the Agreement of the previous December.

However, the Federal Government did not take immediate action to clinch the matter with the reciprocal Act that still was needed. One imagines, during the interval that followed, the feelings of those South Australians who strongly opposed the whole transaction. It appears that the Federal authorities may have wished to allow time for second thoughts, or at least for the sharp edge of bitterness to become blunted. If this were so they were probably wise, for when at last in 1910 moves were made to finalise the matter, trouble broke out at once.

Someone asked W.M. Hughes, the Federal Attorney-General, for an opinion respecting the interpretation of the clauses in the Act that concerned the transcontinental railway. The future Prime Minister and war leader expressed the view that the terms as stated did not bind the Commonwealth to keep the whole course of the railway between Darwin and the northern border of South Australia within the boundary of the Territory.

Immediately opponents of the Act cried "breach of faith"! The door, they claimed, was being opened for a diversion of the line through Queensland, via Camooweal and Birdsville. Some even said that a plan was afoot to extend it to Brisbane and Sydney and thus rob South Australia entirely of the fruits of enterprise and of her manifest rights.

Tumult broke out in Adelaide. Emergency meetings were called. The State Attorney-General was approached for an opinion and appears to have had little consolation to offer. He felt that the wording of the railway clauses was capable of other interpretations than the one most South Australians desired.

All this happened in July, and August seems to have been spent in more discussion and a determined attempt to stiffen the resolve of waverers. Then in September an effort was made to reverse the position entirely.

A notice of intention to repeal the Northern Territory Surrender Act was filed in the South Australian Parliament.

But the move failed.

So in November the Federal Government ratified the original agreement in The Northern Territory Acceptance Act, described as "An Act to provide for the Acceptance of the Northern Territory as a Territory under the authority of the Commonwealth and for the carrying out of the Agreement for the Surrender and Acceptance." The preamble itemised the relevant happenings from the grant of the Letters Patent, through the Constitution Act to the Agreement of 1907 and concluded, "Be it therefore enacted by the King's Most Excellent Majesty, the Senate and House of Representatives of the Commonwealth of Australia as follows—".

The Act then elaborated the Agreement to the extent of nineteen clauses and a Schedule.

Disregarding the great detail and involved verbiage of many clauses, the essential provisions were:

(a) That the Commonwealth accepted responsibility for South Australian loans for the development of the Northern Territory by agreeing to recompense the State annually for the amount of the interest, by establishing a sinking find to redeem the loans on maturity, and by paying the deficit incurred by the State in respect of the Northern Territory;

(b) That—at some unstated future date—the Commonwealth agreed to build a railway southwards from Pine Creek to a point on the northern border of South Australia;

(c) That the Commonwealth agreed to purchase the Great Northern

Railway from its starting point at Port Augusta to its terminus at Oodnadatta, and to build an extension to the northern border of the State to link, eventually, with the railway from the far north.

Both the Northern Territory Surrender Act 1907, and the Northern Territory Acceptance Act 1910 came into force by proclamation on 1 January 1911. Six practical results emerged from this legislation:

(i) South Australia received the sum of £2,239,462 in payment for the Great Northern Railway;

(ii) South Australia was relieved of the burden of the continuing heavy losses incurred in operating the railway;

(iii) The Commonwealth undertook to benefit South Australian trade by building a railway from Oodnadatta to the Territory so that the production of the southern part of the Territory would pass through Port Augusta and Adelaide;

(iv) The Commonwealth assumed responsibility for the Territory at a cost price of £3,931,086;

(v) South Australia was relieved of the heavy liability of developing and administering the Territory—apart from loan transactions, the revenue in 1911 was £47,000 while expenditure was £123,000;

(vi) South Australia was relieved of its sense of responsibility in respect of the completion of the north-south line, though the Commonwealth undertaking in this regard was entirely indefinite.

Yet another agreement was made between Prime Minister and Premier. Because no Commonwealth Railways Department yet existed, it was arranged that the South Australian Railways Commissioner should continue to work and maintain the railway on behalf of the Commonwealth. So the state resumed the railway from the Federal Government at a yearly rental of one peppercorn. The effect of this agreement was set out in the South Australian Railways report for the year ended 30 June 1911. "As from the date of transfer, this railway has been leased by the Commonwealth to the State and is now worked as part of the South Australian railways system, the receipts being accepted as the return for working the line, the Commonwealth Government, however, bearing all extraordinary maintenance charges."

Discounting the "humiliation"—it appears that the word was used for long afterwards—South Australia would seem to have driven a shrewd and advantageous bargain. The State had advantage from Commonwealth expenditure on railway works within its borders, while it continued to benefit from a material portion of Territory trade.

Those people who had strenuously opposed the Acts are said to have smiled sardonically when the burst of activity with which the Commonwealth opened its administration in the Territory foundered on economic rocks. But they had no sound grounds whatever for the "shame" which they claimed to have suffered. Through more than forty years South Australians had fought valiantly to support their obligations and to carry a burden too heavy for a small population. But many were unable to take consolation from this knowledge.

Meanwhile Europe was moving towards war. The Agadir incident made headlines. But few who read with interest of the activities of the German gunboat *Panther*, cruising off the Moroccan coast, can have foreseen that these would have any effect on the fortunes of the Great Northern Railway. Yet this news was an early straw in an ill wind which was to affect life even in the Lake Eyre region.

In 1913 the South Australian Government found that the working arrangement into which it had entered was operating to the disadvantage of the State. During the first twelve months under the new order, expenses on the line had amounted to £69,367 whereas receipts had totalled £57,939. The State was paying for losses on property it did not own!

In the ensuing wrangle the State Government practically refused to continue the agreement. This placed the Federal authorities, who still lacked a Railways Department, in a quandary. Eventually, in December 1913, yet another Agreement was drawn up. This provided that losses should be borne by the Commonwealth, and that in future interest should be paid on the capital value—estimated at £143,000—of South Australian rolling-stock loaned to the railway.

In the meantime an extension of the Palmerston railway to the Katherine River had been authorised. After the passing of the Pine Creek to Katherine River Railway Act 1913, work began as a combination of day labour, piecework, and small contract. This line was completed to Emungalan on the north bank of the river. But it was not carried over until May 1917.

Now occurred an event that must have reminded elderly Port Augustans of the memorial, prepared thirty years before, to press for a railway north-westwards to Phillips Ponds. A survey began from a point 113 miles west of The Port and moved northwards towards Coward Springs.

By this time work had begun on the East-West Railway, then known as the Kalgoorlie to Port Augusta line. The thought had come to the Commonwealth Minister of State for External Affairs that, since a standard-gauge line soon would cross the Nullarbor Plain, a logical move would be to convert the Great Northern Railway to the same gauge and thus make it possible for identical rolling-stock to run anywhere between Kalgoorlie, Port Augusta, and Oodnadatta. And then the

Minister had had a further thought. There would probably be little difference in cost between the operations of reconstructing the existing line and building a new and more direct one from a suitable point on the east-west route. Should this alternative idea be adopted, the engineering difficulties of the Pichi Richi and Mernmerna passes would be eliminated.

In the upshot, the Federal Government had decided to make a preliminary survey, and The Pines (Pimba) had been chosen as the starting point.

So now, in March 1914, Nathaniel Chalmers, a member of a firm of contracting surveyors, set out from a spot where east-west rails would soon be laid, crossed the Eucolo Tableland, and worked his way northwards to the west of Lake Torrens. Broadly speaking, this was the plan that the long-forgotten memorial had proposed.

From Coward Springs Chalmers went on to re-examine the country that Graham Stewart had travelled nearly a quarter of a century earlier. Then from Burt's Creek he carried the preliminary survey to the Katherine River, approximately 1,700 miles from Adelaide.

On his return he recommended that the proposed line should start from Kingoonya, ninety-seven miles west of Pimba, and move direct to Oodnadatta. In this way twenty-eight miles of sandhill country would be avoided.

This proposal, made more than sixty years ago, is interesting in the light of today's survey from Tarcoola.

The Federal Cabinet approved a Kingoonya–Oodnadatta survey. The report, submitted four months later, said that the line—approximately 176 miles long—would cross good pastoral country, that the ruling grade would be 1 in 100, that heavy earthworks would not be needed, and that bridgework would be light. The cost of a standard-gauge line was estimated at £882,000. And there the matter rested, because war had broken out in Europe. But, war apart, the Federal Government had enough on its plate for the time being in major construction work on the Nullarbor Plain.

While the new survey was in progress an event of railway importance occurred at Port Augusta. The goods sheds and sidings, together with the old railway wharf, which had been built to handle the vast wheat export anticipated as a result of the farming drive to Wonoka, passed from South Australian to Federal control.

The first World War had startlingly immediate effects upon South Australian railway traffic. Within a month the thriving trade with Broken Hill ended because of the closing of the metal market in Germany. In August the output of ore averaged 21,000 tons weekly, in September 1,000 tons.

To loss was added the drag of serious drought. Special water trains had to be run on the Great Northern. Many emergency bores were put down, but the water obtained turned out to be unsuitable for use in locomotives, and unscheduled repairs to engine boilers and travelling tanks became necessary. Extra pumping loaded working costs. The tonnage of wheat handled dropped from 300,579 in the previous year to 49,673. Economies were made by reducing train mileage, and by placing staff on five-sixth time.

Originally the Federal Government had regarded the leasing of the railway to South Australia purely as an interim measure, but wartime problems—important among these rolling-stock shortage—caused the arrangement to be extended. Much development work was halted. In August 1916 the Public Works Committee wished to extend the far northern line from Emungalan to Mataranka, a distance of sixty-four miles. But, though the work was authorised, no action followed because materials were unobtainable.

Meanwhile expenses mounted. Today, in a period of constantly escalating costs, some of the problems of those years may seem slightly absurd. For instance the Chief Mechanical Engineer of the South Australian Railways, reporting for the year ended 30 June 1917, noted that whereas on the south-eastern line the outlay for fuel and lubricants on narrow-gauge locomotives was at the rate of a fraction over 6d per train mile, on the Great Northern this item of cost amounted to almost 7½d. Poor man, his troubles were not eased in October when the Federal Government took over the Port Augusta passenger station. For though, in future, Commonwealth staff would control the entire railway business of The Port, the management of the northern line still remained a South Australian responsibility.

None the less, increases in major costs were solid. Before the war the cost of constructing one mile of standard-gauge line was about £6,000; at the end it was approximately £9,000. The upward trend was reflected in levies. In July 1919, the South Australian Railways increased passenger fares and freight rates.

Justifying this action, the Commissioner drew attention to rising costs overseas—in British countries an over-all increase of forty per cent; in France 140 per cent; in Belgium 100 per cent; in Portugal fifty-seven per cent; in Holland seventy per cent; in Switzerland 180 per cent; in Norway 150 per cent; in Sweden 200 per cent; in Austria and Hungary 300 per cent; and in the United States forty per cent. Information from Russia was unreliable, but reports spoke of an increase in goods rates of 3,000 per cent.

This action by the State discovered inequity in the Agreement of December 1907. It had been laid down that the Commonwealth would

"Give, and continue to give, to the State and its citizens equal facilities at least in transport of goods and passengers on the Port Augusta Railway to those provided by the State Government at the present time, and at rates not exceeding those at present in force." This clause had been incorporated in both the subsequent Acts, and included in the 1913 Agreement.

Thus the Commonwealth was forced to continue the freight rates and passenger fares of 1907, no matter how great the loss incurred.

The Commonwealth Railways Commissioner raised this matter in his report of 30 June 1918. "Some time since the South Australian Railways Commissioner increased goods rates over the State Railways by 10 percent, and introduced a system of single passenger fares with increased rates. On account of statutory provisions, however, the freights and fares could not be increased on the Oodnadatta Railway. Thus the people using the Oodnadatta Railway are charged less than the freights and fares operating on other railways in South Australia, and the Commonwealth is not receiving in revenue the amount that would be received were the railway owned by the State . . . The Commonwealth is also adversely affected in that it cannot reduce the train service below the service that was in operation at the time the Agreement was entered into in 1907."

The final point constituted a special grievance. During a recent coal strike the South Australians had drastically reduced train services, but the Commonwealth had been unable to make any change. The Commissioner concluded: "Steps have been taken to admit of the Commonwealth charging rates and fares at least equal to those in operation on the South Australian Railways. It is urged that the matter be finalized with the least possible delay."

However, nothing was done, and in the following year the Commissioner raised the matter again, this time in some irritation. "On several occasions I have asked that steps be taken as would admit of the Commonwealth charging the rates in operation in South Australia, and as would admit of our reducing the train service when trade slackens or as may be necessary for other causes." He added that the time had come when the Commonwealth "should seriously consider the question of calling tenders for the necessary rolling-stock and taking over the working and maintenance of the railway".

At last the situation was remedied by means of a legal instrument entertainingly described as "An Act to ratify an Agreement for the Variation of the Agreement for the Surrender of the Northern Territory and for other purposes"—The Northern Territory Surrender Act Amendment Act. This Act came into force by proclamation on 20 December 1919. The additional revenue it obtained for the Commonwealth amounted to about £1,000 a month.

Now, as though wishing to suggest that the Commonwealth could not reasonably expect that a profit should be made on the Great Northern line, the South Australian Railways Commissioner drew attention in a report to the loss incurred in the working of most developmental railways. He said that in the United States it was accepted as axiomatic that territory with fewer than 300 people to a mile of line did not invite railway construction. He pointed out that South Australia had an average of only 204 people per mile of line, and listed nine South Australian lines which, after allowing for working expenses and interest payments, showed a combined loss of £196,348. How then could the northern "desert" railway be expected to pay? "When compared with settled countries such as Great Britain, where the average was, in 1919, 1,943 inhabitants per mile of line open, it will be seen what a difficult problem is constantly faced by the management of the railways in endeavouring to make lines of development in any way remunerative. The average number of inhabitants per mile of line open in South Australia is one of the lowest in the world."

Dissatisfaction was expressed in the Commonwealth Railways report for the year. Under the heading "Oodnadatta Railway", the Commissioner remarked: "This railway is worked by the South Australian Railways Commissioner for and on behalf of the Commonwealth. The financial position is unsatisfactory. The railway has been consistently worked at a loss." He then gave figures showing the excess of working expenditure over revenue for the three previous years—£53,075, £37,481, and £60,460. "Under ordinary conditions, the loss for the year under review should have been much less. The season was good, and, with the aid of increased fares and freights, the revenue reached £112,091, an advance over the previous year of £37,381. The expenditure, however, amounted to £172,552, an increase of £60,361. The cost of working per train mile for the previous year was 8s 6½d, as against 10s 9¼d for the year under review."

Clearly he considered that the loss would be greatly reduced, if not turned into profit, were the lease terminated and the line run by Commonwealth staff. Two years later, when the loss had mounted to £69,411, he made his feelings abundantly evident. "The existing arrangement was made prior to the inauguration of the Commonwealth Railways Department. This Department, however, is now well-established, and has officers located at Port Augusta operating the Trans-Australian Railway, who could also control the Oodnadatta Railway. Control by the Commonwealth Railways would avoid the South Australian Head Office administrative charges, and reduce the costs incurred at Quorn, where there are workshops, and a distinct controlling staff for the Oodnadatta railway. The agreement requires that 12 months notice be given when the Commonwealth desires to take over the working of the railway."

Evidently some feeling existed for he continued a little sharply. "The taking over could have been effected some time since, but agreement could not be arrived at with the South Australian authorities concerning the value of rolling-stock proposed to be transferred for the working of the railway. Several conferences were held, but agreement satisfactory to the Commonwealth could not be reached. It is proposed to invite tenders for the rolling-stock, and provision has been made accordingly on the Loan Estimates for the current financial year."

During the years that had passed since the transfer, the Federal Government had considered the matter of extending the railway on a number of occasions. But the war and, perhaps, caution prompted by the failure of over-precipitate action in the Territory had prevented plans from maturing. Now impatience appears to have built up in South Australia. Just when was the railway to be constructed?

While admitting that both materials and labour had been in short supply during the war, many people argued that the north-south line should have received the priority in fact given to the East-West Railway.

Concern was not confined to South Australia. By 1920 the idea of a north-to-south transcontinental railway seems to have taken country-wide hold on public imagination. The subject was featured in the Press of all States. It was pressed on the Federal Government in representations made by many societies and leagues. Out of much argument emerged the fact that views respecting the best route for the railway differed very widely indeed. In the circumstances the South Australian Press felt it necessary to stress that the Act left no room whatever for argument, that the route the railway must follow was laid down clearly—a direct north-south line.

The issue that presently was joined turned upon sub-sections (b) and (d), the clauses on which the Federal Attorney-General had expressed an opinion that did not support the positive South Australian view. These sections laid down that the Commonwealth should:

(i) Construct or cause to be constructed a railway line from Port Darwin southwards to a point on the northern boundary of South Australia proper;

(ii) Construct or cause to be constructed as part of the Transcontinental Railway a railway from a point on the Port Augusta Railway to connect with the other part of the Transcontinental Railway at a point on the northern boundary of South Australia proper.

TOP: As it was in the old days—a rake of cattle trucks on the way south (*R. D. Kempe*).
BOTTOM: Waiting for the Ghan—far northern passengers on the way south (*R. D. Kempe*)

Many interested persons in other States argued that, obviously, the wording of these clauses allowed a route that crossed the northern border of South Australia at a point near Birdsville and reached the Katherine River by way of Boulia and Camooweal.

Again the cry "Breach of faith" was heard in Adelaide. The only permissible route under the Act ran from Oodnadatta to Alice Springs and so north.

At the time when the first Agreement had been drawn up the transfer of the Territory dominated the minds of the framers. In the circumstances, perhaps no one thought through the railway angle in all its possible aspects or, for that matter, foresaw that such differences of viewpoint might arise that opinions would be sought from many eminent legal men. But this is what happened.

The argument was soon dubbed "The Battle of the Routes". The Commonwealth Railways Commissioner remarked: "The railway will be provided under statutory provision, so as to link the North and the South, and will afford comparatively rapid transport between those points. The wording of the agreement, however, does not appear to me to provide for a direct route, and so long as there is fulfilled to the State of South Australia the spirit and intention of the agreement, and a comparatively direct connection afforded, the route should be settled in the best interests of the people of the Commonwealth generally." This view was supported by the Premier of South Australia, who stated in the House of Assembly that his Government would not stand in the way of a deviation, if it could be shown that this would be in the best interests of the country as a whole.

In an effort to show that a deviation to the east would be in the interests of the nation, certain of those in favour of a loop line through Queensland drew up a report comparing the direct or western line with the route they desired.

Greatly compressed, this report set out that the direct route:

(a) Would tap country where only 61,000 cattle and 12,000 sheep were depastured;

(b) Would pass through vast areas of sand and spinifex country where little or no traffic would be available;

(c) Would be incapable of linking with the railways of the eastern States;

(d) Would not develop the best part of the Territory, unless a branch line were built, at heavy extra cost, to Camooweal from Newcastle Waters.

On the other hand, the Queensland route:

(a) Would tap country where 650,000 cattle and 4,800,000 sheep

TOP: A camel string being loaded at Oodnadatta for the journey to the Centre in the early 1900s (*R. D. Kempe*). BOTTOM: Bejah Dervish, perhaps the best-known cameleer. He worked for many years from Hergott Springs up the Birdsville Track into Queensland (*Mrs B. N. Bejah*)

were depastured;

(b) Would permit direct connection with railways from Townsville, Rockhampton and Brisbane;

(c) Would pass through regions of higher rainfall;

(d) Would develop cattle country in north-eastern South Australia, and fulfil the agreement by crossing the northern border near Birdsville.

As, of course, was to be expected, people having ideas bearing only indirectly on the main issue took advantage of the opening provided by the controversy to press their wishes.

One day a deputation representing the North Australian Railway and Development League waited on the Commonwealth Treasurer in Melbourne. The members asked for the help of the Federal Government in developing the north-western region of Western Australia. An expedition to collect first-hand information on a little-known area had been organised and it was proposed that a representative of the Commonwealth Railways should accompany the party.

Accordingly George Alexander Hobler, Engineer of Way and Works, Port Augusta, accompanied the expedition, which covered some 2,500 miles by car and motor-boat. Out of this journey arose a proposal for a railway to run north-west from Meekatharra to Halls Creek and on to Newcastle Waters, there to make junction with the proposed transcontinental line.

This was one of a number of railway development schemes that were advanced at this time.

Eventually the Federal Government decided to investigate the situation in depth, even though this meant delaying a decision.

So on 25 November 1920, in the House of Representatives, the Minister of State for Works and Railways moved: "That in accordance with the provisions of the Commonwealth Public Works Committee Act 1913–14, the following work be referred to the Parliamentary Standing Committee on Public Works for its investigation and report thereon; (i) Northern Territory Railway, extension from Mataranka to Daly Waters, and (ii) Port Augusta–Oodnadatta Railway, extension from Oodnadatta to Alice Springs."

In each case the matter was resolved in the affirmative.

Earlier that day the Minister had obtained the consent of the House for the construction of an extension of the Pine Creek to Katherine River Railway southwards to Mataranka, or Bitter Springs, a section that had been surveyed and pegged in 1914.

In instructing the Standing Committee on Public Works to investigate two specific proposals, the Minister expected the enquiry to throw up particulars of numerous alternative proposals, for example, of the already widely-canvassed "Queensland loop".

One may wonder why the Darwin to Katherine River Railway was given priority over the far longer and seemingly more important Great Northern Railway. It seems that a change in viewpoint had come about in 1911, the year of transfer. Whereas in the beginning South Australia, building northwards, had regarded the line between Port Augusta and Wonoka as the first section of the future transcontinental railway, after transfer the Federal authorities, established in the Territory, viewed the stretch from Darwin to Pine Creek as the commencement. Instead of moving northwards, the transcontinental railway was now to be viewed as advancing southwards towards the northern border of South Australia.

In the new year the Committee planned its procedure. It decided that the Government would be served best if enquiries were made in such a fashion that a report could be prepared on the question of the railway as a whole. To begin with, a sub-Committee of three members was sent out to make a journey of investigation with the especial duty of studying the country, in both east and west, along the proposed routes. The sub-Committee left Melbourne early in June and, on arrival at Quorn, was joined by G.A. Hobler, who was to act as technical consultant.

Meanwhile the Committee proper opened the general enquiry. Starting in Perth on 28 January 1921, it finished in Melbourne on 11 September 1922. During this period it took evidence in Adelaide, Sydney, Brisbane, Rockhampton, and Townsville, examining in all 136 witnesses, including railway engineers, traffic managers, surveyors, geologists, miners, battery managers, pastoralists, Ministers, and Members of Parliament. Additionally, old and new reports were examined as well as documents bearing on railway and Northern Territory problems.

The journeys made by Committee and sub-Committee totalled nearly 20,000 miles.

The enquiry naturally turned upon the interpretations put upon the controversial sub-clauses (b) and (d) of the Act. A railway could be built either to the east or to the west of Lake Eyre and the Simpson Desert, and still cross the northern border of South Australia. Was the eastern route permissible?

On this matter witnesses clashed. A Member of the Legislative Council of South Australia, who had worked on the staff of the *Register*, said flatly: "I say that, under the Agreement, the Commonwealth Government are absolutely bound to build the line from Oodnadatta. There is no escape." Again, a witness who had been Clerk to the

House of Assembly at the time of transfer told the Committee: "I think that only a direct line was in the minds of Members."

These views were supported by certain witnesses from other States who were of the opinion that, under the terms of the Agreement, the intention was clear and the Commonwealth was committed to the construction of this line and this line only.

Those holding the contrary view were just as positive. Alexander Hobler who, as an expert witness, was called on eight separate occasions, was emphatic. "I think the intention was to leave the Commonwealth to decide the route. Even if the agreement was to build a line on the western route, if—after the lapse of so many years and with the altered conditions now prevailing—it is considered better to build the line along the eastern route, the agreement should be mutually altered. Two wrongs do not make a right . . . If it is found that the western route is not the better route, that it is not likely to be so good for the development of the country as the eastern route, and that it will be a greater burden on the taxpayer it is wrong to carry out the agreement. In that case, it is up to the country, or the parties concerned, to alter the agreement."

Another witness recalled that Senator McGregor, when introducing the Northern Territory Acceptance Bill to the Senate in 1910, had said: "There is no intimation made that it is to be a straight, or a crooked, or a triangular line. There will be every opportunity for the line to be taken in the direction which will be in the interests of the whole people of Australia."

The Commonwealth Railways Commissioner, when examined in Melbourne, said: "In considering the construction of a developmental railway, we should put aside any thought as to what authority owns the railways. We should look upon them as Australian railways, and a new route should be fixed with a view to the benefit of the whole of Australia rather than the benefit of any particular State system. If the whole of the railway system of Australia were under my control, I would build the proposed new railway on the eastern route because, by so doing, I could connect much more readily with the other portions of the system under my control . . . I have not obtained a legal opinion on the agreement, for it appeared to me that if it could be shown that the eastern route was much more in the interests of Australia than the western route would be, the route should be selected, notwithstanding anything that might be contained in the agreement. I think that South Australia would agree to a deviation from the direct North and South route if it could be shown that such deviation would be in the interests of Australia as a whole."

Some witnesses cancelled each other out. One group quoted extracts from speeches to show that the purpose in the minds of the framers of the Agreement had been to allow the Commonwealth freedom to route the line through Queensland, provided always that it was brought back to the northern border of South Australia to make junction with the railway to Port Augusta. Another group quoted the same sources to show that there was no such intention.

Yet others recalled the Northern Territory Surrender Act Amendment Act and argued that, since the principle of altering the Agreement had been established, it was wise for Parliament to consider the construction of any line of railway which would make for the better development of the Northern Territory and of Australia as a whole.

Conflicting legal opinions were quoted freely. But here the Committee took a decided stand. It set all such evidence aside, arguing that where eminent legal authorities disagreed it did not feel qualified, or called upon, to make investigation.

As the enquiry advanced, opportunities occurred for interested persons to urge other and very different routes. Queensland railway officials pressed the desirability of a line—already several times suggested—that would link Emungalan with Bourke in New South Wales. Though this route would not pass through South Australia at any point, the Queenslanders urged that it would permit direct links with the ports of the eastern seaboard. It would also provide an insurance against drought over a very wide area, because it would enable stock to be moved quickly into watered country.

The Committee did not take this proposal seriously into account, however. It was far from their terms of reference. For the same reason, other suggestions not directly relevant were ruled out.

After amassing a great quantity of notes filled with fact and opinion, the Committee found itself in a quandary. Every scheme proposed involved substantial annual losses!

Finally, having disallowed a motion by a member that the time was not ripe for further development of any kind, the Committee arrived at its recommendations. Summarised, these were:

(i) That the Port Darwin to Katherine River Railway be extended to Daly Waters on the understanding that it is to form part of a line eventually to pass through Newcastle Waters to Camooweal;

(ii) That a light line be built from Oodnadatta to Alice Springs with sixty-pound rails and low-level bridges;

(iii) That these lines be regarded as providing sufficient railway development for the Territory for many years;

(iv) That, as the evidence shows such a wide divergence of opinion, the Committee considers that at present no decision is possible as to which through railway route will be in the best interests of the Commonwealth; and that when the time arrives for the construction of a through transcontinental line, negotiations be entered into with South Australia to permit of the alteration of the Northern Territory Acceptance Act 1910 to allow of such line being constructed on the route then shown to be in the best interests of Australia.

Eight minor recommendations dealt with gauge, sleepers, bridges, Darwin wharves, non-European labour, and a progressive policy for the development of the Territory.

In final form the report devoted no fewer than 301 closely-printed double-column pages to minutes of evidence. This voluminous document was signed by Senator John Newland, Vice-Chairman of the Committee, in Parliament House, Melbourne, on 5 October 1922.

Three years and three months were to pass before the take-over was finally accomplished, despite an earlier intention.

On 30 June 1924 a Commonwealth Railways report gave the loss on the Great Northern Railway for the previous year as £71,587. "In terms of the Agreement, notice has been given the Government of South Australia that the railway would be managed by this Department as from 1st January, 1925, and arrangements are being made accordingly . . . Negotiations were entered into with the South Australian Railways Commissioners regarding the purchase of rolling-stock from that service, but apart from the purchase of five vans, one sleeping-car, and one steam motor, no business resulted."

So other arrangements were made. Contracts were signed for thirty-eight open goods wagons, thirty-two cattle wagons and much else—in all a total of 156 vehicles. In addition, an order was placed for fourteen locomotives, more powerful than any previously in use on the railway.

Eventually the new engines improved performance, but at the outset they were the cause of a provoking delay explained in the next annual report. "It was intended that the Commonwealth should take over the control of the railway as from January 1st., 1925, but as the locomotives were not available, and as an arrangement could not be come to with the Government of South Australia to hire the locomotives which hitherto had been employed on the railway, it was necessary to postpone the date of taking over."

Passenger carriages, brakevans, and other types of rolling-stock were built in the Commonwealth Railways workshops at Port Augusta. These vehicles were ready for use at the times arranged. But troublesome delays occurred in deliveries from contractors. For example, a number of

4,000-gallon water-wagons promised for the end of October 1924 were not delivered until the end of the following April. The conditions of contract, both in respect of locomotives and rolling-stock, provided for penalties in the event of late delivery and these penalties were enforced.

Negotiations between the Commissioners drew out. But on 22 December 1925, an agreement was signed. This laid down the conditions under which traffic would work from Commonwealth to State railways and vice versa, an understanding respecting running rights, jointly-owned rolling-stock, joint use of Quorn junction, methods of accounting, and so on. It included an arrangement whereby a number of State employees such as drivers, firemen, gangers, fettlers, and cleaners were retained by the Commonwealth for agreed periods after take-over.

Now the way was clear, and on 1 January 1926, after leasing the line to the State for fourteen years, the Commonwealth Railways Commissioner assumed management and maintenance of the Great Northern Railway as a part of the Commonwealth Railways system administered from Port Augusta.

Perhaps it was inevitable that a measure of friction should occur at take-over. Understandably, many South Australians felt strongly about the State ceasing to control the railway it had nursed into existence. Equally understandably, the management of the Commonwealth Railways was annoyed at Press criticism of new arrangements. It seems that adverse comment at first was directed largely towards the alleged late running of the Slow Mixed between Quorn and Oodnadatta. In the Commonwealth Railways annual report one encounters this indignant comment: "The running has been at least the equal of what it was prior to our taking control." And again, "The Commonwealth Government having determined to take over the railway, it is only fair to this Department that the people should accept the control as it now is."

Difficulties were greatly increased by the drought conditions that prevailed at the time of take-over. Sand-drift was general along the line, but north of Marree the situation became so serious that gangs with special sand-clearing trains had to be sent out.

Removing the sand from the line and then shovelling it into trucks or trolleys was trying work in summer months. A sand-clearing machine was introduced. This device consisted of scoops fixed to an outrigger attached to the train which travelled to and fro in cuttings at a speed of about four miles an hour. The scoops, each of ten cubic feet capacity, were tipped at the ends of the cuttings. "The position was exceedingly troublesome," remarked the report with some restraint.

Then, suddenly, exceptional rains ended the drought in wild washaways. Traffic was halted at Copley. Beyond, the line was impassable for many days. Three weeks passed before normal train services to Marree and Oodnadatta were resumed. Even then, special work trains were kept in service for a fortnight, and one continued for ten weeks. In the report this work was described as "extraordinary maintenance". The bill for repairs to the line amounted to £14,000.

The permanent way then included rails of light, medium, and heavy weights—forty-one pounds, fifty pounds, and sixty pounds—with the medium weight predominating. The light rails were in bad order and had to be renewed in large numbers. Some were old iron rails that dated from the time when the line was first laid. Many sleepers, too, were worn and over 4,300 were renewed.

Sand-clearance, storm damage, and large-scale renewals of equipment spelled heavy expenditure. Financial returns for the year of take-over were unsatisfactory. Costs had risen, being described as "outrageous", in comparison with years gone by. The basic wage had mounted from 8s a day to 14s 3d. Coal charges had increased by 106 per cent, and other necessities had gone up in proportion. In consequence, passenger fares were increased by thirty-three per cent and freight charges by forty-eight per cent. So the year—half under South Australian, half under Commonwealth management—showed a loss greatly in excess of that for the previous year. Working expenses exceeded earnings by £105,186.

13

OODNA INTERLUDE

Save for the magnificent performance of a grand horse, the murder would have been forgotten long ago. But Browl's great ride to the railhead became famous. Talk of Paul Revere!

The sordid killing occurred in country beyond Dalhousie Springs Station some weeks after the line reached Angle Pole. Browl rode to report the facts to the mounted constable newly posted to the district.

Though the scene of the crime was more than eighty miles distant, the messenger made the journey in under nine hours—surely a notable feat, even in a region where great horses were bred! This was the part of the tale that was remembered. For the rest, it was recalled vaguely that a murder was the cause of the ride.

The few facts I found were recorded in a newspaper of the time. The murdered man's name is unimportant, for he received no more than his due—by Aboriginal standards. He was a prospector, travelling south. After pitching his tent on the evening of the crime, he sent his Aboriginal boy on ahead to the station. Then he fetched an Aboriginal woman from a near-by encampment and, according to the Aboriginal story, backed up threats with a gun.

It appears that later that night, Tommy, the lubra's man, came silently to the tent. Finding the prospector asleep, he tomahawked him where he lay.

On hearing Browl's story of the finding of the body and the subsequent flight of the Aborigines, the constable saddled up and rode north. But I found no account of Tommy's capture and trial.

At the time of Browl's ride, the settlement at the railhead must have been a pleasant enough spot at which to live. The surrounding country was sprinkled with mulga and desert oak. A few years later, however, no trees remained. All had been cleared by the axes of the settlers. Firewood was obtained for a time—by mortgaging the future.

The outback parson, R.B. Plowman, who went to Oodna from Beltana to work for the Australian Inland Mission, and who later conducted the first religious service in Alice Springs, explained in his book *The Man from Oodnadatta* the origin of the settlement's first European name. Approaching from the north one comes to a low hill where once the camel pad changed direction almost at right angles. This was the Angle Pole. On rounding the corner, one sees the settlement ahead, usually dancing in mirage. The name that was to become famous was chosen by Sir Samuel Way, Chief Justice of South Australia and Acting Governor for a few months in 1877. An adaptation of the Aboriginal word "utmadata", meaning "blossom of the mulga", it suggests the appearance of the district before the railhead was established.

The cameleers of Oodnadatta made tremendous journeys through the outback. It is said that they even crossed the Gibson Desert to Marble Bar.

Their desert mail, a northern extension of the line, was a regular outback service. Two camel strings—one working out of Oodnadatta, the other out of Alice Springs—were timed to meet at Horseshoe Bend, where they exchanged mail-bags and other loads. Then each faced about and returned to base. The pace of the camel being about four miles an hour, the mail-bag going southwards travelled from three to four times as fast when it reached the guard's van.

No man who has not lived in a region is qualified to judge it, and I have not lived in Oodna country. But that outrageous description "the dead heart" has been used so widely that one feels obliged to speak out, qualified or no.

Let me say plainly, then, that I like Oodnadatta, though its busy railhead days are long gone. To the east may be sandhill desert, but to the west is fine pastoral land. To the north-east and north-west gidya and gum creeks afford shade and surface water. From Macumba to Dalhousie Springs and on to Charlotte Waters the country lacks the drought resisters, spinifex and mulga, but it is good for fattening stock—given, say, four inches of rain.

Again, from Alberga and Todmorden to the Musgrave Ranges is good stock country. Well water may be had here at depths of from eighty to 100 feet, and surface water is said to be available in the creeks.

Following drought, the country recovers quickly. One is told that even during poor spells—given careful stocking so that the land is not overtaxed—it may do adequately. Records show this to be so. About twenty years after the arrival of the railway—between December 1910 and December 1912—extreme drought hit the Oodna district and a wide region to the north, as far as the Territory border and beyond. Two inches of rain a year! And that in showers of a few points each.

Fearing disaster, the railway authorities kept trucks in readiness to send to Oodna. They expected to be called upon to move thousands of cattle to pastures in the south. But few beasts were sent away and losses were light. And when the drought broke, the country recovered so quickly that within a year some 40,000 fats were trucked out of Oodna.

Such is the country where the railhead rested throughout the years of the Long Pause; allegedly a desolate and sterile region.

It seemed a good idea to question people who had lived there then.

"Sure! I recollect the take-over," said an old identity who had been a fettler in the latter days of the Long Pause. "Well, o' course I would at my age, mate."

He removed an old bush hat with a tattered brim and rubbed a rough hand up and down a shining scalp, as though the action assisted memory.

"It was shortly before the murder in the railway camp at Algebuckina."

What! Another? I thought, then asked for facts.

He hesitated. "Yeah. That would be it. April! Take-over was in Jan. Well, they was strengthening the bridge to take the heavier locos the Commonwealth was bringing in. So a deviation was built round by the creek bed. Then rains! She come down a banker. So goodbye to the rail. Proper hell's delight. There was a permanent-way gang helpin' on the bridge. 'Bout fifty jokers, I reckon. Well, early one mornin', afore they left camp, there was a quarrel. Don't know what about. All of a sudden one feller runs fer a rifle an' shoots the other through the chest."

He rubbed again, recalling memories. "Plenty in camp at the time, so several saw what happened. A message was sent through to Oodna police, of course. The railway doctor and a nurse went in the car with the constable. But the feller was dead. Young chap, too. The murderer was charged in the police court at Oodna. Taken south on the next train."

In due course, I checked on the old fettler's tale. It seems that the camp at Algebuckina still occupied the site of the one established by the construction gangs thirty-six years previously. The killer was a navvy of fifty-seven; the murdered man a fellow labourer of twenty-one.

Sly-grog was the cause of the tragedy. Attempts were made to conceal this fact when the case was tried at the Port Augusta Criminal Sessions, but the truth came out.

The prisoner, a South African, had worked on the East-West line as well as on the Great Northern. He was known as a "grog-hound". Indeed, cross-examination uncovered the fact that the gang as a whole had been drinking consistently for a fortnight.

The quarrel was at breakfast time. It was a trivial dispute, but the older man sprang up in a rage and presently was heard loading his rifle. He came back, yelling, and shot through a gauze door at the young man who had gone into the kitchen. At once the ganger rang the police, as the old fettler described.

In the interval that followed, the murderer seems to have gone off his head. He went to various of his mates, beating his chest and yelling, "I'm a murderer, Norm!", "I'm a murderer, Bob!", and so on. Then he wandered away into the bush.

Two men who followed lost sight of him for a time, but soon came on him "coiled up like a fox in a dry bush". When he saw them, he got to his feet. "Shoot me, Bob!" he yelled. Then the mounted constable came up and he was arrested.

The defence was that the shooting was an accident. The dead man had threatened violence. "In trying to go away I slid on something hard and slippery, and in trying to keep my balance the rifle went off."

Counsel for the defence was clever. He made much of the unreliability of witnesses who withheld evidence about sly-grog "in order to save their measly jobs at Algebuckina", told the truth only by accident, or were too drunk to remember anything at all. There was evidence to show that the course of the bullet disallowed the prosecution's claim that the shot had been fired with the rifle held to the shoulder. This caused uncertainty. In the end the jury brought in a verdict of manslaughter. The sentence was ten years imprisonment with hard labour.

Recollections of this drama of times long gone stirred the old fettler's memories. He was on his mettle now, determined to justify his self-description, "a bit of a historian".

"There was some feeling in them days," he offered presently. "Lot o' whingeing over the bogie cattle trucks Commonwealth brought in. Proper strife, that was. Well, I reckon." He rubbed again—crosswise this time. "The truckers were used to covered wagons with panels across the middle, yer see. Didn't fancy the new-style, no-panel type. My oath, they didn't. No panel! No bloody roof! Raised hell, I can tell yer. Said no panel meant cattle would bruise worse. But I reckon the idea of no roof hurt 'em most." He chuckled. "Some swore their beasts would take sunstroke. Imagine that! Seemed the idea was they could take the sun on the hoof, grazing like, but not standin' hour after hour in a truck. Seemed crook, that notion. But then, of course, a man likes the things he's bin used to."

He rubbed afresh. By this time the gesture fascinated me. It appeared to follow alternate paths; north-by-south, then east-by-west, and back again to north-by-south. Minutes might separate gestures, but he seemed never to forget which way the previous one had gone.

"Fact was, no roof turned out to be an improvement. Running boards follered the open tops. So drovers could move up and down aloft, roping beasts that got down and were in danger of trampling. Ease 'em up agen, see?"

Actually, the truck that was considered an innovation on the Great Northern Railway had been in use for many years in Queensland, where particular emphasis was placed upon the avoidance of bruising. And there, experience had shown that the removal of centre partitions resulted in less bruising, because animals had more room in which to move and recover from stumbles caused by the jolts and jars of travel.

To convince a deputation of South Australian stock-owners, a test was arranged. Six wagons with partitions and six without were used on the same stock train. Comparison of the condition of the animals at the end of the journey proved that the Queenslanders were right.

Another cause of dispute between the railway authorities and stockmen arose at that time. An effort was made by stock-owners' associations to obtain a reduction in the number of wagons required as a minimum for a special train. Under South Australian management, special stock trains had been run with fifteen wagons north of Marree, and twenty cattle wagons—or sixteen sheep wagons—south of Marree. Under the new Commonwealth management the number of wagons was increased to twenty-two throughout. There was a reasonable explanation for this.

With the introduction of heavier locomotives, fewer engines were provided than hitherto and the greatest possible use had to be made of each. A report said: "The locomotives haul 50 per cent more than those previously in use, and the higher minimum required is to ensure heavier loads and more profitable use of the locomotives. It would not be good business to run trains lightly loaded over the very long distances."

However, since cattlemen with smaller properties at times found it impossible to provide animals enough to fill twenty-two trucks—about 220 beasts—a proposal was made. "It is realized," continued the report, "that it is difficult, owing to the great distances separating the cattlemen of the interior, to combine consignments to make up the required loads. To meet such cases arragements are now being made for a trial series of special trains at fixed intervals. All concerned will be advised as to the time-table."

When work began on the Oodnadatta extension, this situation was eased. Cattle trucks were attached to work-trains returning south after delivering construction material to the camps. So for a time cattlemen enjoyed better facilities for small consignments than ever before.

The old fettler's mind was packed with memories—mostly unclassified. Suddenly, he rubbed from west to east. "The Federals sure copped it in them first few months," he said. "People felt it warn't right giving up their last hold on the old Oodnadatta line. After all, they'd built it, mate."

Here, the point that caught my notice was the description he employed for the railway. Despite the official title, Central Australia Railway, introduced at the time of the take-over, all the old names seem to have been used as before, with the exception of the first and most picturesque, Port Augusta and Government Gums Railway.

Another old name that survived for many years was Goat Halt. Like Port Augusta, Oodnadatta kept many goats in the early days. After the second World War the early description seems to have returned for a while to a settlement grown sleepy during the years following the passing of the railhead. For by that time most cattle raised in the Centre were being trucked at Alice Springs. The name, affectionately ironical perhaps, seems to have been dropped again quite quickly.

In any case it had gone out of use when a friend of mine, David Mercer, arrived in 1948 as a Meteorological Observer with the Meteorological Section of the Department of the Interior. He and three colleagues lived on the aerodrome run by the Department of Civil Aviation with a staff consisting of an airport manager, two radio operators, and two groundsmen. In those days Oodnadatta had slowed down. Gone was the bustle of the railhead times and probably all the young Met. Observers found Oodna very dull. They had little work and much time on their hands. Single men, they lived in a hut on the aerodrome and ate at the pub in the township about a mile distant.

Then, the European population comprised aerodrome and meteorological staffs, two policemen, the railway stationmaster, three or four railway gangers, a storekeeper, a butcher, a schoolteacher, a post-office technician, a publican, the pub cook and waitress, and the families of the married men. In all, about sixty persons. Some fifty migratory Aborigines lived in the usual shanty town near by.

The Ghan, once known facetiously in Oodna as the Limited Express, seems to have provided the highlight of life. Whenever the train pulled in, thirsty passengers would jump from the coaches and swarm into the pub for a few butchers of beer out-of-hours. Everyone dutifully signed the publican's book. In this way each traveller registered himself as a bona fide passenger who had travelled more than fifty miles that day. Always, however, the company in the bar included several locals who, though they might try to make themselves small behind the broad backs of legitimate drinkers, were a serious embarrassment to the young policeman whose duty it was to meet the train.

It seems that in those days the only life in the township was found in the pub. Even there, train days apart, one rarely met more than two men and a dog. However, every now and then a situation developed—usually whenever a party of stockmen arrived in town to "blow their cheques". "I remember an evening when one of these characters collapsed in the bar," said David. "He'd been drinking steadily all afternoon, and when we arrived he was just able to sit upright. Then he tossed down another beer. For a moment, he stared fixedly but then, unable to maintain his seat, he slid off the stool to the floor where he twitched a couple of times and lay still. When the dinner bell rang the diners just stepped casually over him on their way out."

The Oodnadatta weather report forms part of an Australia-wide pattern that enables the forecaster to compile a weather map and make his predictions.

Basically the Met. Observer's job is to take four-hourly observations of temperature, barometric pressure, cloud cover, and wind velocity and direction. "We relayed this information in a coded message to the Weather Office at Alice Springs aerodrome where there was a forecaster," said David.

Important among the tasks of the Met. Observer is to fly a miniature balloon. The object of a balloon flight is to record the velocity and direction of winds at all levels. For this purpose a balloon, approximately two feet in diameter, is filled with hydrogen and released. As it climbs its course is checked by following the path it takes with a theodolite. Between readings, the observer works a slide rule to calculate the wind speed and direction at each level. On sunny days a white balloon is used to show up against blue sky.

Usually the air at Oodna is sufficiently clear for the balloon to be observed at a height between 25,000 and 30,000 feet. Sometimes it may even be observed at a height of 40,000 feet, but then the observer must keep his eye glued to the lens for the final few thousand feet if he is not to lose sight of the balloon. On cloudy days a black balloon is used.

"At night," said David, "we used a balloon with a small paper lantern suspended from it. A stub of candle in the lantern supplied the light. Windy nights we found frustrating. Once you had lit the candle—and this wasn't easy—you had to release the balloon with a steady movement or the candle would blow out. It was irritating to go through all the awkward business of inflating, tying off, attaching the lantern, and so on, merely to watch the light go out at a height of perhaps ten feet! The lantern could be followed to a considerable altitude. But it was hard to sight on a starry night when the balloon drifted slowly."

Goats still infested Oodna. But the beast which opened the settlement, the camel, was seen no more. And of the first encampment—the huts and mosque of the Afghan drivers—no trace remained. However, the old pad was still there, though no longer beaten out by the camel strings. "Never a decent road north of Oodna," the old fettler had said. "I was that way during the war. Must ha' been 1941, I reckon. But mebbe 1940. Anyway, there'd been two seasons of good rain. And, well, there warn't no track to speak of in places. That trip to Alice was mostly skid. My oath!" He slapped a knee. "Should've gone by rail, of course. Reckoned we'd save money, though. Well, reckon we didn't."

Oodnadatta is the terminal point of road traffic north of Marree. Three feeder roads, branching from Oodna, connect with the Stuart Highway to Alice Springs at Mount Willoughby, Wellbourn Hill, and Granite Downs. The region traversed by the track north of Oodna is subject to severe flooding and, since the arrival of the railway, reports have been constant of stretches impassably closed for periods of up to three weeks.

Many people seem to suppose that this sort of thing ended during the second World War, when the much-advertised Stuart Highway was built by defence forces. But this route was built northwards from Alice Springs. No reliable road was driven southwards to Marree.

Until January 1967 the maintenance of far northern roads was the responsibility of the Engineering and Water Supply Department. But on the first day of that year the duty was assumed by the Highways Department, and in 1970 a Highways Department Administrative District Office was opened in Port Augusta especially to control the development of the far northern road system. However, at present the Department has no plans for upgrading the road that runs to Oodnadatta from Marree and on, in less reliable shape, to the Territory border. Naturally, the situation will be considered in the light of the likelihood that the narrow-gauge railway north of Marree will be discontinued before many years have passed. Probably the road through Coober Pedy and Granite Downs will always be considered the main route to Alice Springs, since it passes through comparatively hospitable country with less risk from floods.

Oddly enough the police station seems to me the pleasantest building in Oodna. It is a shady, verandahed house with a magnificent view across vast plains. The staff of six officers has four borders to patrol. Indeed, here is the largest police territory in Australia, some say

TOP: Station transport in early times at William Creek (*Vic Lee*). BOTTOM: Ready to depart—a typical scene, probably at Oodnadatta (*R. D. Kempe*)

in the world.

Oodnadatta is still the rail halt for an important cattle-raising region, some seventy miles to the west. But, unfortunately for the one-time terminus, the future Tarcoola–Alice Springs standard-gauge railway will pass through this district.

What will happen when the new line has been built and the existing narrow-gauge route becomes redundant? Surely, when that time comes, aerodrome, meteorological office, post office, hospital, hotel, store, and the local Highways Department will all pack up and travel across country to form the nucleus of another township beside a new and far more efficient railway! One must suppose that in, say, ten years from now, Oodnadatta will have joined the large and mournful company of ghost towns of the outback. But perhaps then the desert oak and the mulga will return.

TOP: A carriage of 1911–12 with seating accommodation for 60 passengers and including a lavatory (*South Australian Railways*). BOTTOM: The arrival of the first diesel-electric locomotive at Alice Springs (*G. L. Stirling*)

14

THE ROAD TO RUMBALARA

The decision to build a railway to Alice Springs was reached shortly before take-over.

On 18 September 1925 the Governments entered into yet another agreement. Under this an understanding was arrived at that matters concerned with the route, starting point, and gauge of the new line should be subject to the final decision of the Federal Government. But only two courses were left open to choice. The railway should either continue from Oodnadatta as a narrow-gauge line; or start entirely afresh from a spot near Tarcoola as a standard-gauge line.

This agreement—as in the cases of earlier understandings—was made subject to the approval of the Commonwealth and State Parliaments and, on this occasion, to the grant by the State of the consents necessary for the construction and working of the railway within State borders.

Provided all details had been settled by 30 June 1926, the Federal Government agreed to start work within six months of that date. Furthermore, subject to interruption caused by circumstances beyond its control, the Commonwealth undertook to complete the railway in time for traffic to open on 30 June 1929.

Having obtained agreement in principle to these proposals, the Federal authorities proceeded to examine the position. Meanwhile the Commonwealth Railways Commissioner and the South Australian Railways Commissioners made a separate agreement in respect of methods of co-operation in working traffic on the Commonwealth and State lines in South Australia. This agreement was signed three days before Christmas.

There ensued the usual complicated legislation. Two Acts—Nos 2 and 3 of 1926—were introduced in the Federal Parliament. The first, The Railways (South Australia) Agreement Act, simply approved the terms of the agreement. The second, The Oodnadatta to Alice Springs Railway Act, provided for "the extension of the Port Augusta Railway by the construction of a railway to Alice Springs".

Thus the Federal Government adopted the recommendation of the Parliamentary Standing Committee on Public Works. The direct, western route was to be followed, at least as far as the MacDonnell Ranges. It was felt that this line, in conjunction with the extension (already approved) of the North Australia Railway, would, as the 1922 report had suggested, provide adequately for the foreseeable future. And Parliament, not being clairvoyant, doubtless decided that the foreseeable future was all for which it could reasonably be expected to cater. Both Acts were assented to on 15 February.

Meanwhile, the South Australian Parliament convened a special session at which the North-South Railway Agreement Act was introduced. This Act ratified the new agreement and granted the Commonwealth Railways Commissioner "all the rights, powers and authorities which the State or the South Australian Railway Commissioners would have in respect of the purpose aforesaid". This Act was assented to on 26 February.

Owing to heavy rains the start of the survey was delayed for some weeks. But two parties moved out from the railhead on 8 April. The first began work from Oodnadatta; the second from a point 100 miles north, or about twenty miles south of the Territory border. Simultaneously, minor survey parties left to site reservoirs along the route.

Estimated costs of £1,700,000 provided for a ruling grade of 1 in 80, and sixty-pound permanent-way material.

The standard rails then in use by the Commonwealth Railways Department were of sixty pounds, eighty pounds, ninety pounds, and 100 pounds. The sixty-pound rail was regarded as a serviceable light rail. But should traffic require a heavier rail then it was considered uneconomic to use one of less than eighty pounds. Probably, at that time, the seventy-pound rail was not rolled in Australia.

But the heavier the rail the better the running, the lower the maintenance costs, and the greater the safety. So clearly the engineers in charge did not consider that the Centre would develop rapidly, or that there would be heavy traffic on the extension for many years. However, it should be remembered that the degree of safety also depends to some extent upon the number of sleepers used to the mile.

Each in its turn, numerous settlements on the Great Northern

Railway had experienced the temporary consequence of being the head of line. But generally importance had departed as soon as the railhead moved on. Thus several names, briefly famous, are long forgotten. A few spots, however, enjoyed local advantages that ensured continued prominence. Both Farina and Hergott Springs were focal points on principal stock routes and so, in themselves, were places of mark. But usually the temporary railhead dropped out of the news and became just another lineside halt as soon as the plate-laying gangs moved on.

Now, though the prestige of thirty-six years as terminus of the line ensured the settlement's survival and continued reputation, Oodnadatta's turn had come.

The ceremony of turning the first sod took place on 21 January 1927, hastened a little perhaps by concern expressed by the South Australian Premier that the start of work had been delayed. But, since the permanent survey was approaching completion and the Department of Works had assembled materials for the construction of the twenty-one miles of line to link Oodnadatta with the base camp at Wire Creek, the Federal Government considered that work had in fact started, and said so plainly.

Now the polished shovel, already used on two important railway occasions—turning the first sod of the Port Augusta and Government Gums Railway on 18 January 1878, and turning the first sod of the eastern portion of the Trans-Australian Railway on 14 September 1912—flashed in the sunlight of a scorching day. The Minister of State for Works and Railways performed the customary motions. But the occasion appears to have evoked little enthusiasm. Apparently, no celebration was held in the hotel. And, since insufficient accommodation was available in the township, the visiting party lived on the Ministerial "special", which soon steamed away. Thus, quietly, was the extension to Alice Springs inaugurated.

But if the turning of the first sod caused few headlines, the Press carried some surprising stories from Oodnadatta at this time. One, for example, described the arrival of a large party of men who had "walked through from the Northern Territory terminus and arrived in a sad condition". These men had assumed that work in plenty would be available in Oodnadatta.

To tramp 1,000 miles through the heart of the continent was a remarkable feat, and the disappointment that awaited the men when, finally, they reached their destination, must have been hard to take. But the Department had no work to offer.

Since other men, all expecting to obtain employment on the workings, reached Oodnadatta from various places down-line, the gathering of navvies must have been considerable. Reports gave a total at well over a hundred. This situation led to a tragedy that took place one night in the Oodnadatta railway yard.

Two mates, George and Bill, having failed to obtain work in the Department's gangs, tried elsewhere in the township without success. So they decided to leave by the next train. They spent the evening drinking. Then they went to the railway yard, where Bill lay down on sacks in an empty truck. But George threw his sacks on the ground under the truck and proceeded to use a rail for pillow.

Realising what had happened, Bill swore at his friend, calling him a fool for such behaviour. When this had no effect, he climbed down and dragged George clear of the line. But five minutes later George was back in position. Again Bill pulled him away.

According to a subsequent statement this procedure was repeated on four or five occasions. George must have been very drunk indeed. He insisted obstinately that no train would run that night and that if shunting started in the morning he would waken in time to get clear. At last Bill put a coat under his head, covered him with a sack and, climbing back into the truck, went to sleep.

When he awoke, the truck was moving. He scrambled down. Running back a few yards, he came upon a ghastly sight. George had shifted in his sleep, for there he lay with his head and body on a sleeper and his legs, or what was left of them, across a rail.

He was taken to the hospital of the Australian Inland Mission, but died in a few hours. The coroner considered an inquest unnecessary.

For some time after the turning of the first sod, the railhead remained at Oodnadatta. No one appears to have been in a hurry to start work seriously in midsummer heat. The plan was to use departmental labour as far as the construction depot then being prepared at Wire Creek. When the linking line was complete, contractors were to take over and build the major part of the work, 272 miles of permanent way.

Prior to the railway invasion, Wire Creek had consisted of a shed standing by a bore that supplied a 20,000-gallon iron tank, which in turn fed a galvanised-iron trough where camel strings were watered. Far out in a northerly direction a dark green, flickering light would hold the gaze of travellers. This was no mirage. The flicker marked the line of the wide, sandy bed of the Alberga River with its fringe of gum trees, where fresh water was always to be had either in waterholes or soaks.

On 18 March a report in the *Transcontinental*—which had succeeded the *Dispatch* in 1916—stated: "We understand that the railhead is already a mile beyond Oodnadatta." Scarcely rapid advance!

Labour troubles had caused delay. An agreement between the Commonwealth Railways Commissioner and the Australian Workers' Union had fixed the rate of pay and conditions of employment of the construction navvies. This provided for a basic wage of 18s a day, the rate to apply throughout the section from Oodnadatta to Alice Springs only, for in the south the labourer's pay was then 16s a day. The agreement also determined rates in higher grades, the marginal differences above the basic wage being those granted in Award No. 94 of 1926, which covered construction workers on the Trans-Australian Railway.

However, the Union was dissatisfied, and since the agreement provided that either party might (within a reasonable time) approach the Court for revision of the basic wage, it made application. It now demanded a basic wage of 20s a day with appropriate marginal advances. But the Court disallowed the claim, fixing the rate at 18s a day. The decision did not end labour unrest in the north, and a sense of ill-usage persisted.

One day a gang of twenty navvies downed tools and refused to resume work until a mate, dismissed by the ganger-in-charge, had been reinstated. The local authorities refused to submit to this ultimatum, so the men shifted their stand, saying that they would not continue work under the ganger. The dispute seemed likely to spread throughout the workforce.

The impasse continued for over a month. Then, on 13 May, a report headed "Oodnadatta Strike Settled" said that work had been resumed, the Department having transferred the ganger to other duties.

Perhaps it is not surprising that by the end of June only fifteen miles of line had been laid. However, the depot at Wire Creek had been completed and now awaited the construction materials, which could be received and stacked only when the linking railway was finished.

At this time 9,000 tons of rails and 135,000 sleepers were stored in Port Augusta. The sleepers were Powellised jarrah and karri timbers from Western Australia, and ironbark, tallow-wood, grey gum, and white mahogany beams from New South Wales.

Tenders for the construction of the railway from Wire Creek to Alice Springs — invited in April — were returned on 30 June. Two offers were received. These, together with an estimate prepared by the Department, were handed to the Government. The tender of the Victorian Construction Proprietary Limited for £695,320 was accepted, and the contract was signed on 11 August.

Under the terms arranged, the Department became responsible for the provision of all basic materials, the supply of water, and the erection of station buildings and engine sheds.

An important condition required that the line should reach a point 170 miles north of Oodnadatta by 30 November of the year following. This point, Rumbalara— "rainbow", an Aboriginal attempt to describe the appearance of the country after rain —lay on the old camel pad to the Centre. The date for completion to Alice Springs was 30 June 1929.

The Department-built line to Wire Creek was finished on 29 August 1927. At once the contractors moved in and construction trains began to shuttle backwards and forwards between Port Augusta and the new railhead.

By this time supplies at The Port had been built up to quantities approaching the totals needed, and the materials now carried north included 31,700 tons of rails, 709,000 sleepers, 2,018 tons of fish-plates, 1,081 tons of dogspikes, 227 tons of fishbolts, and 368,000 spring washers.

To move this great mass of materials from Port Augusta to Wire Creek, a distance of 480 miles, called for more rolling-stock than the Department had available. A number of sub-contracts were therefore let. Important among these was one for eight more locomotives of the NM type, for this engine had been adopted as the standard class for the railway. Under a different description, it had been used for years on Queensland railways. Modified to suit conditions on the long arid stretches crossed by the Central Australia Railway, the twenty-two engines ultimately owned by the Department were to be known as NM 15–28 and NM 31–38. Double-heading when necessary, these worked out of Port Augusta for many years hauling construction traffic, and then "Ghan" and "Flash Ghan".

Now, however, for a time the engine situation was difficult. Unavoidably the firm in Castlemaine, Victoria, which held the contract to build the new locomotives, failed to meet the delivery date, 23 March. The general strike that had broken out in Britain prevented them from obtaining certain essential parts, so delivery was delayed by some weeks.

Meanwhile the workshops at Port Augusta built various types of rolling-stock — composite brakevans, combination sleeping vans for train crews, and a number of passenger cars. As soon as completed, all new rolling-stock was hurried into service.

Unfortunately, several engines were usually laid up, undergoing renewal of tube plates and crown stays in Port Augusta yards. This was largely because reservoir supplies became exhausted and bore water had to be used. A bore was sunk near Brachina at this time, and though the water flowed at over 1,300 gallons an hour it contained scale-forming solids. So sometimes great difficulty was experienced in providing locomotive power to meet an increasing demand.

Earthwork-building gangs moved out from Wire Creek in mid-September 1927. At the end of the month, when these were some seven miles ahead, the plate-laying parties started in pursuit. By this time, 650 navvies were working on the line. All had been engaged in Port Augusta. The order was advertised widely. Yet men continued to arrive at Oodnadatta, confident that they would be engaged on the spot. None were, and some ill-feeling resulted.

To begin with, work advanced rapidly. Ten years previously, in reports prepared for the Commonwealth Railways Engineer for Construction and Maintenance, J.J. Waldron of the Department of External Affairs had variously described the country that the track-builders now faced as "easy construction", "moderate construction", and "moderate-to-difficult construction".

Wishing to show that the problems of railway construction in the region had been exaggerated, he pointed out that Oodnadatta was on the same parallel of latitude as Brisbane, and that the MacDonnell Ranges were no further north than Rockhampton. It was absurd, he felt, that anyone who visited Alice Springs should be looked on as an explorer "while he would be a suburban commercial traveller who had not been beyond Rockhampton".

Later the construction gangs were to encounter difficulties greater perhaps than any Waldron visualised, but for the time being all was easy going.

Old-timers sometimes describe the men who now worked their way northwards from Wire Creek as the usual nondescript construction worker. This they doubtless were, but all were fit, hardy men. Here was no repetition of the experience of forty years previously when many of the men recruited from the unemployed had been totally unsuited to heavy labour. Nevertheless, far more care was taken than hitherto to provide adequate medical attention for the camps.

Prior to the take-over, a special medical fund had provided for the health needs of northern railwaymen. This had been financed by a levy of 1s from the weekly wage packet, a contribution that covered the cost of medicines and the salary of a railway doctor stationed at Oodnadatta.

This doctor's duties were now extended to include attendance at Wire Creek Depot. But the system was changed at about the time when the contractors' men moved out. Thereafter the medical officer gave all his time to the depot and camps north. And railway employees stationed between Oodnadatta and Mernmerna became entitled to treatment and accommodation, either in the hostels of the Australian Inland Mission at Beltana and Oodnadatta, or in those of the District Trained Nurses' Society at Farina and Marree. Serious cases were taken to the Port Augusta District Hospital.

On the workings, most of the labour was still done with pick, shovel, and barrow. Horse-scoops were of great assistance in clearing cuttings blasted with explosive. But, by and large, there was little advance on the methods used in building the Port Augusta and Government Gums Railway. Here and there a few Keystone excavators and Marion shovels lightened the labour where embankments had to be built. But no machine power-tools were yet in use.

Tented camps sheltered the workers. Most of the tents were square in shape and ragged in appearance. Cook-houses usually consisted of rough timber sheds that could be easily dismantled in sections, loaded on trucks, and re-assembled at the next camping site. Meals were taken either inside tents or at long trestle tables, flanked by benches or packing cases.

Tatterdemalion settlements, lacking in military precision, appear to have been established at intervals of eight to ten miles. But there seems to have been no rule in the matter. Probably spacing depended upon the difficulties encountered along the way.

Men who were present, whether as navvies or as construction-train crew, all speak of the good conduct in the camps. But then, as an afterthought, most add that of course alcohol was not permitted on the workings. Well—perhaps! But substitutes were not wanting. It seems that hop beer was made all along the way from Wire Creek to Alice Springs, and when the brew was prepared in tins over camp-fires, copper coins were tossed in to add strength to the liquor, just as in the old days. And all accounts say that whenever a man went down-line, his mates expected him to smuggle in drink on his return. However, officially, the ruling was enforced by police officers, who made regular visits of inspection.

Gambling—principally two-up—was general. One pictures the scene after sunset. The ragged camp huddled at the trackside in the midst of wilderness. The stacked tools. The occasional brazier. And then the tent with the open fly, and the figures grouped about a packing-case lit by a hurricane lamp.

From Wire Creek the survey line ran close to the old stock route. As far as the Finke River the stock route lay a little to the east. At the Finke it crossed the path of the rail, continuing to the west as far as Rodinga, where it wound to the east once more, only to re-cross at Deepwell and then continue on the western flank to Alice Springs.

So at times the navvies must have paused, leaning on their shovels, to watch mobs of cattle plod by, or to stare at heavily-laden pack-camels padding deliberately between horizon and horizon.

At this time, when the ship of the desert was preparing to bow out—though not because of the advance of the rail—the camel freight rate between Oodnadatta and Alice Springs had risen to an astonishing £17 a ton. Until the period of the Arltunga gold boom in 1903, when more than a thousand diggers went north, the charge had remained steady for many years—£7 a ton. But then it had jumped to £13. And after the first World War it rose again. Then in 1920 the cameleers, who had considerable payments to meet on the road for watering their beasts, endeavoured to push up their rate once more. But this time agents refused to pay.

Eventually the Afghans had their way, but it was their last burst of prosperity. For a time strings were to continue to work the country from Alice Springs to Newcastle Waters, and north-eastwards from Marree to Birdsville and on into Queensland. But generally speaking their work was done. The motor-truck was proving an invincible competitor.

Towards the end of 1925 an Act was passed authorising landowners to destroy trespassing camels. The completion of the Trans-Australian Railway had exerted a depressing effect upon camel business. Drivers lost more and more trade and then came a time when they could not give their beasts away. Some took their animals to the edge of the desert and released them there to roam at will. Herds formed, multiplied, and became a menace to pastoralists, for fences did not stop them, and the water they drank represented a heavy toll on the supplies of many stations.

Under the Act a landowner, before he might destroy camels on his property, was obliged to follow a definite procedure. First, he had to insert an advertisement in the Government *Gazette*, then two notices—at intervals of a week—in each of two daily newspapers, and one more in a weekly, all giving warning of his intention. Not until this obligation had been observed in full might he take steps to clear his land—and then for a period of three months only.

However, for a little while longer the strings were still a common sight in the north, and railway navvy and cameleer exchanged rough banter.

Through torrid summer heat the gangs worked on into the bitter cold of winter. It is said that many of the navvies would not believe at first that if a basin filled with water were left out overnight it would be found next morning with a thin coating of ice. Particularly hard to bear must have been the south-east wind that may blow continuously all day and every day for days on end, dropping only at sunset. Descriptions remain of camel drivers reluctant to ride the leading beast in their string, because of the numbing cold of a bitter south-easter that made a nonsense of blankets. The navvies must often have thought longingly of the camp braziers they would light when, at last, the wind dropped.

By 30 June 1928, the earthworks had been pushed on to a point 122 miles north of the depot, with a further ten miles partially cleared. This meant that they had reached the district of the Finke River. The plate-layers had lost a little ground in relation to the leaders.

They knew the Finke to be a great flooder and so a high-level bridge of ten spans was built. This crossing was destroyed by flood in 1930, after which the track was laid on a length of stone pitching in the river bed, for by this time it was known that the Finke drops back quickly to a depth of about two feet, continuing to run at that level for weeks.

Steam engines could cope with a crossing where not more than two feet of water covered the rails. The modern diesel-electric locomotive, on the other hand, is halted in such conditions. The effect of water on sophisticated electrical equipment prevents the engines from passing through a depth of more than three inches. So today the Finke River crossing consists of a reinforced concrete causeway which allows floodwater to pass through culverts. This permits the diesel locomotive to move as soon as the peak flooding is over.

But in the days when they built the line to Rumbalara, the diesel-electric engine—though invented in principle in 1890 by Herbert Akroyd Stuart—had not been considered for use in Australia.

At this stage the contractors were working to schedule and a railway report remarked with satisfaction: "The work is well in hand, and from present indications it is evident that the conditions of the contract will be complied with." Indeed just then the Department had every reason for gratification. "For the year under review, earnings met working expenses and contributed £17,858 towards interest. This is the first time since the Commonwealth Government took over the railway from South Australia in 1911 that earnings have met working expenses. Every other year large sums have had to be contributed to meet the difference between the earnings and working expenses . . . Under the Commonwealth management the financial position has greatly improved. For the first full year after assuming control the loss, excluding interest, was £6,574 as against £105,186 for the previous year."

The situation was the more satisfactory since £13,000 out of earnings had been spent on repairs to the permanent way. Unfortunately the following twelve-monthly period was to show a loss again, this time of £12,283.

Perhaps it was optimism engendered by an improved financial position that caused the Department to consider for the first time the possibilities of tourist traffic to the Centre. A modest test tour was planned in conjunction with the South Australian Railways. The itinerary included Wilpena Pound, St Mary's Peak, Paralana Springs and other beauty spots in the Flinders Ranges. It was a beginning. The chief obstacle to the development of this source of revenue was an almost total lack of suitable accommodation in an undeveloped region.

Now the path of the construction gangs left the gibber plain and moved into sandy country of mulga and desert oak. The sandhills ran west of north and, here and there, were varied by patches of stony tableland.

At this point, Rumbalara was only twenty miles distant. Perhaps the sandhill country caused delay. However, progress slowed and the railhead arrived in mid-December so that the contract time was slightly exceeded.

The section was taken over for traffic two days before Christmas 1928.

15

MAIDEN'S BREAST

Late afternoon and Rumbalara!

"All change for Horseshoe Bend," said the guard facetiously.

Now Horseshoe Bend is not on the line, and I wondered why he mentioned it at all. It was, of course, the spot where the bags of the desert mail were exchanged between camel strings which then made a right about-face, returning north and south respectively. But this was not the kind of recollection to induce so whimsical a grin. Then I remembered the story of the he-man character of Horseshoe Bend.

The tale dates back over half a century to times when The Bend is said to have had a great reputation for he-men and for general perversity. It seems that one inhabitant above all others was considered to typify the "spirit" of The Bend. When he died, as even the most he-man-minded do, friends planned a special mark of respect. But what might they lay on that was different?

Then someone had an idea which was promptly adopted. They buried the most outstanding he-man of them all in a coffin made out of whisky cases—the only really common timber in the district! Or so the story goes. And perhaps it suits a countryside where the flat crowns of table-top hills remain rugged even when neighbouring lands, smiling under good rains, are lush with grass and a delicate blue flower like a periwinkle.

It had been a journey filled with interest. One hundred and seventy miles of unusual stories—beginning with the tale of a hold-up at Wire Creek.

Bob Kempe first told me of the robbery at the construction depot. At second hand, however, for at the time he was a child on Macumba Station, where his father was then manager.

That day the paymaster held a large sum in cash—navvies' money. Armed men just walked in and took it all. They made a successful get-away, travelling northwards, probably heading for Alice Springs. But their staff work seems to have been poor. Their car broke down.

Perhaps they were without the spare parts they needed; perhaps the damage was too extensive to repair in the bush. Whatever the facts, they abandoned the car and set out to walk.

By the time they reached the neighbourhood of Hamilton Bore, they had decided that escape would be impossible if they kept possession of the loot. So they planted the money in holes in trees, doubtless intending to return for it. Then they got away, just how is not known. The obvious theory—that they were navvies who, on the failure of their attempt, slipped back to their jobs, losing themselves in the gangs—has no supporting evidence. Later, part of the money was found.

The Slow Mixed stopped, and men came running. A name-board said "Alberga", and this meant we were twenty-six miles north of Oodna. Just then one part only of our long train interested the runners—the pay van. I wished I might take a place in the queue. Probably everyone whose money arrives irregularly knows a feeling of envy of those who enjoy the clockwork rhythm of the pay-packet.

The pay van has the usual fittings of a pay office—counter, grille, and money tills. Perambulating the outback, it still is just a bank—the Commonwealth Bank. However, there are points of difference between it and a city branch. It is also a post office, though the pay clerk may not transact business at any halt where a branch post office exists. Then it doubles as a book shop, the counter being flanked by racks where paperbacks and magazines are displayed.

Despite the general bank atmosphere, I had thoughts of a village store and looked round for a table with writing pads, pens, rubbers, and paper-clips. Instead, through a door into a small back office, I saw a safe that stood open.

Thinking of hold-ups, I asked the pay clerk if a gun lay in the drawer from which he had just taken a folder of stamps. He grinned, shaking his head. After all, in the absence of construction gangs, where might a robber find anonymity in such lonely parts?

A fettler, having transacted the important business of the morning, strolled down the track to give us good-day. He talked of his "caulis" and tomatoes which apparently flourished like marrows on a compost heap. And well they might, for the garden plot was hard by an artesian bore. I asked why he gardened, when all needs were delivered at his door. He looked surprised. Clearly, a foolish question! "Reckon you know the old Chinese saying?" I asked if Confucius had been busy again. He ignored that. "It goes this way. 'To be happy for a day, get drunk; to be happy for a week, kill a pig; to be happy for a month, get married; to be happy for life, make a garden.' Seems that's bonzer whether you live in Peking, Swatow, or—Alberga."

So! A desert philosopher who had travelled! "You talk Mandarin or Pai-hua?"

He grinned. "Merchant seaman talkee-talkee—as a kid." One meets all sorts by the desert rail.

Five fettlers are stationed at Alberga, and they have a fine house.

"Cool day, eh?" Another man strolled up, tucking in notes as he came. I learned later that the thermometer inside the house registered 83°F.

This fettler had two dogs, Queenie and Ringo Dingo, the first a full collie, the other a wild dog cross. Queenie, it appeared, was hot on snakes, a fortunate circumstance since copperheads infest the region; no fewer than six had been killed in and about the house during the previous week. Queenie had bailed-up one in the shower at midnight. Usually a silent dog, she had begun barking furiously. "Where, Queenie?" She had led the way to the curtain.

Queenie's owner said that a fettler's life is pleasant and not over-strenuous—often just a matter of being on hand when needed. Nevertheless, unlike his gardener mate, he was restless. Posted to Alberga some months before, he had enjoyed life there, but planned to return to a job on the oil rigs in Timor, where, it appeared, work was phased—a fortnight on, a week off.

Many cattle are raised in the region and the fettlers spoke of a paddock near the line where Brahma cattle are brought to mate.

Alberga is open country. To the north lies a scrub-covered, sandy region. At Mount Sarah halt a six-man queue formed smartly by the pay van steps. Here, long before the railway, came John Ross. A Scottish explorer and pastoralist, Ross is thought to have accompanied Charles Bonney on his overland trip in 1838. Later, while working as a drover for Thomas Elder, he explored the Macumba region north-west of Lake Eyre. Amid such loneliness, it was natural that he should think of his people and he gave family names to a group of hills—mounts Sarah, Rebecca, Alexander, and John.

Here was fine horse-breeding country; some would say the finest; that here horses can be raised to beat the world. That is as maybe. But in the days of the British Raj, the Indian Government bought thousands of horses from this region, mostly remount and gun horses, strong, heavy animals.

This country may become green, surprisingly green from the angle of the townsman who has heard much of its aridity. Heaven knows, at times, the Hamilton River at Pedirka (the next halt on the railway) gives an efficient impression of aridity. Yet George Stirling told of an occasion when floods held up his train so effectively that food had to be flown in to the stranded passengers and crew. The country is a network of rivers and water channels, which for years on end may be bone dry. But two inches of rain in the catchment area sends the river down a banker.

Thus floods occur in one or two places in a season, briefly cause havoc, and then dry out to sand once more. For instance in March 1972 the Todd River ran amok, washing away rails and embankments, and running in places seventeen feet deep. Yet a month later, though the Ghan still crept cautiously across washaway areas, the river bed was dust once more.

Fortunately the rivers do not flood all at one time. George Stirling told me that during twenty-two years as a driver he had been held up at the Finke on some twenty occasions.

My friend the pay clerk was just as popular at Abminga, some eleven miles south of the Territory border, where one may see relics of the days of steam—a water sleeve beside a bore, a coal bin that has begun to fall apart, and so on. They stand by a siding where once engines and tenders backed in for supplies.

Abminga means "tracks of the snakes", and a short trip in the neighbourhood will convince you of the aptness of the description. Here kangaroos, when seen, are found to be as red as the sands of the near-by Simpson Desert. They were numerous once. So too were bustards, formidable if feckless birds. It was here that George Sitrling caught the turkey chick that was to become a household pet. They had stopped the freight train on sighting turkeys, the usual procedure in days more leisurely, perhaps more satisfying than our own. And at once Stirling spotted a young bird that he contrived to capture alive. Taking the little creature home, he reared it on chopped steak.

When that chick grew up it earned its keep, for it turned out to be better than a watch dog. A friend of the family, the bird did not end its days on the Christmas table, but was given to a private zoo.

Abminga was a camp on the old camel pad. And until the start of the second World War, one could see the majestic, supercilious beasts passing by in strings of forty or more on the way to some lonely station or, perhaps, to some new gold strike far off beyond the sunset.

During the building of the extension to Alice Springs, engines broke down on a number of occasions, usually as a result of the use of bore water. George Stirling, who was born in 1896 at Bunbury, worked for many months in the Abminga region, driving the construction train that carried sleepers, rails, and other materials to the head of the line. Once his engine failed north of Abminga. There was nothing to be done until new parts were brought up-line from Oodnadatta. So he, the fireman, and the guard spent the night under a gidgee tree with a tarpaulin for covering. Next day, when the parts arrived, repairs were made on the spot, and the heavily-loaded work-train continued the journey to the railhead. This, it seems, was a typical incident of building days.

Abminga was the starting point of the Simpson Desert Expedition. C.T. Madigan and his Adelaide party left the train here to meet Jack Bejah who was waiting with nineteen camels at Charlotte Waters, the old telegraph repeater station. In those days the halt consisted of a shed, a ramp for loading cattle, and a water-tank with a fettlers' camp near by.

Though situated on a featureless gibber plain, Abminga is a place of many stories, partly because of its proximity to Charlotte Waters. But the tale that fascinates me most concerns an early explorer. The astonishing incident began in a report that was a canard—or so many people decided. But was it a hoax? There appears to be some room for doubt. These are the curious facts.

One day, some ten years after the completion of the Rumbalara section, a surprising story was told in an Adelaide bar. A stockman, mustering on the fringe of the Simpson, was said to have come upon seven human skeletons lying near a spot where, many years previously, a fire had burned between sand ridges.

People talked, jumping to the conclusion that this was Leichhardt's last camp, and that a ninety-year-old mystery had been solved.

Ludwig Leichhardt, a German scientist, made a number of expeditions inland from a base at Moreton Bay. In 1848 he set out with six companions—four European and two Aboriginal—to travel across the continent from the Darling Downs to Perth. None of the party was seen again.

Now that seven skeletons had been found, some people said that coincidence was out of the question. When sceptics pointed out that the spot—near Muckarinna waterhole in the bed of the Finke—was off the route that Leichhardt had proposed to follow, there were many who recalled that an associate of the scholar-explorer had written that the German was no leader: that, in fact, "He had not enough commonsense to keep away from the business end of a mule."

So the matter was argued. In 1938 the South Australian Government organised an expedition to investigate the discovery. Specialists, among them an anthropologist, joined the fortnightly express that then ran to the Centre. They reached Abminga at 3.30 a.m. on a cold, dark day.

Crossing the gibber tableland to the Finke River, the party reached the scene of the discovery and pitched camp. But as soon as the scientists saw the spot they knew that the "bones" were not skeletons at all, but the roots of dead whitewood trees about which calcareous deposits had formed. True, there was a close superficial resemblance to long bones, but these were not human remains.

This decision seemed to end the matter. But the stockman was not satisfied. Though forced to accept the experts' finding, he insisted that a camp had been here in the long ago and that, if search were made, relics would be found to prove his statement.

Probably with little enthusiasm, the scientists agreed to stay for a few days. They set up sieves for a planned "dig". They would examine the sand in the immediate area in ten-foot squares to a depth of six inches.

Work began with, one imagines, little expectation of results. It was then that, in rapid succession, some astonishing finds were made.

Most of the discoveries occurred at the six-inch level, a circumstance which disallowed a suggestion — made some time afterwards — that the area had been "seeded" with relics. In any case, as will be seen, this suggestion was absurd.

First a human tooth was found; then pieces of a skull. Iron fragments came next. Then scraps of leather. Finally two coins were dug up and these posed a puzzle which still remains unsolved.

The first was of silver, and was dated 1841. It turned out to be a Maundy threepenny piece. About 3,000 of these little coins were minted for Queen Victoria to distribute to the poor on Maundy Thursday. How was it that this rare coin, designed for use in England only, had reached the fringe of a Central Australian desert?

Some people claimed that this find alone proved that Leichhardt's last camp had been discovered. Had he not passed through England in 1841? And had he not been the type of man to keep the threepenny piece for its rarity? And if not Leichhardt, who else could have brought this rare Maundy piece to the Simpson Desert?

The second coin was as great a surprise. A half-sovereign, dated 1817, it belonged to the first issue of half-sovereigns of which 1 million only were minted. When, later, the Mint authorities were consulted, it was learned that the average life of the half-sovereign was seventeen years. Thus, if the coin was carried by Leichhardt in 1848, it had already exceeded by fourteen years its estimated period of use. Yet, so far as is known, no white man other than John McDouall Stuart—and he in 1868—came within 100 miles of the Muckarinna waterhole until the 1880s.

In all, fifteen objects were unearthed in the immediate vicinity of the "bones". Then the expedition packed up and went home to Adelaide in the confident expectation that a second and larger "dig" would be organised. They argued that it would be reasonable to suppose that other finds would be made if an area four times as great were investigated. Unfortunately the South Australian Government made no further move.

Is it too late to take action today? If, humanly speaking, Leichhardt's fate is far beyond remedy, historically it is of importance still.

As to the location of the finds—apparently unlikely in relation to Leichhardt—it has been suggested that the explorer, meaning to follow a route to the north of Sturt's Stony Desert, was halted by the Simpson and moved southwards in search of water. If this was what happened, the party, following the Mulligan River, could have reached the southern edge of the desert, moved northwards up the Macumba, and so arrived at the Finke.

The suggestion that the old camp was an Aboriginal camp and that all the articles found had been stolen, seems too far-fetched to consider. All the evidence suggests that here was a European camp. Then, having regard to the dates of the coins, if not Leichhardt's, whose? Who carried to the Simpson Desert a half-sovereign and a Maundy threepenny piece, both minted in the first half of last century? Surely the interest attaching to this mystery would justify the cost and effort of a further "dig"!

Many odd stories are told of spots on or close to the railway in the region where it crosses the Territory border. Unusual among these is one associated with the poem *Childe Harold* and its author, Lord Byron.

The permanent pool at the famous telegraph repeating station near Abminga was named after Charlotte Harley, the Ianthe to whom the poem was dedicated. Charlotte, the daughter of the sixth Earl of Oxford, was an exceptionally beautiful child. Byron met her when his poem was already in the hands of the publisher. A person of impulse, he at once sat down and wrote the famous dedication. Then he commissioned William Westall, R.A., who as a young man had sailed with Matthew Flinders, to paint the girl's portrait. The engraving appeared in all editions of the work.

One day in 1871, three surveyors—all working under Charles Todd—camped in the Abminga district. Coming upon an unusually clear pool, the senior member of the party named it after Charlotte. For this seemingly inconsequent action there was a direct connection.

Charlotte had married Major-General Anthony Bacon, a veteran of the Spanish Wars and of Waterloo and, in 1860, had settled in Adelaide.

Her son, Harley Bacon, became Todd's storekeeper in the Finke River district during the building of the Overland Telegraph Line. Apart from Charlotte's fame as a beauty, this circumstance probably accounts for the naming of Charlotte Waters.

Harley Bacon's duties included the management of the flocks—some 2,000 sheep—pastured on the Finke River between the repeater station and Rumbalara, a corner of an undefined area called "Larapinta Land" by the Aborigines.

Larapinta was the ancient name of the Finke River which, for the greater part of its course, runs in a high-banked channel. But at the railway crossing the banks are not high, and when the river enters desert, the channel grows shallow. Here, during monsoonal floods, the stream spreads widely in alluvial flats because, except in exceptional seasons, sandhills prevent the water from bursting through to Lake Eyre. In the river basin, in the region crossed by the railway, one of Australia's rare earthquakes occurred in June 1941.

Rumbalara halt is twenty miles north of Finke. One of the principal known deposits of yellow ochre exists in the district. Consequently, the area has long been frequented by Aborigines, probably from ancient times. Here is Simpson Desert country, which in this fringe region resembles the South African Karroo because of its many flat-topped hills. And like the Karroo it can be a place of beauty. After rains the desert blossoms: yellow and pink flowers shoot up; butterflies flutter against red sand.

My introduction to the name of this important halt was unparliamentary. At the time of an early visit to Port Augusta, when I was looking for old identities willing to tell their railway tales and recall those of their fathers, I met an old man who chatted freely of the line north of Oodna. He had not worked on the railway, but as a youth he had been a jackaroo on some station in the region.

Early in our brief acquaintance, it became clear that the old fellow's memory was a function upon which little reliance might be placed. He imparted information with a garrulity that inspired no confidence. While I awaited an opportunity to escape, he began to talk of a place where, he said, a pause in building had occurred. But the name had slipped his memory. He cracked his fingers, swore mildly. He was an irascible old party. "Know it like me own street," he said. "Anyways, it don't matter. Gin's Tit, or some'ut to that effect."

You will perceive his style. Then he went on to tell a spun-out yarn of no consequence.

As may be imagined, his description enlightened me not at all. Indeed, I forgot the incident until one day, quite suddenly, the penny dropped. I learned that sometimes Coulson's Peak, a conical hill to the east of Rumbalara, is known as Maiden's Breast, and that the halt was known by this name when Rumbalara was the railhead. Then the association of ideas in muddled thoughts became clear. For the testy old party, Gin's Tit was near enough. Probably that is how he still thinks of Rumbalara and its pointed hill.

Of course, the breast analogy is used the world over in naming hills with smoothly-rounded summits that terminate in pinnacles. In Natal, for example, twin peaks are known locally as Sheba's Breasts.

A range of flat-topped hills near Rumbalara is characteristic of many seen from the railway. In places, two are joined together in the likeness of a giant saddle. For the rest, Rumbalara offers desert oak, mulga, and spinifex. But to my way of thinking the special country lies westwards—through Erldunda, Angas Downs, Curtin Springs, and Mount Conner to Lake Amadeus and the Olgas.

I was told of a New Zealander who has worked on the northern railway for over thirty years. With four dogs for companions, he goes up and down the line checking books. "He has taught his dogs all manner of tricks, hoop jumping and what not," said my fettler informant. "He reckons his job is a real good life."

I agree with that Kiwi.

16

ON TO THE NORTH

Following the completion of the line to Rumbalara, there came a pause.

From a dot on a surveyor's map of sandhill country, Rumbalara now became the advanced depot for the supply of the construction gangs. Materials were brought forward in quantity from Wire Creek and stacked according to type in readiness for a fresh beginning. And when, presently, the clearing, grubbing, and earthwork gangs moved out once more, the railhead was a busy place. It remained so for eight months, until traffic was opened to Stuart.

At that time people spoke of the point for which construction now headed as Stuart or Alice Springs—indifferently. But the names referred to two entirely separate places and Stuart, two miles south of Alice Springs telegraph station, had been chosen as the northern terminus for the current stage of the southern section of the transcontinental railway. And there a station had been laid out.

The settlement at Stuart began about ten years after the telegraph station by the springs had been established. A ruby rush opened in the district and Charles Todd's telegraph staff could not provide for all the strangers who arrived. So a camp was established. This was named Stuart after the explorer, though in fact the route he had followed lay well to the west.

A centre for the ruby-miners and later for the gold-miners of Arltunga, Stuart—at the time when the rail advanced from Rumbalara—consisted of a store, a boarding-house, some huts, several hundred tents, and a Chinese market-garden that supplied the district and the camel strings passing north and south on their journeys between Oodnadatta and Newcastle Waters.

The new railway terminus was named after the township. Four years later, on 26 January 1932, the day on which the post office moved to Stuart, the name of the terminus was altered to Alice Springs. The change was made because the authorities realised that as soon as the postal centre had been transferred to Stuart it would be impossible any longer to dissociate the newer from the older settlement.

On moving out from Rumbalara, the gangs entered a belt of difficult country between thirty-five and forty miles wide. Though construction had reached the fringe of the Simpson Desert a little north of the Finke River crossing, the district beyond Rumbalara presented greater problems. But some very heavy going, involving increased engineering hazards, was not the sole hindrance encountered in this region.

Strong winds that, through many ages, have played a part in eroding the land surface still blow. But, fortunately, only when these are particularly boisterous do they raise dust storms that sweep the country. When normally strong, however, they cause sand, resembling smoke, to rise high into the air from the tops of ridges.

The navvies of the construction gangs suffered great hardships. At the time they arrived, drought exacerbated normal conditions, and sand drift was unusually high. Reports of the day speak of the men's sore eyes and rasped throats, discomforts caused by the driving sand that was whipped constantly from the crests of the great naked red ridges among which they toiled.

The prevailing winds blow towards the east and south-east, and fine sand may be carried for hundreds of miles, occasionally to districts as far distant as Bourke in New South Wales. It is said that the red colour of the sand of the Simpson Desert is due to a coating of oxide of iron, the basis of rouge, and that if one boils a handful of red desert sand in acid, the result will be a handful of ordinary white sand. If you enter the desert to the east of Rumbalara, you will find that the colouring becomes even richer.

So the navvies toiled in a tormenting red haze that came and went with the gusts. Long before, in the days when the line approached Hergott Springs, surveyor C. Winnecke had described this country. He called the Simpson—then the Arunta—"a perfect desert" and added that he felt sure that it had never been visited by Aborigines, an assumption in which, almost certainly, he was mistaken. Old bushmen speak of finding the remains of fires built by Aborigines when making dashes into the Simpson in the Wet to collect pituri, a narcotic that grows there. Chewing pituri has an effect similar to that produced by opium.

Now, in the dry season, the advance of the construction gangs dragged. For a time, daily progress slowed to little more than a quarter of a mile. Day after day the navvies worked in great discomfort. Strained nerves caused tempers to run high. Quarrels were frequent, and fights occurred. Often these arose out of trifling matters.

An old-timer, then a member of a supply-train crew working out of Wire Creek, tells of entering the store at Rumbalara just as one of these clashes began. "When're you paying me for those eggs?" demanded the storekeeper of a ganger who was fingering a pair of work trousers. "I'm not. Most were rotten." The storeman growled. "That's a lie. All right, then. Don't pay and not only won't you get any more eggs, but you'll get a hiding right now." But the ganger merely made impolite noises. So the storeman leapt the low counter and a fight was on.

But if the men quarrelled and sometimes fought, they did work, despite the trying conditions. Gangs competed against one another. Wagers were laid, which meant that every man strove to achieve that little bit extra. Accounts agree that the navvies took pride in their jobs. Always the work came first. And that is a refreshing recollection in the light of much present-day experience.

Odd characters were met; odd incidents occurred up and down the workings. It appears that, here and there, shanty stores dispensed, from under the counter, liquor somewhat stronger than the hop beer that was general. One owner was known as "Willing" Corn. His name was Cornelius and he was willing to take reasonable risks in meeting his customers' tastes. Another appears to have suffered from a divided house. His wife's views on thirst differed from his own and so business was discouraged. The story goes that once when a navvy came to the counter, the woman looked him up and down and then said shortly, "I've a pretty good idea what you're after, and it ain't tomato soup." The man grinned. "No, ma'am, I want a drink." She snorted. "Well, Jim's out, and I never handled an alcoholic drink in my life. You'll have to wait."

Drought persisted that year. The situation became critical, not only in the sand-ridge country, where the workings struggled forward in great heat and in sand-filled furnace winds, but also in country far to the south. A railway report spoke of one gale that "caused the rails in upwards of thirty cuttings to be covered to depths varying from nine inches to eight feet for distances of from one to twelve chains". No sooner had the sand been cleared sufficiently to permit trains to pass, than fresh winds rendered the track impassable again. The removal of the sand necessitated the employment of large numbers of extra men. Sand-drift became a serious problem on many sections of the railway.

Drought cost the Commonwealth Railways dearly. That season the loss on livestock traffic alone amounted to more than £35,000. Only fourteen special stock trains ran between Oodnadatta and Marree as compared with ninety in the previous season.

Such were the conditions in which the construction gangs worked north of Rumbalara. Grubbing and clearing parties had advanced a little beyond the midway mark in the sand-ridge country, when they came abreast of a distant landmark which John McDouall Stuart had made notable in a railway context sixty-eight years before.

Situated on a hilltop, a huge sandstone pillar, more than 100 feet high, and perhaps fifteen feet square at the base, dominates the sandhills of the Finke and Hugh rivers, which make a junction about seventy-eight miles north of the Territory border. Stuart remarked that, from one angle, this pillar had "the appearance of a locomotive" and the railway analogy has been remembered, for this was certainly the first occasion on which anyone thought of railway engines in Central Australia. The native name for the column is Idracowa; the explorer called it Chambers Pillar.

Leaving sand-ridge country behind them at last, the navvies began to make up for the long delay. Now, at times, they advanced by as much as two miles a day.

Meanwhile on the North Australia Railway, the southward push from the Katherine River to Daly Waters—authorised at an estimated cost of £1,545,000 under the Enabling Act (the Northern Territory Railway Extension Act, No. 2 of 1923)—advanced slowly. The work of bridging the Katherine River, a difficult feat of engineering, had been completed in May 1926, and the line to Mataranka, a stretch of sixty-four miles, in July two years later. But now the Government decided that advance must stop short at Birdum, because of a need to limit loan spending.

The decision to halt construction forty-three miles north of Daly Waters necessitated storing about £137,000 worth of steel rails, sleepers, fastenings, and telegraph equipment, the balance of materials bought months earlier. Moreover the cost of the labour expended already on clearing and grubbing south of Birdum had to be written off.

Today, travellers watching from carriage windows as the Ghan moves between Rumbalara and Alice Springs notice, at long intervals, lonely trackside graves. Sometimes these graves are marked by small crosses, sometimes by portions of old iron bedsteads that do service as surrounds.

Pitiful in their isolation, these burials can seldom be identified. One or two may mark the final resting place of railway builders. But not all. Stockmen, prospectors, and even some explorers died in this region, long before the coming of the line. Over the years many men have succumbed to the rigours of the outback. Five died during the construction of the Overland Telegraph Line, but none of them in this district. In early days men in difficulties usually cut the telegraph line, an action that ensured the arrival of help. But one is known to have died because he did not understand this. Another, too weak to climb a pole, died at the foot.

An incident showing how men came to die in the bush was described by R.B. Plowman. One day a swagman (a word seldom heard in the Centre) set out to walk from Old Crown Point store to Horseshoe Bend. He carried a canvas water-bag. Perhaps, when taking a drink, he dropped the bag, losing water in the dust. In any case, he ran short of water and then seems to have lost his judgement and wandered off the track in a vain search. Exhausted, he found his way back to the road and collapsed under a bush. There he died. The irony of the story lies in the fact that the bush stood just below the crest of a rise from the top of which he would have seen the station buildings at Horseshoe Bend.

In 1891 the *Dispatch* drew attention to lonely bush burials in regions traversed by the railway. "The fact that friendless unfortunates found dead in the bush are buried as paupers by the Government irrespective of any property they may possess opens up a field for investigation." A dead man had recently been found and his wallet contained a cheque for £42.

Incidentally, one lonely cemetery on railway land near Strangways Springs was described in the *South Australian Railways Officers' Magazine* at the time when the line was pushed north from Wire Creek. This burying place was said to contain the graves of many railway workers who died during an outbreak of typhoid fever. Sanitary arrangements in early railway construction camps were greatly inferior to those provided when building moved on from Oodnadatta.

Early in May 1929, a report said: "Railhead is now only eighteen miles from Stuart, which will be the northern terminal point, and rails are being laid for two and a half miles daily." At this rate of progress the line should have reached the terminus during the week following. Yet, a month later, another report announced: "Only another ten miles of track to be laid." Eight miles in four weeks! The cause of the slow-down was not given, but was probably the result of a last-minute delay in the delivery of supplies.

However, the completed line was taken over for traffic on 2 August 1929.

Four days later the first passenger train from Adelaide steamed into the new station, then by far the most substantial building in Stuart. Seven years were to pass before specialist shops began to be built, the first being a women's clothing store in Todd Street.

It appears that by early morning the entire population of Stuart and Alice Springs—save only the duty telegraphists—had assembled. In all, there were some 200 persons. The number of navvies had been reduced since the gangs moved out of Rumbalara and so the total labour force, now about to be thrown out of work, numbered 500 men, many of whom were scattered along the line between the terminus and Rumbalara.

Soon word went round among the assembled people that a long delay must be expected before the train would be seen making smoke as it steamed into Heavitree Gap. Delay had been caused by boiler trouble south of Oodnadatta.

Arrival time had been fixed for 9.30 a.m. In fact, the train arrived shortly after 2 p.m.

Most of the waiting crowd appear to have spent the interval discussing likely developments in the pastoral industry of the region, now that the railway had come at last. Talk turned on the departure, two days previously, of the first cattle train to leave Stuart for Terowie. It had been a memorable event, and station-owners and stock agents alike agreed that never again would the Centre suffer cattle losses such as those of the five years just past. This first stock train, everyone said, must have passed the first north-bound passenger train, now awaited, at about the half-way point on the railway.

There was talk, too, of navvy unrest caused by the fear of approaching unemployment. Recently in the House of Assembly a Member had raised the matter of "the small army of workers" shortly to be discharged by the contractors. He had enquired if action had been taken to find work for these men. Now it was recalled that the Prime Minister had asked for notice. Of course, nothing had been done. Well, there was little for the men to do in the Territory now that the line was complete.

And then, while they still waited, news came over the wire that the Commonwealth Railways Department had announced that Wilson would be closed on 6 September, and in future would be worked as an unattended siding. For old-timers present this decision must have stirred memories of the days when construction was being pushed across the Willochra Plain and there was much talk of a great wheat-growing future for Wilson and its neighbour, Gordon. Now Wilson was to be no more. The news must have brought shadows to the thoughts of many gathered to celebrate the completion of the railway, which, in the beginning, had brought Wilson into being.

On the whole, however, the gathering appears to have been optimistic regarding the future. Even a few head-shaking old identities, who felt an obligation to make gloomy forecasts, admitted that never before had they seen so many white people gathered together in the Territory.

At last the train, driven by George Stirling, steamed into the terminus.

When the passengers—among whom was a party of scientists from the University of Adelaide, come to collect facts about the disappearing tribes of the Centre—had descended, the local people climbed aboard. Great interest was taken in the novelties included in this new and much-advertised train. The parlour coach and dining-car were attractions. But the feature which caused most comment was a bijou bathroom. A bathroom on a train! Here was a novelty suited to the importance of the occasion! It was a luxury train for those days. Australian throughout, it had been built in the railway workshops at Port Augusta.

Then, the first-class through fare from Adelaide was £12. This included sleeper and meals from Quorn, where the journey was broken to make the change from South Australian to Commonwealth lines.

Timed to leave Stuart at 1.30 a.m. on 7 August and to reach Quorn at 4 a.m. two days later, the Flash Ghan connected with an express which delivered passengers in Adelaide at 7.58 p.m. Similarly-timed limited mixed trains were scheduled to run at fortnightly intervals. Ordinary mixed trains were run at economy rates, but these did not provide sleeping or dining-car accommodation.

At a gathering in Stuart following the arrival of the first train, a number of speeches were delivered. Some of the remarks of the speakers make odd reading today. The Government Resident said that, as a result of the coming of the railway, the cost of living in Central Australia would be greatly reduced. The charge for the carriage of groceries would drop at least £20 a ton from the current £53, and the price of petrol would be halved from 6s 3d to 3s 2d a gallon.

The Government Stock Inspector stressed the change that must take place in living conditions. Many station-owners—some of whom possessed hundreds of square miles of land—had lived merely in camps or wurlies, for the cost of transporting building materials to their properties had been prohibitive. But now iron and other building needs would be brought from Adelaide at supportable expense. So, in future, families would live on stations where, hitherto, there had been no white women.

The new railway opened with one encouraging windfall. It happened that its completion coincided with the arrival at Stuart of 3,000 head of cattle belonging to Sir Sidney Kidman. Twelve trains were needed to transport this large mob to Terowie, where they were transhipped for Adelaide. Freight worked out at a little under £4 a head.

17
TERMINUS

Though hitherto unheard in the Territory, "tourist" became a familiar word there soon after the railhead reached Stuart. For now Waldron's view that anyone who visited Alice Springs need not be an explorer quickly became true.

By April 1930 railway travel to the Centre was fast becoming the "in thing"—for men!

The Department had made an announcement on the matter. Tours for men, with membership limited to sixteen persons, would be of three weeks' duration at an all-in cost of £65.

If the authorities felt that they were on to an easy thing that called for no special arrangements, they became disillusioned in short order. For, says the record, very soon they were pestered by indignant women. What absurd notions did the Department entertain concerning Australian womanhood? It should know that whatever brothers and husbands might find tolerable in respect of accommodation, the modern woman could and would sustain.

Perhaps the initiative shown by the wife of the Governor of Victoria precipitated this avalanche of protest. In 500 miles of travel through the MacDonnell Ranges "by motor, camel and donkey", Lady Somers seems to have set a pace that certainly disconcerted the railway authorities. The emancipated women of those times were not to be denied. What a Governor's wife could do, they too could do. So in due course a further announcement was made. "The Railway Commissioners, acting on advice received from Alice Springs, are prepared to accept bookings from women who wish to join in tours to Central

Australia during the winter months."

Of course, woman interest spelled revenue. Nevertheless that second announcement had a half-reluctant ring, the savour of retreat.

In June, *Table Talk* had this to say on the matter: "Lord and Lady Somers having set the fashion by going off on a pioneer trip to Central Australia, it is expected that the tours organized by the Commonwealth Railways this winter will be well patronised. At first the Department put its foot down firmly and said 'No women'. But what is the firmness of a Government Department compared with the determination of the Sex? Nothing! Poof! The firmness is gone."

Tours were well patronised but, over the line as a whole, during the financial year 1929–30, about 13,000 fewer passenger bookings were entered than during the previous twelve months. This loss of revenue, together with a fall in returns from livestock traffic—some 46,000 head—accounted for a decline of about £84,000 in gross earnings.

Something had to be done. And tourism promised to be a useful money-spinner, for "unknown" Central Australia gave opportunities for attractive advertising. So tourism was encouraged. But the early travellers probably constituted a nuisance in the Centre in those early railway days.

Predictably, a proportion of the sudden spate of visitors were dissatisfied. Despite the insistence with which they were warned in advance regarding the living conditions they must anticipate, some people were "surprised" by the accommodation they were offered.

Of course the situation had its reverse side in the feeling of the local inhabitants, who sometimes were unflatteringly direct in their comments. One hotel-keeper remarked sardonically, "They come with a ten pound note and one shirt and don't change either."

That year the climate was everyone's enemy. Nobody could foresee or guard against the afflictions that beset many visitors accustomed to associate railway travel with security and relative comfort. If construction from Rumbalara had been carried out in conditions of extreme drought, now traffic operated in totally different circumstances. The northern rivers, in particular the Finke, chose the opening of tourism as the time to stage especially temperamental displays. The Finke had not flowed for fifteen years, but now, following rains that the newspapers described as "torrential downpours" it carried a stream seventeen feet deep and in places more than a hundred yards wide.

The railway crossing was swept away, and a long section of line had to be rebuilt. A report said: "Arrangements have been made to carry the mails by raft across the swollen river." A permanent deviation, nearly three miles long, was constructed. The service beyond Finke was suspended for six weeks. These rains cost the Commonwealth Railways about £20,000, for washaways caused heavy damage at other places on the new extension.

An Adelaide businessman who remembered the occasion spoke with feeling. "I don't believe that anyone in authority in the middle 'twenties fully realised the river situation. Else, surely they'd have carried the line in a wide loop north-westwards from Oodnadatta across the headwaters of the rivers? For my part, I'd grown so used to hearing of dried-up stream beds blowing dust that I had the shock of my life that time I saw the Finke running a banker."

Describing the occasion, he said the north-bound was halted by the flood. No one could tell how long the delay would last. A young member of the train crew swam the flood with a line, then a wire rope was hauled across and drawn taut between trees on either bank. Next the engine-driver and fireman crossed in a flying-fox. On the north shore, beyond the reach of the flood, they climbed on to a fettler's trolley and set off for Rumbalara, where a spare engine with a carriage and brakevan waited in the siding. They lit up the locomotive and returned.

When the water-level dropped sufficiently, flat-top trollies carrying the passengers were towed across. Then everybody packed into the short train and the journey to Alice Springs was resumed.

Some tourists accepted such experiences as a bonus in a holiday that was also an adventure not expected to conform to the standards of a seaside vacation. But not all!

Now the pattern of the future became apparent. At irregular intervals, but sometimes for weeks on end, northern traffic would be disrupted and heavy costs incurred. The Federal Government must have wished that a decision had been taken to build anew from a point on the Trans-Australian Railway, their alternative proposal in the 1925 agreement. Such a railway would have avoided the lower courses of rivers which, though normally dust beds, occasionally came down in floods that carried the countryside before them.

Despite the perversity of the rivers, tourism to the Centre increased. But the financial benefit to the railway failed to compensate for the adverse situation that now developed. The result of the year's working was extremely unsatisfactory—a debit balance of £95,292. This was depressing indeed, especially following upon the optimism of two years earlier, when a substantial credit balance had been recorded.

In part the adverse return was attributable to the fact that graziers had made extensive use of special drought rebates granted in respect of the carriage of starving stock; in part to the circumstance that the construction traffic which for three years had been passing between

Port Augusta and the head of the road had now ended. But a general decline in trade was mainly responsible.

By this time all claims and adjustments between the railway management and the contractors had been settled, and the final payment made. It was now known that the extension had cost £1,713,179.

Naturally, the Department hoped that the coming year would reverse the financial position. And, in fact, working costs were reduced by nearly one quarter. But earnings dropped by over eleven per cent; and in the year following that by a further ten per cent.

Seasons with good general rains returned, but ironically this circumstance did little to help the railway. For world depression had taken firm hold.

But the Depression and its effects apart, the Department felt that it had cause for grievance. In his 1932 report, the Commissioner remarked: "This railway serves pastoral country, and consequently the carriage of live-stock forms a large portion of the business. In the year just closed the earnings from live-stock traffic decreased 35·77 per cent. With an improvement in the purchasing power of the people, both here and abroad, it is expected that the live-stock traffic will recover. Nevertheless, it is evident that the pastoralists — to assist whom the extension of 293 miles 20 chains from Oodnadatta to Alice Springs was undertaken — are not making use of the railway as expected, for in many instances they have walked their cattle along the stock routes parallel to the railway for several hundred miles."

If pastoralists did not sufficiently support the railway for which they had clamoured, the reason probably was that they could not afford to truck their mobs for the whole distance at current Adelaide prices. To make ends meet, many were forced to send their beasts on the hoof to Marree, or even Farina. The animals lost condition on the long journey, but in the circumstances this could not be helped.

At this time railway freight charges from Alice Springs were such that to sell a steer in Adelaide cost between £3 15s 0d and £3 17s 6d. If a good price, say £10, were obtainable, the railway rate could be paid. But if a lower market price obtained, then full distance rail costs could cripple the industry.

Although — most provokingly from the point of view of the Department — mobs were being walked southwards, still the line had to be maintained. This work required the full-time employment of 143 men divided between twenty-four gangs — thirteen flying gangs, and eleven serving fixed station lengths. Motor section cars were used everywhere. The cost amounted to a trifle over £64 per track mile per annum. In addition to this basic charge, costs were incurred in clearing drift sand, and in re-laying track following washaways.

From one cause and another, the vigorous policy the Federal Government had initiated in 1926 had gone into decline. In 1911, when the Commonwealth took over the Northern Territory, an outside estimate in South Australia for the completion of the transcontinental railway had been twenty years. And it is likely that the line would have been extended both from Alice Springs and Birdum had not the build-up for the second World War, following upon world depression, acted as a drag upon Federal enterprise. To engage upon huge undertakings in such times must have seemed the extreme of folly. So, as had happened to Oodnadatta in the early 1890s, now Alice Springs became the terminus.

In 1939 the population of the township was about 700 persons. Among these were a number of once well-known Afghan camel-drivers, men such as Abdul Mudgee and Saidah Saidal, who had settled down at last to sell fruit by the Todd River.

On the outbreak of the second World War, the Central Australia Railway at once became one of the nation's chief communications links. In September 1940, the army occupied Alice Springs. The terminus was established as military railhead for the Centre, and troop reserve base for the far north.

At the height of the war, railway arrangements, in addition to providing for normal civilian needs, afforded an each-way traffic of four service trains a day. This meant that the railway was extended to capacity. The terminus and the junction at Quorn worked twenty-four hours a day.

When the army left, though the permanent population had grown by only 300, Alice Springs held a position very different from that occupied by Oodnadatta after thirty-six years as the railhead.

During the greater part of the war, the terminus had been the jumping-off point for army convoys travelling the road to the north. From the beginning, means of rapid contact with northern and western areas, where sparse settlement rendered the continent especially vulnerable, had been an urgent need. No co-ordinating authority then existed. However, the emergency caused the States to drop domestic road work and combine their strength.

In February 1942 the Allied Works Council was formed to co-ordinate operations, and the nation faced up to the formidable task of constructing at speed a military road to link the railheads of North and Centre.

Thus, the Stuart Highway, sixty feet wide, was built to Larrimah, just north of Birdum, under great pressure and with hurriedly collected equipment. Later it was extended to Darwin, a total length of 950 miles. And when tourism began again—with the chief hotels even in the southern cities advertising single and double accommodation at 7s 6d and 15s daily—the Stuart Highway was in good condition throughout its length.

But, still, the Department had not organised its own road transport between Alice Springs and Larrimah, except perhaps to operate a low-loader to transport heavy rolling-stock. In the late 1940s, when the road remained in excellent repair, many carriers were running services to Darwin. This circumstance did not help the business of the Commonwealth Railways, for the privately-owned companies travelled backwards and forwards all the way, thus by-passing the North Australia Railway. So eventually the Department established the Co-ordinated Road-Rail Freight Service. The chief purpose of this move was to retain for the benefit of the North Australia Railway the revenue from the carriage of goods consigned to Darwin that had already been transported from the south by the Central Australia Railway. In short, it was planned to keep railway business within the railway family.

Periodically since then the Department has invited tenders from firms interested in running this service. The haulier appointed works under contract, loading his road-trains in Alice Springs station yard and off-loading at Larrimah, 622 miles distant. Simultaneously he provides a secondary service for goods consigned to Mount Isa and other western Queensland centres. On this run, road-trains leave the Stuart Highway for the Barkly Highway at a point fifteen miles north of Tennant Creek.

An average Commonwealth Railways road-train on the Highway consists of a prime-mover, measuring thirty-four feet and weighing ten-and-a-half tons, and three trailers. The maximum legal over-all length is 147 feet. This means that when a "train" runs at capacity length one small trailer must be used, since the standard trailer is forty feet long.

Loads consist of perishable foodstuffs, building materials, new and second-hand motor-cars, machinery, ale, general merchandise, and rails and sleepers for the North Australia Railway. The standard trailer weighs rather more than eight tons. On the southbound run, copper concentrates may be loaded at Tennant Creek. But this business will end when a smelter to produce blister copper is built at the mine site.

Some 37,000 tons of goods are carried annually to Larrimah by road-trains. The southward haul is much smaller, about 4,000 tons. The corresponding figures for the Mount Isa run are approximately 2,500 tons and 400 tons.

Goods are transferred from railway wagon to road-trailer by means of overhead gantry cranes and forklift trucks. At Alice Springs there are two fifteen-ton cranes and a twenty-ton capacity forklift; at Larrimah, one thirty-ton crane; and at Mount Isa, one twenty-five-ton crane.

An average run between Alice Springs and Larrimah occupies

thirty-four hours—twelve hours driving, ten hours resting, and twelve hours driving again. In all, twenty-two operators are employed. The transfer staff varies with the traffic flow.

Truckies on the Stuart Highway have a responsible job, especially in the Wet, when a loaded semi-trailer may smash through the road surface and become bogged.

Some eight years after the first road-train pulled out on to the Highway, a day came when the Ghan drew into Alice Springs behind the first diesel-electric locomotive to reach the Centre. This occasion was second in importance only to the great event when the train first arrived behind a steam engine. Again, George Stirling was present.

Describing this affair, Stirling said that the train stopped about five miles out of Alice Springs to allow Lady McLeay to climb into the locomotive and sit in the driver's seat. For the arrangement was that the wife of the then Minister for Shipping and Transport should drive the first diesel-electric engine into Alice Springs.

At that time, Stirling had been an Inspector for some years. And now, having received the temporary driver, his job was to explain to her just what should be done, and generally oversee proceedings. As things turned out, perhaps it was as well that he kept an eye on what happened. His pupil was "so busy waving to spectators of all colours" (which, of course, was an action everyone expected of her) that it was he who chose the moment at which to apply the brake.

Thus was Alice Springs recognised for the second time as the northern terminus.

18

STANDARD GAUGE AT LAST

Had it not been for the second World War, the Leigh Creek coalfield would probably not have been developed. And had it not been for Leigh Creek, the southern section of the railway—Port Augusta to Marree—would probably not have been converted from narrow to standard gauge. Rebuilding to standard gauge from a point on the Trans-Australian Railway had long been an odds-on chance.

Early in 1940 South Australia's electric power system was threatened by a shortage of coal. Hitherto the State had drawn large supplies from New South Wales. Now, suddenly, these were available no longer in the quantities required.

The Government urgently sought a local source, and Leigh Creek, long known for its sub-bituminous deposits, seemed the only practical one. A disadvantage was that this coal was unsuitable for use in large quantities in boilers designed for high-grade fuel. Furthermore the field was 350 miles from Adelaide, where the power stations were located.

In spite of these drawbacks, emergency alone brought about large-scale mining at Leigh Creek.

Railway engineers had discovered the coalfield in 1888, when construction had reached Strangways. A railway dam was being built near Copley siding and dark bands were noticed in the walls of the pit. Engineers checking the work of contractors reported carbonaceous shale. Similar traces were found elsewhere in the district during well-sinking operations.

Suspecting the presence of an extensive coalfield, the Government geologist, H.Y.L. Brown, examined the area closely. He drew a rough sketch-map showing the probable extent of the field.

Shortly afterwards, the Leigh Creek Coal Mining Company sank a shaft, but abandoned it when water was struck at seventy-five feet. Elsewhere, boring discovered a forty-eight-foot seam. This was at a depth of 1,500 feet, however.

Another shaft, the Old Main, provided coal at 240 feet. Then the Telford siding was laid and 200 tons were raised and trucked to Adelaide for tests. Although the report was discouraging, mining was continued, largely owing to the insistence of dissatisfied shareholders. But then the Angepena gold rush occurred. Promptly, the colliers downed tools, and Leigh Creek was abandoned.

Later, however, a briquette-making plant was installed, an experiment that soon failed. Attempts to interest the Government at this time also failed, principally because the railway engineers would have nothing to do with Leigh Creek coal. Efforts to find a market in Adelaide were equally unsuccessful.

To all intents and purposes, the mine closed in 1894. By this time some 5,000 tons had been raised.

Twelve years passed before the coal-bearing region became news once more. In 1906 the lease passed to a director of the Broken Hill Proprietary Co. Ltd. He sold to the Tasmanian Copper Company, which had interests in the area, including the Sliding Rock Mine. This company raised about 12,000 tons which were distributed in Adelaide, Port Augusta, and some country towns. But before the lease expired in 1908, the Company abandoned its South Australian properties. Then the coalfield was withdrawn from the operation of the Mining Act.

However, the Government carried out exploratory drilling near the Old Main, raising 700 tons. This coal was refused by the railways. It was then decided that the only bed worth mining lay at too great a depth for economic development so the workings were abandoned and soon became derelict.

This was the position at the time of the Battle of Britain, when the State Government understood that coal shortage would continue indefinitely.

Forced to consider the use of low-grade coal, the authorities again began drilling at Leigh Creek in search of shallow deposits. Then, north of the Old Main, the principal seam was struck at sixty-nine feet.

Now the Engineering and Water Supply Department began serious development. In 1942, 600 tons reached Adelaide. After that, production mounted fast, until at the end of the war over 100,000 tons were being raised annually, supplementing greatly-reduced deliveries from New South Wales.

The railway was busier than it had ever been. And now a decision was taken that was to affect its future dramatically.

In 1946 the Electricity Trust of South Australia was formed. On assuming management of the new coalfield, the Trust decided to build a power station specially designed to use Leigh Creek low-grade coal, and thus render the State independent of imports from the east. The site chosen for this station was by the sea at Port Augusta. It was little more than a swamp with high tidal variations, and so thousands of wooden and concrete piles were driven into the bed of Spencer Gulf to build up an island that would be sufficiently substantial to carry the great weight of buildings and plant. An earthen road-and-rail causeway was added to link the station with the land. In this way was found the permanent, deep, cold-water supply needed to run the condensers of the steam turbines.

It was planned to install generating equipment of 90,000 kilowatts capacity, using three 30,000-kilowatt turbo-alternators. Two 132,000-volt transmission lines were to carry the power to the Adelaide metropolitan area and, through major sub-stations along the line, to rural areas as well.

Known as "A" Station, this project was destined to place a heavy additional burden on the old narrow-gauge line: a huge coal delivery to Port Augusta.

When the South Australian Government informed the Federal authorities of its intentions, the Commonwealth Railways Department decided that the only way to meet the situation was to build a standard-gauge railway to Leigh Creek. In December 1949 the Commissioner submitted a report recommending that this railway should follow a new route across the western plain joining the old track through the Flinders Ranges at Brachina, and that later it should be extended to Marree.

However, unexpectedly the situation advanced a long step further. Extended surveys at the coalfield discovered large new deposits.

Revised estimates of the coal reserves available caused the Electricity Trust to decide upon a second power station of twice the capacity of the first. Now the output planned for Port Augusta greatly exceeded the combined pre-war output of the two Osborne power stations that had been served by New South Wales coal. The State Government announced the revised intentions in 1951. Now a figure of 2 million tons a year was suggested as the probable amount of coal traffic that would be ultimately involved, although later this estimate was modified. Thus, from a coalfield of no significance, Leigh Creek had become a fuel source of great importance.

In the railway context, the need for a standard-gauge line became urgent. "B" Station would make the situation impossible. In the foreseeable future, the old railway would be burdened with a task wholly beyond its capacity. At least a million tons annually, and this in addition to its original duties, passenger, goods, and livestock traffic! Already the line was taxed to the utmost. Immediate action was necessary.

The Commonwealth Government had approved the Commissioner's recommendations without hesitation, but the consent of the State Government was needed before railway construction could begin in State territory. In the circumstances it seemed reasonable to expect that this consent would be given automatically. But now it turned out that the State authorities considered the standard-gauge railway should follow the route of the narrow-gauge line throughout its course, the road being re-aligned and re-graded as necessary. They had no objection to the section between Brachina and the coalfields, where the proposed route, with minor deviations to allow of easy grades and curves, followed the track of the existing railway very closely. But, they said, the section between Stirling North and Brachina must lie along the existing route through the Ranges, and be regarded as part of the scheme for the eventual standardisation of the whole of the Central Australia Railway previously agreed upon. Perhaps the interests of the towns—especially Quorn—lying along the old route in the hills materially influenced the State's determined attitude.

The Commonwealth would not yield the point. The gradients in the Ranges were very severe. The ruling grade—which is the gradient over the heaviest section that limits the load locomotives can haul—was 1 in 46, and the radius of the sharpest curve was six-and-a-half chains. So to haul a coal train of, say, 400 tons gross trailing load required double-heading in the Ranges. The steep gradients in the Pichi Richi Pass, and the hairpin bends between Hawker and Hookina severely restricted the loads of trains and the speeds at which they could travel. The maximum gross load of a double-headed train, whether hauled by steam or diesel-electric locomotives, was 600 tons. And then at Quorn a special "push-up" engine often had to be added to a heavy coal train for the stiff climb to the summit at the head of the Pichi Richi Pass.

A line across the western plain would save thirteen miles in distance and at least three hours in steaming time.

But argument failed to reconcile the conflicting viewpoints. At last the Governments agreed to the appointment of a Royal Commission to resolve the impasse.

The Commission consisted of a Judge of the Supreme Court of Western Australia as Chairman, and two railway members, the Chief Civil Engineer of the Commonwealth Railways, and the Assistant Commissioner of the South Australian Railways. It met for the first time in Adelaide in July 1951.

Meanwhile the first moves were made in respect of the section north of Brachina, where no conflict of opinion arose.

Taking two bites of a railway cherry, the Governments introduced enabling legislation. The Federal Parliament passed the Brachina to Leigh Creek North Railway Act, and the State Parliament gave agreement in the Brachina to Leigh Creek North Coalfield Railway Agreement Act.

The survey in this region started in the month after the Commission began its sittings. But even here, where all seemed plain sailing, a hitch occurred. When, eleven months later, the final survey was complete, the Electricity Trust pointed out that the route chosen crossed the centre of the coal basin, and that the presence of the railway might result in the loss of more than 5 million tons of coal. An agreement was reached whereby the railway was diverted a little to the east, the Trust undertaking to foot the bill for the extra earthworks involved, the Commonwealth that for the increased length of track.

Almost a year to the day after its first sitting, the Royal Commission handed its report to the Governor-General. The findings were made public in Canberra ten days later. The Committee found in favour of the route proposed by the Commonwealth, a new line in the western plain.

The Governments had agreed to accept as binding upon them whatever the Commission might decide. So once more legislative machinery was put in motion and the Commonwealth Parliament passed the Stirling North to Brachina Railway Act, 1952.

Now work was put in hand without delay. Earthworks were formed partly by Departmental day-labour, partly under contract. The laying of sleepers and rails, the erection of telegraph, telephone, and train control wires and certain other tasks were carried out by Departmental labour. But contractors constructed all concrete bridge piers and abutments, supplied stone ballast, and excavated rock and earth cuttings. Unfortunately progress was to be hampered by shortages of manpower and materials, and by climatic conditions, for on a number of occasions heavy rainfall brought floods that damaged bridges and caused serious washaways.

When tenders were called, Farley and Lewers Pty Ltd won the major contract. This company then enlisted the help of partners to carry out work which was to involve the crushing of a million tons of material. The consortium thus formed was known as Farley and Lewers, McDonald Constructions and Morrison Knudson.

Though incorporated in New South Wales, Farley and Lewers were not newcomers to the region. In 1936 the firm had built the standard-gauge line from Port Augusta to Port Pirie. In that case the contract had called for clearing, earthworks, bridge construction, track-laying, the construction of intermediate stations, and the installation of signalling equipment. The consideration was £209,000—a large sum in those days.

Equipment then used had included one of the first drag-lines imported from Britain. Otherwise the work was carried out in much the same conditions as those that obtained when Barry, Brookes and Fraser had built the P.A. and Gee-Gee line.

The construction methods employed when work began at Stirling North were markedly different. Whereas the pick, shovel, and horse-drawn scoop had been the chief means of grubbing, clearing, and earth-handling, now mechanical equipment performed in hours work that would have occupied an old-time gang for weeks. A full range of power tools was used.

Typical of the new equipment was the "bridge-launching nose" used in the construction of crossings of which there were many, from small ten-foot culverts to the Willochra Creek Bridge, 984 feet long.

Designed by railway engineers and built in Port Augusta, this new device enabled gangs to place bridge spans in position quickly and with great economy of labour. The steel spans, all fabricated in Port Augusta, were standardised at twenty-two, thirty-one, and forty-one feet.

Most of the permanent way sleepers came from Western Australia. Jarrah and karri timbers, they were shipped in sling-loads to simplify handling at the break-of-gauge at Parkeston, the freight transfer station outside Kalgoorlie. Some 660,000 of these sleepers were used between Stirling North and Marree, the majority being bored for dogspiking at Port Augusta.

The raw material for the production of ballast, concrete aggregate, and sand was won from dry river beds. Ballast used was ten inches deep throughout the track between Stirling North and Leigh Creek but, later, when the line was extended to Marree, only eight inches deep. In all, three quarries were used for crushing rock. The first of these was situated at Depot Creek, some twenty miles from Port Augusta. When the plant was shifted to the next, a pit near Brachina, nearly a quarter of a million cubic yards of ballast had been placed on the permanent way.

The third crushing depot was situated at a spot just south of Copley. Here the contractors had intended to quarry a hillside, but instead they found stone of an acceptable quality in a dry river bed which they mined extensively. Nearly three-quarters of a million cubic yards of ballast had been laid by the time the line was finished.

One of the brightest ideas advanced during the building of the standard-gauge line was proposed by G.W. Paully, the Commonwealth Railways earthworks engineer. Paully suggested welding forty-five-foot rails into lengths that could be laid in long strips from flat-top trucks. This plan was adopted and a flash butt rail-welding depot was set up in Port Augusta. The procedure was to weld six rails into a single length of 270 feet. Then work-trains, made up of flat-top trucks, each carried enough welded strips to complete half-a-mile of track. On arrival at the railhead, a train would back up to the end of the line where the lengths of rail, two by two, would be hauled off the flat-top by a tractor in such a fashion that they settled on sleepers laid in readiness.

Later, a welding gang advanced along the newly-laid line and welded each length of rail to the next. Thus the permanent way between stations became strips of continuously welded track.

Many of the men who worked on this project were New Australians. For instance, the contractors employed about 150 labourers, most of whom were immigrants allocated by the Commonwealth Government. The majority were Italians, and there were some Germans. Only about a quarter of this section of the workforce were Australians, and most of these came from the surrounding region.

The contractors' men were concentrated at the ballast depots, especially at the base camp south of Copley. But small groups employed on bridge construction were strung out in camps along the route of the line. All lived under canvas.

This was not always the case with Department employees. And one of the more picturesque features of the operation was "Paully's Circus", a town on wheels.

The Commonwealth Railways were accustomed to provide huts for fettlers. These huts were made of timber, were about ten feet by nine feet and had galvanised-iron roofs. At the time many were stored at Port Augusta.

Paully had the idea that two or three of these huts arranged on flat-top trucks would make convenient living quarters. So the experiment was made. To begin with the huts were bolted down, two to a truck, with the doors facing and perhaps six feet apart. Later, they were arranged in groups of three. Each group constituted a "house" and included a dining-room, sleeping bunks, and a shower. Electricity was laid on.

A number of flat-top trucks adapted in this way made up a mobile camp. Spur lines were laid near the railhead and the "town" was shunted into position. It was convenient for the navvies, and it was in nobody's way. After a time a work-engine would arrive to haul the trucks away to more advanced spur lines. Then the vacated rails would be torn up and laid afresh two stages ahead.

Such was Paully's Circus. It became famous. Today one may see the idea still in use wherever a number of navvies are needed at one place for a considerable period of time.

During this construction the men were allowed a "wet" canteen. A sensible decision, for the sly-grog seller was unknown. Perhaps partly on this account, conduct on the camps was generally good, despite the diversity of types employed. Morale was high, for a friendly rivalry grew up between gangs. This was an excellent development, as teams competed one with another, and at times when the going was relatively easy the railhead advanced at the rate of nearly two miles a day. Yet the labour was heavy. The formation of earthworks for the reconstructed line involved shifting a total of more than 5 million cubic yards of earth, and more than 210,000 cubic yards of rock and rocky soil.

Life in these railway camps must have been considerably more volatile than it was in earlier days. The infusion of New Australian labour, especially Italian, introduced an atmosphere of lighthearted gaiety. However, the ganger's task in overseeing the proper performance of detail may well have been more onerous. The difference between the Anglo-Saxon and Latin temperaments!

The rails reached Brachina on 28 May 1955, and the standard-gauge line was opened for traffic on 10 June.

The Commonwealth Railways now introduced a feature unique in railway practice—the "pickaback" train. The question arose of how to transfer freight and livestock swiftly from the narrow-gauge railway to the superior standard-gauge link that had been made available between Brachina and Port Augusta and Port Pirie junction, and so relieve the seriously overtaxed line to Quorn. Experiments proved successful, and the "pickaback" system was introduced on 4 June. It avoided the troublesome break-of-gauge alternatives—transhipping or changing bogies. In particular it provided a means of handling Leigh Creek coal cheaply and fast. Indeed the first traffic handled by this unusual means was a trainload of coal delivered to the power house at Port Augusta.

The idea was simple; its execution difficult. Train sets of sixteen standard-gauge flat wagons, approximately 800 feet long, were strengthened and then fitted with ninety-four-pound narrow-gauge track. The forward end of the track was fixed in place by dogspikes welded to bearing plates, which in turn were welded to the decks, but the rear end was free to move slightly. The standard-gauge train was backed up to a "match truck" permanently fixed to a ramp fitted with narrow-gauge track. A special locking device fastened train and truck so firmly that movement was impossible. Next, a narrow-gauge engine shunted the train that was to be carried pickaback to the foot of the ramp. When all was ready, loading was accomplished smoothly and quickly. The narrow-gauge train was simply propelled up the ramp and across the matching truck directly on to the track laid on the standard-gauge train.

At the front of this railway on a train a buffer was welded to the deck. Here the narrow-gauge car first in line was locked firmly. But this was merely an additional safeguard against movement. The chief precaution was that the airbrake pipes of both trains—the one that was carried as well as the one carrying—were linked with the engine. Thus whenever the driver applied the brake, the pickaback train was held just as firmly as the main train. Additionally, hand brakes were kept in the "on" position.

To handle pickaback trains, several sidings were built in the yards at Brachina.

All coal from Leigh Creek to the Port Augusta power house, most of the cattle from stations north of Brachina, and much other traffic was carried pickaback. Diesel-electric locomotives were used to haul the trains. They gave higher speeds and much smoother running. A GM-class diesel-electric engine could haul a 650-ton narrow-gauge train pickaback across the standard-gauge line between Brachina and Stirling North in less than eight hours, including the time spent in loading and off-loading, and, in the process, save the Department about £200 on the round trip.

However, pickaback working could be regarded as a temporary measure only. It was discontinued on the completion of plate-laying to the coalfield and the installation at Copley of transfer facilities for livestock and freight.

The railhead reached the Leigh Creek coalfield loading bins at the end of May 1956. Trains ran to Telford a month later, the new station being opened on the day when the old halt, two miles to the west, was closed. The problem of the transport of coal to the power stations had been solved.

Recalling the building days, Mr M.D. Farley writes: "Generally throughout the region dust storms were prevalent. The whole area was subject to high winds. On many occasions camps were flattened, and always tents were guy wired to hold them against the wind. When it did rain, roads became impassable and all work stopped, sometimes for up to a week. The normally dry creek beds were always hazardous. Rain falling up in the Flinders Tablelands, sometimes a week before, would flood down these creeks without warning. Telephone communication was mainly through the railway system and, in those days, unreliable. Radio-telephone was used to some extent, but those were the early days of this type of communication and the area did not lend itself to good transmission. Water was carried by rail tanker from Port Augusta, and from the old narrow gauge line by road transport over very inadequate roads to the camp sites. But I think all who lived and worked in the country learned to appreciate it. The heat in summer and the cold in winter compensated by the magnificent colours, clear skies and brilliant and beautiful wild flowers of the spring!"

After 13 August all passenger and freight services were routed over the new line across the western plain. This was an historic event for it marked the closing of the narrow-gauge line between Brachina and Hawker, which had been in use for seventy-five years. No more would awed passengers look out at the crags and magnificent scenery of this section of the old railway. It was a nostalgic moment.

However, most journals of the day appear to have devoted little attention to this aspect of the situation. Instead they remarked regretfully upon the change that the construction gangs, about 300 men in all, had brought about in the fauna of the region.

Before building began, kangaroos, emus, scrub turkeys, donkeys, and camels had been common throughout the country traversed by the line. But the men appear to have been irresponsible and thoughtless of the future. They seriously depleted, by shooting out, the wildlife of the entire district.

The standard-gauge line reached Marree on 29 June 1957, a little more than seventy-three years after the first historic arrival. The opening ceremony took place on Saturday 27 July. A special train—a streamlined, fifteen-coach maroon-and-silver marvel, described at the time as "one of the world's most luxurious air-conditioned diesel-electric trains"—had left Port Pirie junction on the previous evening with some 200 V.I.P.s on board. It was hauled by twin locomotives GM13 and GM20.

Sir Arthur Fadden, the Acting Prime Minister—supported by Sir Thomas Playford, the South Australian Premier—drove the final dogspike and declared the line open.

The countryside had turned out, people from surrounding stations and from places as far distant as Birdsville. Among tall cattle men, some of them old-timers of the heyday of droving, a small figure stood out: an eleven-year-old girl with a young cockatoo perched on her shoulder. This was the daughter of Jack and Nora Bejah, grand-daughter of Bejah Dervish, who had died recently in Port Augusta Hospital. The little brunette represented a stronger link with the early days of the railway in this region than most of the people present. At the time when the first line reached Government Gums and Hergott Springs, Bejah Dervish may not have been actually on the spot, but he was not far away. It was suitable that Margaret Bejah (now Margaret Williams) should stand in the front row of spectators when the Prime Minister spiked the last rail of the new standard-gauge line.

The hit of the brief proceedings that followed the opening ceremony was a surprise parade of New Australians. A contemporary account speaks of "Nearly a hundred happy, excited young Italian railway construction workers proudly waving 'viva' banners which they had hurriedly painted that morning and the previous night." The banners shouted "Viva C.A.R.", "Viva Hannaberry", "Viva Paully", and *viva* many a popular construction boss. They marched past, cheering and laughing. Any solemnity that had previously invested the ceremony was gone.

Afterwards, the leader of the march explained the parade to a representative of the *Advertiser*: "We wanted to show Mr Hannaberry how happy we are to have helped Australia, our new country, to build the great railway so quickly," he said. "And to show that we would like very much to help build more standard-gauge railways quickly for Australia."

They had their wish for, shortly, the earthworks plant and crew moved on to level out grades between Oodnadatta and Finke.

One would have expected the visitors to spend the day in Marree. But soon the return journey began and ironically, in view of much talk of fast standard-gauge travel, the train was debarred from exceeding fifteen miles an hour on most of the trip between Marree and Leigh Creek. The result was that three-and-a-half hours were occupied in covering sixty-one miles. The reason for the restriction was that the track was still unballasted.

A prolonged stop was made at Neuroodla, where an impressive coal train awaited inspection. This train was made up of eighty bogie wagons and a brakevan, in all 5,630 tons hauled by twin 1,750-horsepower diesel-electric locomotives. The train filled a siding three-quarters of a mile long.

Despite slow travel on the first stage of the journey, the special reached Port Augusta ahead of time. This was convenient for everyone, for an official dinner had been arranged in the Flinders Hotel.

Now the old line, built with such difficulty through the Pichi Richi Pass in 1878, was closed. In future it would be used only by rolling-stock sent for repair to the Port Augusta workshops from the Quorn to Hawker line, which would remain in service for another fourteen years. That this was a sad event for many South Australians and for that matter for people throughout Australia, is shown by the recent formation of the Pichi Richi Railway Preservation Society, which has for its basic aim the continuance of the last remaining link of the Quorn–Stirling North section of the old narrow-gauge railway.

The final step in the construction of the standard-gauge line came within a few days of the opening ceremony, when the break-of-gauge transfer point was moved from Copley to Marree.

19

DISASTERS AND DIFFICULTIES

Were you to enquire of some member of the railway staff concerning accidents to the Ghan, the chances are that he would hesitate and then reply that, though the train has been plagued by flood and sand-drift, it has been almost disaster-free. As an afterthought, he might say that, of course, there was the Copley smash.

Apparently in early days no official records were kept, other than annual reports. Later, when the railway changed hands in mid-course, tradition was broken. All of which may account for the fact that today little is remembered. However, research shows that those who suppose that the railway has run throughout the years nearly without catastrophe are mistaken.

Old books provide a few facts about accidents. *The History of South Australia*, by Edwin Hodder, mentions a collision in Pichi Richi Pass in October 1883, when several hundred sheep were killed and damage was done to the extent of £4,000—a large sum in those days. But the files of contemporary newspapers afford the surest source of information, and these record the details of accidents and setbacks sufficient in themselves to fill a book.

The first major catastrophe appears to have taken place one Saturday in January 1883, when part of the Slow Mixed from Quorn to Government Gums blew up near Edeowie.

When the train pulled out of Hookina, all had seemed to be in order. Then a passenger—he was the Leigh Creek blacksmith—happened to put his head out of a carriage window and saw smoke and flame belching from a truck loaded with sacks of chaff. This was serious enough, but the blacksmith remembered that explosives were being carried that day.

No alarm-cord gave communication with the guard. So the blacksmith, followed by one or two fellow-passengers, climbed out of the carriage and shuffled along foot-boards towards the burning truck while the wind fanned the fire.

Arriving at the chaff truck, the blacksmith climbed up through the smoke. Later he described what happened to a newspaper reporter: "I dowsed the fire with water passed along by other passengers while the train was in motion. Then I looked ahead again and saw another truck burning and realized that this was the powder magazine that was on fire. I made tracks back and gave the alarm which was taken up by other passengers."

Someone scrambled along to the rear of the train. The guard confirmed that the smouldering truck held dynamite and gunpowder. But his only means of alerting the driver was to apply the brakes. This he did—violently.

Slackened speed warned the driver that something was amiss. He stopped the train. Then the guard ran along the line yelling to the passengers to climb down and run for their lives. Few needed this urging; they were already on their way.

Somehow the truck containing the explosives had to be isolated. The report said simply: "The guard succeeded in doing this. The train continued a short distance." It seems likely that the feat was accomplished in two operations. First, the guard, helped by the driver, the fireman, and the assistant guard, uncoupled the rear of the train from the burning wagon and the front portion was pulled forward for some distance. Then the explosives truck was uncoupled from the front portion and left standing by itself, mid-way between the two sections of the divided train.

Shortly after this had been accomplished, the dynamite detonated in four heavy explosions.

The noise was heard twenty miles away. Horsemen from Edeowie galloped down the line supposing that "an engine had burst".

Fragments were scattered over an area with a radius of a quarter of a mile, and the line was wrecked for some distance in either direction. There and then the passengers took up a collection for the train crew.

When the story was known, angry letters reached the newspapers. One writer declared that it was "time the public asserted themselves and caused the pompous bosses who muddle things to see in future that the railways are made for the public and not for the special delegation of Government officials". One assumes that the word he sought was "delectation", though why Government servants should have relished the chance of being blown sky high is hard to fathom. But he had his point when he added, "Steps should be taken so that passengers could have communication with the guard . . . This explosion is not the first time an accident has been averted by passengers going to the guard by the foot board, not a pleasant thing to do when the train is going fast by persons unaccustomed to it."

In the following August a gathering that passed almost unnoticed took place in the Council Chamber in Port Augusta. Four bashful railwaymen listen to a speech in praise of their courage and resource. The Mayor, it appears, excelled himself. He closed his remarks with an expression of regret that the subscription raised in recognition of the men's devotion to duty was not larger. But they must remember, said he, that times were hard. The amount that had been collected was £33 7s 0d. And the Government had given pound for pound. So the total sum allowed each man £16 13s 6d. Since they had benefited from the collection taken up on the spot, they may be considered to have done reasonably well for those days.

Another railway explosion occurred at this time between Stirling North and Saltia. On that occasion an engine did burst. The boiler blew up, and scalding water and steam sprayed locomotive and tender. Several people were burned, but again nobody was killed.

The first fatal accident took place on 21 April 1886, when five navvies were killed and several injured. The *Dispatch* gave the story. "A ballast train ran into a mob of cattle at the 38th mile post. The accident occurred near the Finniss on the Hergott–Strangways line now being constructed by relief work. It happened at 8 o'clock as the ballast train was returning with 30 navvies in eleven trucks to the Finniss Camp. The trucks were in front of the engine, the guard being in the foremost. At a place where two falling gradients meet on an embankment 20 feet high a curve in the line takes place and here a mob of Mundowdna cattle were met too suddenly to allow of the train stopping in time. Three animals were killed and seven trucks ran off the line, falling over the embankment and killing the five men who were not thrown clear. Three others were injured. At the inquest, the railway construction authorities were exonerated. But the suggestion was made that a brighter light than a guard's lamp should be provided in front of night trains."

Many accidents happened to sheep and cattle trains, though perhaps not so many as in Queensland. In a cattle truck the centre of gravity is high, and the truck must be wide in order to accommodate the animals crossways. So speed is not possible, especially on curves. In early days, the maximum speed was thirty miles an hour, the average probably about fifteen.

When cattle vans became derailed, the animals were released on the plain. This is still the practice. The beasts need to be freed from prolonged confinement in small space. And the procedure helps in re-railing for it saves the men from the unpleasant experience of jacking up a truck from which there is a noxious discharge.

Shortly before the Finniss disaster, catastrophe befell a special loaded with sheep. The train was hauled by an X-class locomotive with a W-class engine as pilot. It stopped for water at the top of a slope, and before the leading engine was uncoupled to go down a spur line to a supply tank, the hand brakes were set on several trucks. But, as soon as the pilot engine was freed, the train rolled back down the incline.

To warn the driver of a contractor's ballast train coming up behind, the guard swung up to the roof of his van and stood there, signalling frantically. His effort failed. The trains collided, the contractor's engine being overturned, while the guard's van and five trucks were wrecked. It appears that the driver of the X-class engine was drunk and failed to ensure that sufficient brakes were set to hold the train after the pilot engine had been uncoupled. Surprisingly, nobody was killed.

Head-on collisions were rare, but one took place between Farina and Witchelina in January 1889. A report said: "The train from the south left Farina at 7.30 p.m. and in 2¼ miles ran into the line-repairing engine returning with a number of trucks and navvies. Owing to dust, a misty atmosphere and curves in the line the drivers did not see each other until too late."

According to the account, on the cry, "Jump for your lives", both trains erupted with leaping figures. The repair train had four trucks in front and the navvies in these needed no warning. Passengers in the train from the south scrambled through windows when they heard the yell. The first truck of the repair train split, the sections dropping over an embankment, and the second smashed and up-ended. The engine of the passenger train left the rails.

The report ended with a comment which is hard to accept. "The cause of the catastrophe is said to have been the strong south wind which kept the repair engine back and prevented it arriving in Farina at the proper time, it having been arranged that if the engine had not returned to Farina by 7.30 p.m. the train should go on from that station for Hergott."

In early days the Brachina Plain was the scene of a number of accidents and narrow escapes. At this spot, some ten miles from the Range, the line was often flooded. After heavy thunderstorms over the high hills, floodwaters—flowing fast across flat lands—would sweep away the rail near Brachina siding. On one occasion a train, caught in the flood, plunged into a washout here and was wrecked. The driver was killed, his mate maimed. After that, train crews grew accustomed to scan the hills for signs of any departing storm that could have dropped a flood which, even then, might be rushing across country to destroy the track ahead.

Thumbing through newspaper files, one might pick out two score reports of railway accidents of various kinds. So one's choice must be arbitrary and brief, for to tell all would be to give a long and repetitious account.

At the end of the first World War, a bizarre incident took place near Alberrie Creek, west of Callanna. The Marree Mixed, double-headed, left the road when travelling fast. Tearing up the permanent way for 200 yards, the train veered away from the track and bumped off across the plain, wrecking rolling-stock and playing havoc with freight. Much damage was done. But, though the passengers received a great shaking and some nervous shock, none was injured.

On the same section of line some years later James Sharp, Superintendent of the Great Northern Railway, was killed in a somewhat similar accident. The *Transcontinental* reported the tragedy. The Superintendent's party was travelling in "a Dort railway car which, when coming out of a cutting, capsized and fell down an embankment". All members of the party escaped with a shaking, except for the Superintendent. He died that day from his injuries.

A unique derailment occurred in this region. One day a truck filled with sand ran off the rails and was dragged for more than five miles. Then it re-railed itself, most conveniently just before reaching a bridge where, if off the line, it would have wrecked the train. More than a thousand sleepers were broken, some shattered in pieces.

The Copley disaster must be described at somewhat greater length because of the unusual circumstances that attended it.

This smash happened on 11 May 1944 at a spot between Puttapa and Copley. Both the trains involved were travelling northwards, one behind the other. The first, No.453, was a troop train; the second, No.455, a freight. An hour apart, they passed in turn through Quorn and moved slowly up the line.

At about 10.30 p.m., the train controller at Quorn telephoned the duty porter at Beltana and instructed him to hold the freight until he received further orders. This he did, because Copley had not reported the arrival of the troop train, which therefore must have been delayed somewhere on the line.

The situation was complicated by the presence of a southbound train, which both 453 and 455 were timed to meet at arranged crossing places. Both these operations were performed safely and so, though the third train was in the area at the time of the smash, it may be disregarded.

At 11.30 p.m. the porter at Beltana allowed the freight to continue its journey. This was the first mistake. But, following routine, he reported to Quorn. Instantly the train controller demanded to know why the order to hold the train had not been obeyed. It transpired then that a number of other messages had been received at Beltana. The situation had become confused. In short, the porter had forgotten the instruction.

By this time the troop train was at a standstill. On coming to a steep grade at Quarry Hill, just north of Puttapa, the engine, a T-class locomotive, had stalled. The war had caused a decline in maintenance standards. In this situation the driver could follow one course only. He ran his train back down the slope, built up steam, and tried again. Once more the engine failed. But on the third attempt it made the summit and the train began to descend on the other side.

Now further trouble developed and the driver pulled up at the foot of the slope and signalled the guard.

Workshop handling was needed to correct the fault. While the men discussed the situation before deciding what to do, the freight train climbed Quarry Hill.

The fireman first noticed the light at the summit. He shouted. Then the guard ran back waving his lantern.

The freight train consisted of twenty-three trucks, a load of 328 tons. Seeing the warning light, the driver jammed on the brakes and reversed the engine. At that moment, his train was travelling at perhaps thirty miles an hour.

Because of the slope, the train could not be stopped quickly enough. It skidded for nearly 300 feet, then struck the rear of the troop train at a speed of about five miles an hour. The bump—for the collision can have been little more—had a disastrous effect upon old rolling-stock brought back into service to meet wartime shortages. In the troop train, several carriages of the type known to railwaymen as "Short Toms" were telescoped. Four soldiers were killed, and twenty-seven injured.

Complicated legal proceedings followed. These have no place here, but they have been described in detail in the Journal of the Australian Railways Historical Society. Train controller, drivers, and porter were all involved. However, no action was taken against anyone.

Asked the railway's chief troubles aside from accident, a fettler replied emphatically, "The Dry and the Wet, mate." Most railwaymen would agree, though some would say "The Wet and the Dry", for which of these ordeals is the more trying is a matter of personal feeling.

The Dry brings dust storms and drifting sand. In the cabs of their engines, drivers and firemen used to muffle their heads in cloths during dust storms, while passengers sat in discomfort in coaches that leaked fine particles of sand, hard-driven through crevices.

A story is told of a mob of 5,000 cattle that drovers walked southwards in 1897. The beasts must have been divided into separate herds, but a storm that lasted days swept over all. Most of the animals were stifled. The remainder stampeded in the darkness of the dust and, rushing towards a salt-pan, became bogged.

Today rolling-stock is more or less sand and dust proof. And the engine driver, sheltered in his closed cabin, needs only to shut a window when storms blow up. But the trials of drift sand remain. The region between Marree and Edwards Creek has been called "the drift country". Beginning in the Callanna district, drift occurs through Alberrie Creek and Coward Springs, and on through Strangways, William, and Anna creeks.

Ridges in the red sandhills show how the drift travels, backwards and forwards, westwards-eastwards, in accordance with the direction of the strong winds that sweep the region.

Efforts have been made to prevent the drift from obstructing the line. Here and there one sees the remains of sand breaks built out of discarded sleepers, of fences put up to protect patches of sand-binding vegetation from creatures that grub up roots.

On stretches particularly exposed to the gales lie boulders collected in an effort to stop the movement of sand from the crests of ridges. In some places the entrances of cuttings have been widened in the hope that the winds would sweep through and thus keep the line clear of drift.

Only partial success has been obtained.

In March 1926, the *South Australian Railways Officers' Magazine* said of the drift country, "The patrol gangs on this section are often called on to work continuously from 20 to 30 hours clearing the rails for the passage of trains . . . A refusal to work is unknown, although the temperature may be twenty degrees over the century and the wind still blowing. Four feet of sand over the permanent way is fairly common and trains have been held up for 24 hours awaiting a favourable opportunity to cross the drift."

Perhaps this comment was called forth by a complaint from a pastoralist who had said bitterly, "Last year I bought three trucks of bulls, and they were hung up at William Creek for seven hours while sand was being shovelled off the line to let the train through." He pointed out that through "railway inefficiency" his animals had remained unwatered from the Thursday morning when entrained at Quorn until the Saturday evening when released at Oodnadatta.

On a similar occasion, when sand-drift delayed a stock train for twenty-four hours, no fewer than thirty-six of the animals died on the train, and twelve more collapsed and died on arrival at their destination.

The disasters of the Wet tend to be more spectacular than those of the Dry, and have often made the news. For instance, in February 1890, the *Dispatch* had this to say regarding the railway approach to the problems of the Wet. "Cheaply constructed railways are all very well till the tug-o'-war comes in the shape of floods and washaways. The experience of last year, as well as of this, should teach the Government a lesson in the actual economical construction of railway lines. One of the most surprising returns would be the repairing costs on the Great Northern . . . A duplicate line would certainly prove a boon during rainy weather."

Of course the final comment—apart from its inconsequence in view of the emphasis on economy—was crying for the moon. Unless carried far to the west, as already had been suggested on several occasions, how could a second line have improved the situation? It must have run into identical watery difficulties.

Generally the heaviest flooding occurs during the northern monsoon, from December to February. Then streams, which are usually dust beds, become raging rivers following downpours over wide catchment areas.

Great disruption of traffic has occurred constantly at the Finke crossing. This might suggest that the most serious washaways have happened since the railway was extended from Oodnadatta to Alice Springs. And, indeed, some people appear to believe that this is so. But early records—chosen more or less at random—show that the floods that occurred in the region of the Flinders Ranges in the days when the railway was young were just as serious, though they may have been of shorter duration.

On the night of Saturday 12 September 1885, the Hergott Mixed was stopped four miles south of Leigh Creek. The driver had seen a red light wave on the track ahead. O'Brien, the permanent-way inspector for the Farina district, had come out to give warning.

Heavy rains had fallen in the Ranges and the creek had come down a banker. Already half a mile of line had been washed away, and more seemed about to go. Foaming waters had destroyed earthworks on either side of the bridge.

Impossible for the Mixed to advance! Impossible for it to return to Beltana! A cattle "special" on the way to Hergott was somewhere on the line behind.

The night was dark, and there was nowhere for the passengers to go. They stayed wretchedly in dank coaches lit by kerosene lamps, while O'Brien, the driver, fireman, guard, and under-guard, together with a few navvies whose railway cottages had been swept away, worked up to their waists in water in an effort to repair the line. The work went on till daybreak.

Eventually the Mixed reached Leigh Creek. But there it stayed. Beyond the halt, the rails had been washed away entirely for eight lengths. At last the resident engineer and the local traffic manager arrived with gangs of navvies and trucks loaded with sleepers. Then they waited at Leigh Creek for the waters to subside. Meanwhile several stock "specials", booked to take cattle down from up-line to Port Augusta, were cancelled.

That storm cost the South Australian Railways £2,300 in repairs, exclusive of the expense incurred in digging a new channel for the creek.

An old-timer, whose father was a ganger on the line at about this period, said that railway workers often suffered great hardship in times of flood. The waters isolated the depots, so that food and drinking water could not reach them.

One may trace the story through the years. Sudden, devastating flood! Dusty, often grassless country, all at once inundated by raging torrents, creeks normally without importance save for the shade provided by a few trees along their banks.

A particularly notable early washaway occurred at the outset of the 1890s. The railhead had just reached Oodnadatta, when the North and South Peake rivers came down in a flood that obliterated the line for over two miles. It is said that in places the waters ran thirty feet deep. The highest spots reached in this monster flood were marked by two white-painted sleepers. Standing on end, one in the north, the other in the south, the posts indicated the extreme limits of the wide section cut out by the waters.

Occasionally there comes a flood that is different—the difference usually being an exceptional destructiveness. In 1938 the Alberga River exploded suddenly in a raging flood. This was a terrifying inundation. A homestead was washed away—entirely! Nothing was left. House, wagons, motor-trucks, livestock, machinery, outbuildings—all went. The station people spent a day and a night in near-by trees. Ordinarily, the Alberga is dry.

More damaging than even the worst northern floods, because it happened in a populous region, was the inundation let loose by the Willochra Creek in the early 1920s. Eleven inches of rain fell in three days, and it is recorded that in places the normally placid stream ran over thirty feet deep and five miles wide. The railway was washed out and for eight days traffic was at a standstill. Even telegraphic communication was cut. The staff of the Willochra siding were forced to leave the flooded buildings, and some families living near the river climbed to the roofs of their houses and there awaited rescue, afraid that the still-rising waters might sweep them away. A large boat for use in rescues was sent up-country from Port Augusta. This flood caused severe damage to the railway for a distance of seventeen miles between Quorn and Gordon.

But, in so far as the Ghan is concerned, the most extreme of all floods in the region occurred in 1950 when a situation arose for which no parallel is found.

The drama may be said to have opened in December 1948, when the northern line was washed out in two places. In the following March floods came again, and in June rivers in both west and east flowed out across the dry, salty bed of Lake Eyre. This rare happening was followed by heavy rains in September and November.

When the chief western rivers—the Finke, the Macumba, and the Neales—flow strongly, their waters may rush wildly across country, but normally they are dissipated by absorption and evaporation. They seldom reach Lake Eyre. The great eastern streams—Cooper Creek, formed by the Barcoo and the Thomson that unite in Queensland; and the Warburton, which north of Goyder's Lagoon is known as the Diamantina—draw water from monsoonal rains that fall on the western slopes of the Great Dividing Range. Rarely they come down in exceptional floods that affect their deltas, but seldom indeed the Lake proper.

During the first year of the great rains the floods made no lasting impression. The water just sank into the parched, cracked surface. However, it saturated the lake bed. So when fresh rains came and the rivers continued to flow, the ground could absorb no more water. Then the Lake began to fill.

In February and March 1950 many trains were cancelled. In June heavy rains fell yet again on the watersheds to west and east. Complete dislocation of railway traffic followed. And Lake Eyre became an inland sea, 3,000 square miles in area. According to one report, soundings taken from a boat—remarkable sight on the great salt-pan!—showed that the water was twelve feet deep at places forty miles from the southern shore of Lake Eyre North.

And then came the birds—many thousands of them! Freshwater fowl of numerous species, and sea-birds, too. From time to time birds are seen about the deltas of the Frome and Clayton rivers that flow with some regularity into Lake Eyre South, which is linked by a narrow passage—a channel normally dust-dry—with the main salt-pan. But they are seen rarely only on Lake Eyre North.

The great flood closed the Birdsville Track. By that time few cattle were walked to the railway by the old route, but two mobs—over a thousand head in all—were held up for weeks near Kopperamanna. At last one drover took a chance. He pushed his mob across a channel hundreds of yards wide and some seventeen feet deep.

In due course evaporation did its work. After a few months the vast volume of water had been greatly reduced. And, despite renewed floods in the following June, when the railway near Alice Springs was washed out, by 1953 Lake Eyre was dry once more.

However, two years later heavy rains in western and eastern catchment areas turned out to be sufficient to refill the still-saturated lake bed. In March that year serious traffic dislocation occurred; and again in June. But the period of phenomenal flooding had passed, and the railway returned to the old annoying routine—delay, expense, delay—brought about by local flooding of first one then another of the chief watercourses in the great network of channels with which the Ghan is involved. For example in 1963 nearly 200 passengers were airlifted from the train, helplessly stranded. But that year the Lake was not affected.

Ironically enough, the first passengers to travel on the new standard-gauge line did so not as a result of railway planning but as a direct consequence of a washaway. Indeed the Department had no intention of opening the service at that time. But on 5 July 1955, a double-headed coal train was derailed near Hookina on a washed-out stretch. So, when the southbound Ghan reached Brachina, it was halted because of the blockage on the narrow-gauge line, which still carried all traffic save construction trains.

To relieve the situation, standard-gauge railcars were sent to Brachina. Ghan passengers transferred to these and so travelled to Port Augusta by standard gauge, the first members of the public to use the newly-built line across the western plain.

Recent newspaper comment not only brings the story up to date but typifies the kind of report that has appeared at frequent intervals for the greater part of a hundred years: "A vital rail bridge over the flooded creek at Callanna north of Marree was said to be swinging precariously"; "The poor old Ghan is in trouble again, this time delayed for twenty-four hours by a freight train derailed near Finke"; "The Commonwealth Railways said yesterday that repairs to the crossing were expected to take two days. About a third of the north side of the bridge at Finke was completely silted up and five inches of water were flowing over the top."

So has it been, and so must it continue to be, until the time when the new railway is built at last and the region of intermittently raging rivers is by-passed in a wide sweep to the west.

Since the April day, nearly one hundred years ago, when a passenger signing himself "Occasional Traveller" wrote to the *Dispatch* to complain of service on the railway recently built to Quorn, the Ghan has been consistently—though, usually, good-humouredly—criticised. "Whose duty is it to clean the passenger carriages of the Port Augusta and Quorn Railway?" demanded this first critic, clearly of the testy kind. "I am led to think that it is no one's duty as the carriage I travelled in today, judging by appearances, has never been cleaned since it has been in use. It was a mere foul den—offensive to the smell, touch and sight. It was only after opening the window that there was sufficient light to enable me to see the extreme dirtiness of the inside."

A week later the newspaper published a letter from "Stab in the Dark", who replied so censoriously that it seems likely that he was a railway official, possibly the one responsible for carriage cleanliness. Amusingly, the editor commented: "We found it necessary to eliminate a few unnecessarily severe expressions."

The matter was closed by the correspondent who, four years later, was to write the controversial letter that opened the discussion leading to the submission of the famous Phillips Ponds Memorial. Now he wrote in typically authoritative style, castigating "Occasional Traveller": "Let us hope that the next time he visits Quorn via rail he will be *compos mentis* and not 'seeing through a glass darkly'. Let me add that I am a constant traveller and can bear testimony to the uniform cleanliness of the carriages referred to."

Later, the ironic manner seems to have become fashionable among complainants. For example, there is the correspondent who wrote: "I have formed the opinion that the railway is a farce." This critic was a pastoralist and his dissatisfaction concerned an alleged failure on the part of engine drivers to give warning of the approach of trains. "I have to pass the fourth crossing on the line from Port Augusta every morning and have never heard a whistle sounded. I pass with about six hundred sheep, and who will pay the damage if the train should run into my flock? The driver might say he was going one mile an hour."

Today the modernised, air-conditioned Ghan is still the butt of those who have nothing better to do than write carping letters, or who just like to see their comments in print. But now the popular line concerns the railway's "incredible dawdling".

Through the years there have been many causes for slow speed. Among these, in the early days, camels appear to have taken a place of some prominence. The beasts seem to have caused constant annoyance to engine drivers, quite as much as to teamsters. One reads a report from Farina: "A camel belonging to the Camel Carrying Company placed himself before the engine on Tuesday night at the crossing near the triangle and, refusing to budge, was shunted into the rail yard where the usual examination took place."

Apparently, one might shunt an obstructive camel but, if it was in any way injured, a report had to be made both to the railway authorities and to the owners. And so, in the very first days of the line, one comes upon a newspaper article which suggested that camels "should travel at some distance from the main track, instead of following it as they now do".

Ghan country, perhaps especially in the north, became known as "The Land of Plenty of Time and Wait-a-bit". This leisurely approach to railway management is popularly supposed to have continued into the present day, and it accounts for jokes like the yarn that tells of a truck of perishables over-carried and dutifully run back while fuming passengers wait. Such chestnuts are recounted today with all the relish customary when they were first told, say, three-quarters of a century ago.

Probably the practice will continue out of long habit until the Ghan, packing up rails and sleepers, migrates 100 miles across country to make a fresh start where the permanent way—not to mention the long-suffering staff—will be plagued no more by flooding waters and much less, it is to be hoped, by drifting sand.

20

GOODBYE TO THE GHAN

So ends the story of the Ghan to date. But a new chapter in the history of the Central Australia Railway is about to open.

In March 1967 Mr J.R.A. Walker, Chief Civil Engineer of the Commonwealth Railways, said that an aerial survey of country far to the west of the existing rail had convinced him that it would be practicable to build a line between Tarcoola and Alice Springs.

Then in May of the following year a South Australian Member of the House of Representatives in Canberra suggested that the new railway should be routed through Coober Pedy. Were the line to follow this course, he said, it would facilitate oil exploration in the region, pass within 100 miles of the Wingellina nickel deposits, and stabilise the opal-mining industry. He asked the Government to make money available so that a survey might be made at once.

To the satisfaction of all progressives, the 1970 Federal Budget allocated $230,000 to a detailed survey for a standard-gauge railway to follow high ground to the west of the existing flood-prone narrow-gauge line.

In due course, the survey teams moved out.

Next, in February 1972, the Minister of Shipping and Transport announced that the Federal Government had approved in principle the construction of a standard-gauge railway between Tarcoola and Alice Springs to replace the existing narrow-gauge line north of Marree.

This firm decision to adopt an old idea at last and build an entirely new railway to Alice Springs appears to have been reached through a series of uncertainties.

After the second World War, the questions of whether or not the Government should build afresh along a route that avoided the regions of great flood, and whether or not the greatly inflated outlay would be justified, seem to have been discussed intermittently for some years. Apparently no conclusion had been arrived at when the Railways Department was confronted with the embarrassing Leigh Creek coal situation.

The subsequent construction of a standard-gauge line in the country of the original railway met the immediate need. But it also diverted Government purpose. Or so it seems.

Since, willy nilly, 150 miles of standard-gauge railway had to be constructed to Leigh Creek, commonsense had compelled the continuation to Marree, for one day the long-mooted Queensland border link would have to be built. With this done, inevitably the point arose that a standard-gauge railway from Port Pirie to Marree covered exactly one-third of the distance to Alice Springs. In the circumstances, would not the most practical and economical course be to continue the conversion all the way to the Centre and shelve proposals for a new line in the west?

For a time, this view appears to have been accepted. In a Commonwealth Railways booklet, *The Stirling North–Marree Railway*, published in July 1957, there is this comment: "It [the new railway] is of special importance also to the Northern Territory as it is the first stage in the ultimate conversion of the narrow-gauge railway to Alice Springs to standard 4 ft 8½ in gauge."

Clearly, at that time, the Government purpose was to upgrade the entire railway, despite flood, despite sand-drift. The proposal to build afresh in the west—argued off and on for over seventy years—would seem to have been set aside indefinitely, perhaps for good.

Probably a number of factors contributed to cause the change in policy. But an important consideration was the deteriorating condition of a large number of creek and river crossings between Marree and Oodnadatta.

North of Oodnadatta there are virtually no bridges, the practice being to run the line over stone-pitched causeways on the beds of the watercourses. To the south, bridges have suffered deterioration in the lime-concrete abutments, and eventually will require reconstruction. But to rebuild these many crossings would involve heavy expenditure. Was it worthwhile to give this very costly face-lift to an old line that was subject to so many disadvantages? In the long run, would it not be wiser and much cheaper to build afresh? Flood and sand had caused tremendous wastage in the past. Future losses that could be avoided might legitimately be taken into account in authorising a bold new step.

The estimated cost of the future Tarcoola to Alice Springs Railway is $70,000,000. But estimates seldom cover ultimate costs, and so the final figure is likely to afford a still more staggering comparison with the expense visualised when the transcontinental railway started out on its journey 100 years ago.

When the new standard-gauge railway has been built, the old narrow-gauge line north of Marree will be closed. The question of building north-eastwards from Marree to a spot on the State border east of Birdsville is a matter of Government policy. So in regard to this nothing can be said except that, in view of current outlays, the long-delayed extension will wait longer yet. For the construction of the Tarcoola to Alice Springs line is planned to take five years—from the date when the customary legislation has passed Commonwealth and State Parliaments.

As for the question of the construction of extensions from Alice Springs and Birdum to complete the transcontinental line, perhaps it is suitable to quote from the Report of the Northern Territory Investigation Committee published in 1937. After outlining the provisions of the Northern Territory Acceptance Act, this report said, "That the north-south transcontinental railway should have been insisted on by South Australia is significant of the ignorance of the time. The spinifex desert country through which most of the uncompleted section of this railway would now have to run would never justify its construction, and if the line were built it would simply pile up heavy losses. The construction of this line is, therefore, no longer within the sphere of practical politics."

That opinion was given long ago. Since then conditions have changed dramatically. Air communication increasingly asserts importance. Yet, at great cost, a new railway is to be built in expectation that the business of the Centre will increase beyond narrow-gauge capacity, indeed, out of present-day recognition.

But what of the Far North where very large sums have been poured out on capital works services, and where money is constantly spent on developing roads to provide access to pastoral, mining, and agricultural areas? It seems that important advances, pivoting upon the North Australia Railway, may bring a day when, after all, the completion of the transcontinental line will become a necessity, road carriage being insufficient to meet a mounting need for ground transport across the "gap". The cost would be great, but in the foreseeable future the air road—though well able to deal with emergency lifts—will scarcely sustain the heavy transport with which a railway copes.

The principal traffic on railways is usually between the terminal points. And should a time come when it is to the national advantage that Darwin should realise the ambitions with which it was founded and become the ultimate terminal, with Alice Springs the half-way stage, then the reference in the 1937 Report to unproductive spinifex-desert country would not amount to a great deal.

It is unlikely that the section of the Trans-Australian Railway that includes the Nullarbor Plain will ever in itself justify the construction of the 1,000-mile line. This stretch of 420 miles simply links pastoral country in the east with pastoral country in the west. It seems possible that, in like manner, the Northern Territory "gap" may one day be bridged.

One can only speculate.

Probably most people expected the nickname "Ghan" to fade out with the coming of the diesel-electric locomotive and the substitution of standard for narrow gauge on the old line to Marree. "Exit 'The Ghan' ", proclaims the title of a newspaper article in June 1954. "The diesel-electric service inaugurated this afternoon takes the place of the leisurely 'Ghan' whose time-tables were only approximate." It appears that many old residents, long familiar with the line, were "overwhelmed" by the new locomotives.

Indeed, it was reasonable to suppose that the ten impressive engines—the first deliveries in an order for fourteen—would end talk of the "Ghan", so different were they from the old "steam wagons". For essentially the name had been associated with trains hauled by engines whose smoke plumes had been the first indication of home for many a wanderer coming in from the desert. With both steam and narrow gauge gone, what remained, save habit, to hold public regard for the old nickname? The answer seems to be sentiment, strong in the people of the outback and its fringes, though probably most would hotly contest the statement.

In the upshot, the name continued in general use. The new locomotives and modernised rolling-stock made up a train unlike the old trundling Marree Mixed. But no matter. So one still heard the old jokes, sometimes slightly adapted, but frequently not. The express due at 6 p.m. limping in at midnight; the driver who complained that he could not persuade either injector to cut in. That the wit was often no longer topical was of no consequence.

So the old name has stuck. But will it survive the fresh therapy that is pending?—complete removal to the west with transformation to standard gauge throughout? Will it jump the 250-mile gap to Tarcoola and blandly resume sovereignty, saddling the new and up-to-date railway with time-worn sarcasms? Or will the occasion when the first train heads northwards out of the new terminus be the day when, at last, everyone will say goodbye to the Ghan?

I hope not. But for us at least that time had come. Silverskin was needed for other duties. And we, like the Ghan, had reached Alice. We climbed down for the last time with reluctance, for there is much truth in the saying "to journey is better than to arrive". A very pleasant interlude had ended.

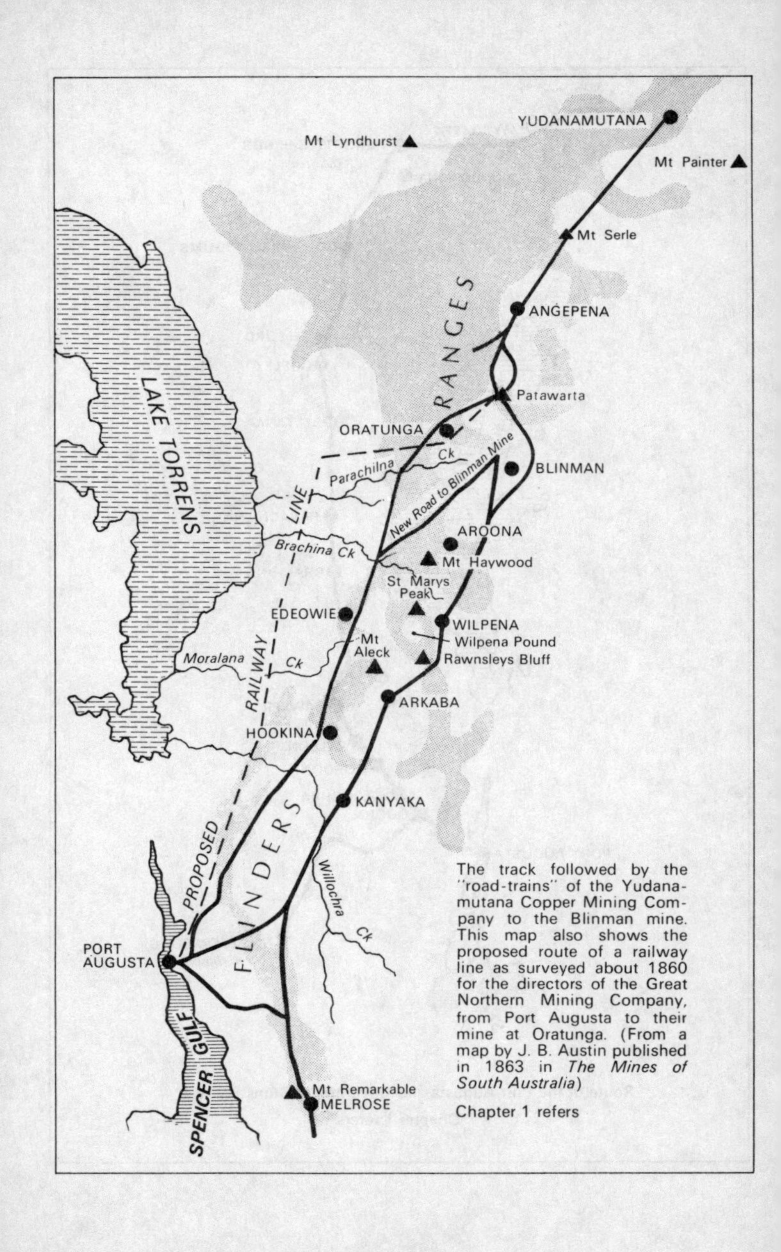

The track followed by the "road-trains" of the Yudanamutana Copper Mining Company to the Blinman mine. This map also shows the proposed route of a railway line as surveyed about 1860 for the directors of the Great Northern Mining Company, from Port Augusta to their mine at Oratunga. (From a map by J. B. Austin published in 1863 in *The Mines of South Australia*)

Chapter 1 refers

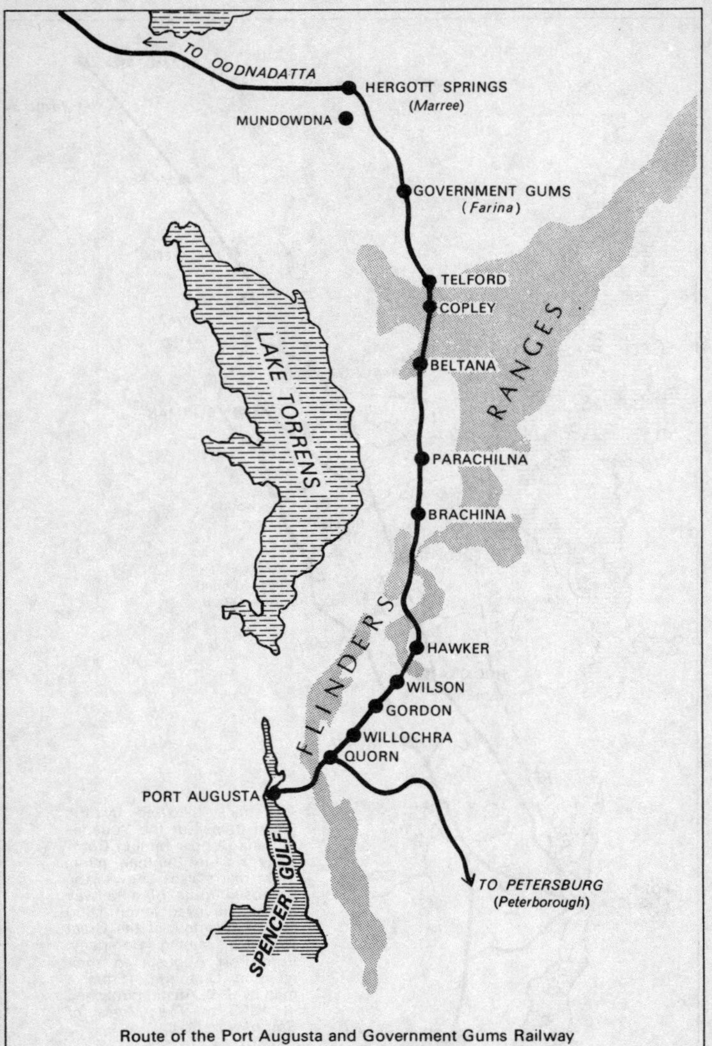

Route of the Port Augusta and Government Gums Railway
Chapter 1 refers

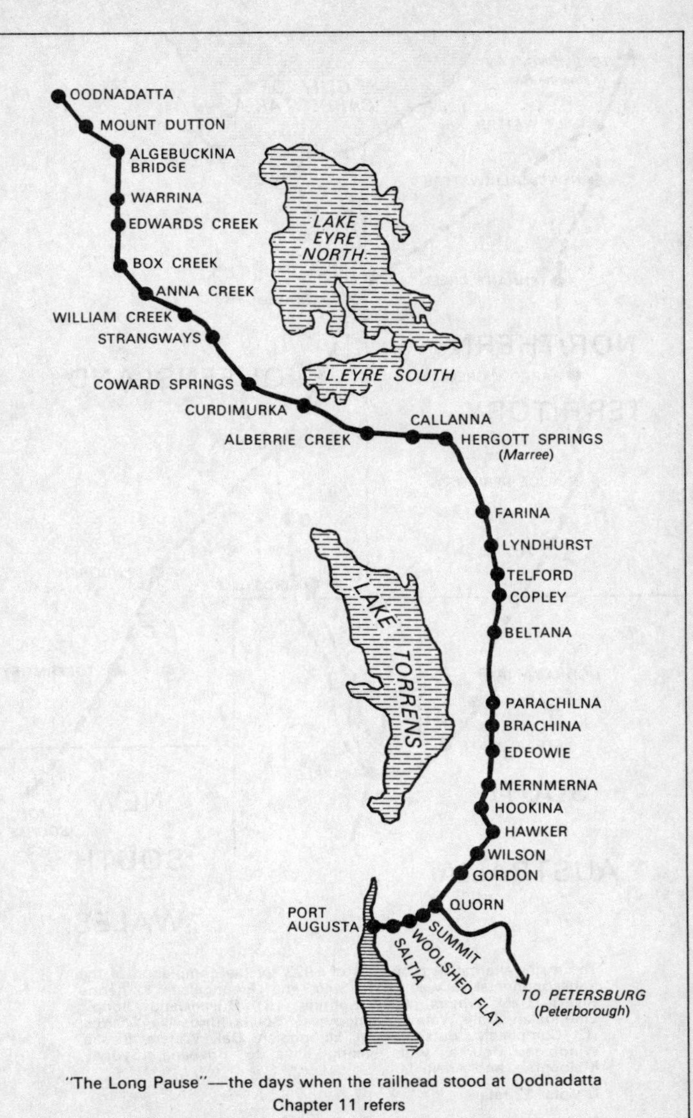

"The Long Pause"—the days when the railhead stood at Oodnadatta
Chapter 11 refers

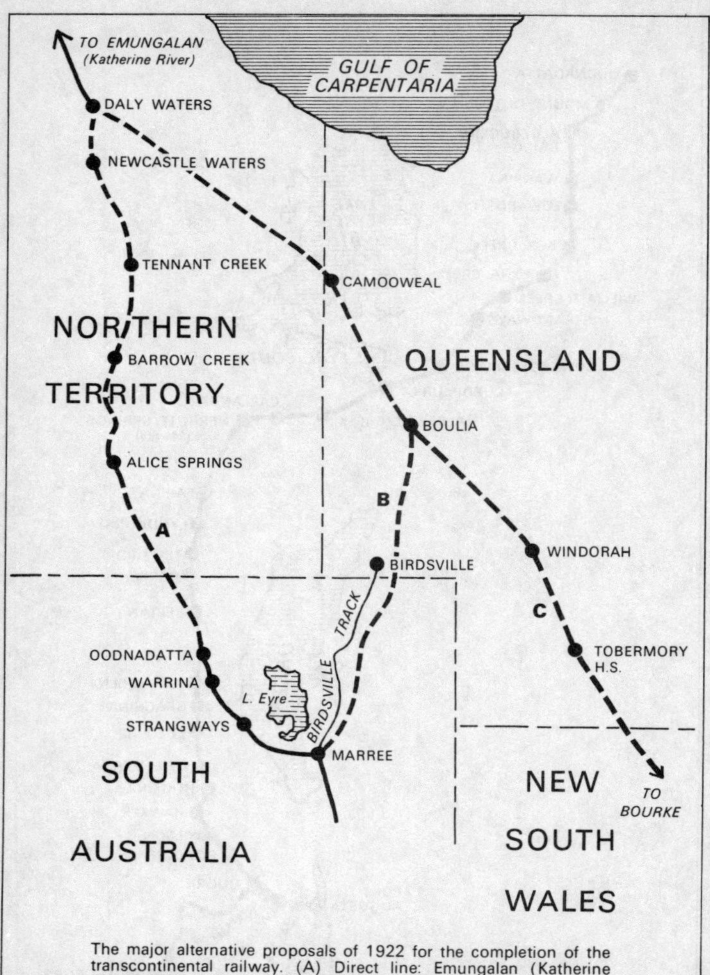

The major alternative proposals of 1922 for the completion of the transcontinental railway. (A) Direct line: Emungalan (Katherine River), Daly Waters, Alice Springs; (B) Queensland "loop": Emungalan, Daly Waters, Camooweal, Boulia, Birdsville, Marree; (C) Completely "outside" line: Emungalan, Daly Waters, Boulia, Windorah, Bourke, with linking lines to Brisbane, Sydney, Melbourne, and Adelaide

Chapter 12 refers

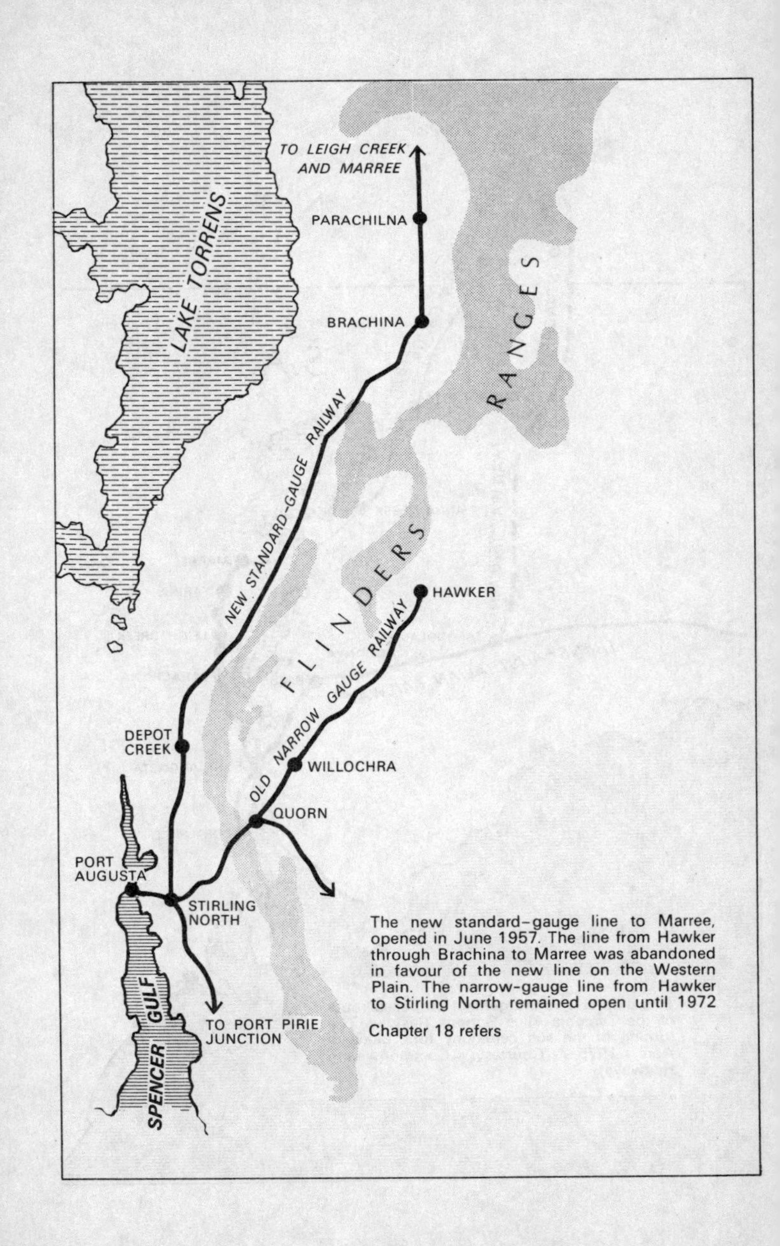

The new standard-gauge line to Marree, opened in June 1957. The line from Hawker through Brachina to Marree was abandoned in favour of the new line on the Western Plain. The narrow-gauge line from Hawker to Stirling North remained open until 1972

Chapter 18 refers

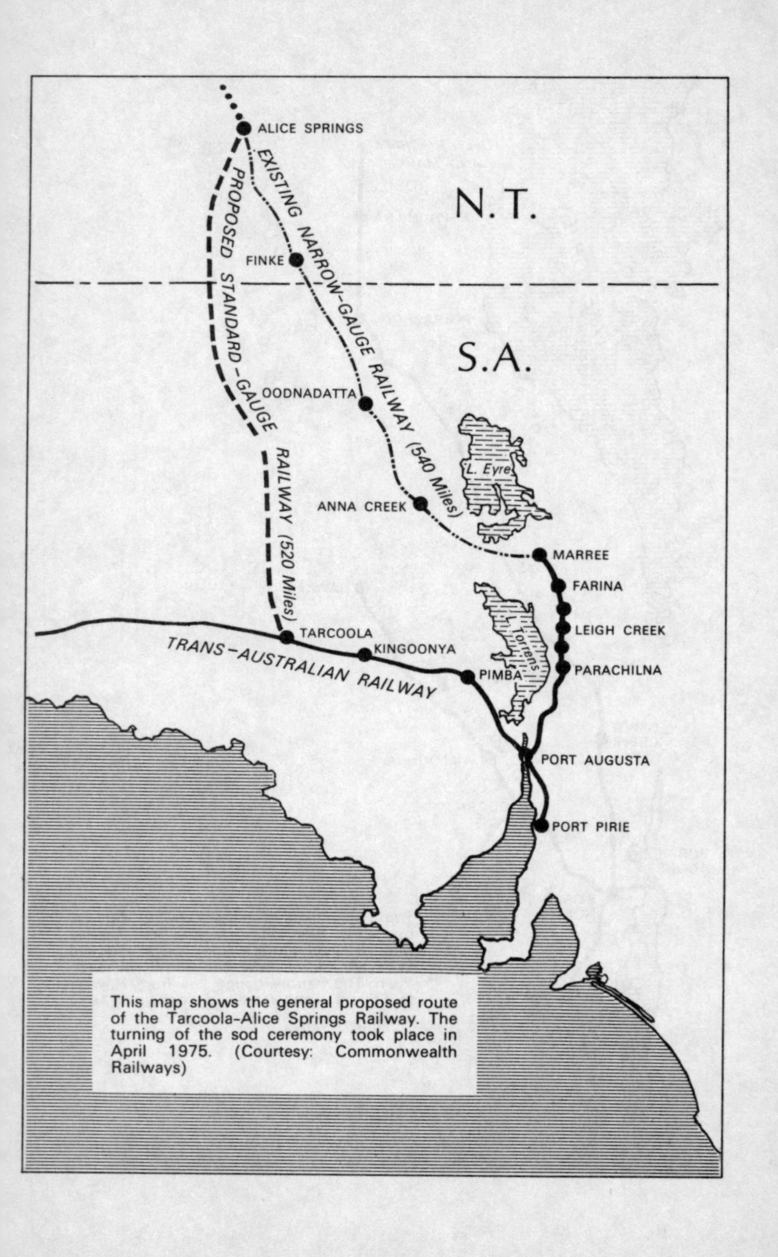

This map shows the general proposed route of the Tarcoola-Alice Springs Railway. The turning of the sod ceremony took place in April 1975. (Courtesy: Commonwealth Railways)

BIBLIOGRAPHY

Books

AUSTIN, J. B. *The Mines of South Australia.*
Australian Encyclopaedia (ed. A. CHISHOLM).
BARNARD, Marjorie. *History of Australia.*
BLACKET, J. *History of South Australia* (1911).
BRADY, Edwin J. *Australia Unlimited.*
BULL, J. W. *Early Experiences & Recollections.*
BURT, J. *The Birdsville Track.*
COCKBURN, A. Rodney. *Pastoral Pioneers of South Australia.*
FENNER, Charles. *South Australia: A Geographical Study.*
GORDON, D. J. & RYAN, V. H. *Handbook of South Australia.*
GREGORY, J. W. *The Dead Heart of Australia.*
HARCUS, William. *South Australia: Its History, Resources, and Productions* (1876).
HILL, Ernestine. *The Territory.*
HODDER, Edwin. *History of South Australia* (1893).
HOLMES, J. Macdonald. *Australia's Open North.*
JESSOP, William R. H. *Flindersland and Sturtland: Or the Inside and Outside of Australia* (1862).
LANGLEY, M. *Sturt of the Murray.*
MADIGAN, C. T. *Crossing the Dead Heart.*
MEINIG, D. W. *On the Margins of the Good Earth.*
MINCHAM, Hans. *The Story of the Flinders Ranges.*
MOOREHEAD, A. *Cooper's Creek.*
MUDIE, Ian. *Heroic Journey of John McDouall Stuart.*
Office Directory and Year Book of Australia, 1884.
PAGE, Michael F. *et al. South Australia.*
PERKINS, A. J. *South Australia, an Agricultural & Pastoral State in the Making.*
PETRIE, Sir Charles. *Great Beginnings.*
Picturesque Atlas of Australasia (ed. A. Garran, 1886).
PIKE, Douglas. *Paradise of Dissent, South Australia 1829–1857.*
PLOWMAN, R. B. *The Man from Oodnadatta.*

PRICE, A. Grenfell. *The Foundation and Settlement of South Australia.*
RATCLIFFE, Francis. *Flying Fox and Drifting Sand.*
SCOTT, Sir Ernest. *A Short History of Australia.*
Statistical Register of South Australia.
STOW, J. P. *South Australia: History, Productions & Natural Resources* (1883).
STURT, Charles. *Narrative of an Expedition into Central Australia.*
TESTRO, Ron. *Pictorial History of Australian Railways 1854–1970.*

BULLETINS, PAPERS, AND REPORTS

Annual reports of the Commonwealth Railways.
Annual reports of the South Australian Railways.
Bulletins of the Australian Railways Historical Society (especially Nos 115, 218, 229, 364).
"Centenary History of South Australia" published in *Proceedings of the Royal Geographical Society of Australasia*, vol. xxxvi.
Parliamentary papers relating to the northern explorations of Babbage, Freeling, Goyder, and Warburton.
Report and Minutes of Evidence respecting proposed Northern Territory Railway (extension from Mataranka to Daly Waters), and proposed extension of the Port Augusta–Oodnadatta Railway from Oodnadatta to Alice Springs, submitted to the Parliamentary Standing Committee on Public Works (1922) of the Parliament of the Commonwealth of Australia.
Proceedings of the Royal Geographical Society of Australasia, South Australian Branch.
Report of the Administrator of the Northern Territory, June 1946.
Report of the Northern Territory Investigation Committee, 1937.

NEWSPAPERS AND MAGAZINES

The *Advertiser* (Adelaide).
The *Chronicle* (Adelaide).
The *Farmers' Weekly Messenger* (Adelaide).
The *News* (Adelaide).
The *North-Eastern Times and Terowie News.*
The *Northern Argus* (Clare).
The *Port Augusta Dispatch.*
The *Port Pirie Gazette and Areas News.*
The *Register* (Adelaide).
The *Sunday Mail* (Adelaide).
The *Transcontinental* (Port Augusta).
Walkabout (Melbourne).

INDEX

THE GHAN LIVES ON

It is over 20 years since the journey of the last old Ghan, and the legend lives on!

In 1975 the Prime Minister Gough Whitlam marked the beginning of construction of a new standard-gauge line by turning the first sod. In 1980 the line was opened by Princess Alexandra. It now runs some 150 km west of the original narrow-gauge line, and avoids many of the streams that flooded so easily when the rain set in. The Tarcoola to Alice Springs section is 831 km long and contains 52 bridges, the longest being over the Finke River. It is at last a truly all-weather track.

The new, standard-gauge Ghan has continued the tradition of containing both sleeping and sitting cars. The facilities are first-class: showers, reclining chairs, powder rooms and restaurants. Certainly these innovations are a far cry from the 'Short Tom' compartments of the old Ghan. The Ghan used to be renowned for its tardiness: a driver once had to kill wild goats to feed his passengers when the train was delayed by flood waters. But the new Ghan can be relied upon to complete the journey well within 24 hours.

The old days are far from forgotten. In Alice Springs in 1980, a group of rail enthusiasts formed a committee to 'preserve, restore and operate a section of the old Ghan narrow-gauge railway line.' By 1988, thanks to voluntary labour, financial assistance from the Northern Territory Government and a Federal Bicentennial Grant, the Ghan Preservation Society saw its dream become a reality at McDonnell Siding, south of Alice Springs. Today the old Ghan labours along its original narrow-gauge track south to Mount Ertiva, recreating the atmosphere of the old days and offering visitors the opportunity to travel back in time, by either steam or diesel. At the siding is a replica, drawn to the original plans, of the railway station of Stuart. It has been meticulously constructed to house the traditional tearooms and ticket box, along with a museum.

In Quorn at the southern end of the track, the Pichi Richi Preservation Society have maintained the narrow-gauge through Pichi Richi Pass in the Flinders Ranges, the first obstacle that the steam locomotives met on their way north. From the restored railway station and the yards in Quorn, one can take a romantic steam trip through the pass to Woolshed Flat.

If Basil Fuller were alive today he would be heartened to know that the old Ghan lives on at both ends of this legendary journey!

Paul Fitzsimons
Alice Springs, 1996